Capitalist Welfare Systems:
A Comparison of Japan, Britain and Sweden

DATE DUE

Capitalist Welfare Systems:
A Comparison of Japan, Britain and Sweden

Arthur Gould

Longman
London and New York

Longman Group UK Limited
Longman House, Burnt Mill,
Harlow, Essex CM20 2JE, England
and Associated Companies throughout the world.

*Published in the United States of America
by Longman Publishing, New York*

© Longman Group UK Limited 1993

First published 1993

ISBN 582 083494   PPR

British Library Cataloguing-in-Publication Data

A catalogue record for this book is
available from the British Library

Library of Congress Cataloging in Publication Data
Gould, Arthur.
    Capitalist welfare systems: a comparison of Japan, Britain and Sweden/Arthur
Gould.
    p.   cm.
Includes bibliographical references and index.
ISBN 0–582–08349–4
    1. Japan—Social policy. 2. Great Britain—Social policy.
3. Sweden—Social policy. 4. Capitalism. 5. Welfare state.
I. Title.
HN17.5.G68   1993
361.6'1'0952—dc20
                                                92-38228
                                                  CIP

Set by 5 in 10/12pt Bembo
Printed in Malaysia by VP

To Andrea, Art and Mag

Contents

Abbreviations

AHA	Area Health Authority
AMS	Labour Market Board
CP	Community Programme
CTC	City Technology College
DES	Department of Education and Science
DHA	District Health Authority
DHSS	Department of Health and Social Security
DN	*Dagens Nyheter*
DRG	Diagnosis Related Group
DsA	Ministry of Labour
EHI	Employees' Health Insurance
EPI	Employees' Pension Insurance
FC	Family Credit
FIS	Family Income Supplement
GP	General Practitioner
IEA	Institute for Economic Affairs
ILO	International Labour Office
JCP	Job Creation Programme
LDP	Liberal Democratic Party
LEA	Local Education Authority
LMS	Local Management of Schools
LO	Federation of Trade Unions for Manual Workers
MHW	Ministry of Health and Welfare
MSC	Manpower Services Commission
NHI	National Health Insurance
NHS	National Health Service
NPI	National Pension Insurance
OECD	Organisation for Economic Cooperation and Development

PFC	Polytechnic Funding Council
RAWP	Resource Allocation Working Party
RFV	Social Insurance Board
RHA	Regional Health Authority
SAF	Confederation of Employers
SAP	Social Democratic Workers' Party
SAU	Social Affairs Unit
SBC	Supplementary Benefits Commission
SCB	Central Bureau of Statistics
SEG	Socio-Economic Group
SKr	Swedish Kronor
SoL	Social Services Act
SvD	*Svenska Dagbladet*
TC	Training Commission
TOPS	Training Opportunities Scheme
TVEI	Technical and Vocational Education Initiative
UFC	University Funding Council
UK	United Kingdom
UN	United Nations
VAT	Value Added Tax
WHO	World Health Organisation
¥	Yen
YOP	Youth Opportunities Programme
YTS	Youth Training Scheme

Currencies

References to amounts of money in different currencies have been kept to a minimum. As a rough guide it may be assumed that £1 = SKr10 = ¥250.

Preface

My interest in the welfare systems of Japan, Britain and Sweden began in 1976 when devising a course for undergraduate students which was to examine the relationship between society and social policy. The students already had a basic knowledge of the British system and it was decided to complement this knowledge with that of two other advanced capitalist countries. Japan and Sweden were chosen partly because they represented clear political polarities but also because of their international significance. Japan was clearly a nation for which superpower status was being predicted, while Sweden was still cited as *the* model for combining economic and social success.

The decision to write a book on the three welfare systems was intended initially to examine developments in the field of social policy since 1973. Only in the process of writing has the final thesis emerged. It was clear that there was substantial agreement that Japan had had a profound impact on other economies. It was also clear that the Western welfare state had experienced some profound changes. Was it possible to argue that there might be a link between the two processes – the Japanisation of Western economies and the trend towards welfare pluralism? The evidence convinced me that it was.

I would like to thank Arnold J. Heidenheimer for inviting me to the annual conference of the American Political Science Association held in San Francisco in 1990, to present an initial paper on the three welfare systems. Critical comments received at that time were severe but welcome. I would also like to thank Andrea Jackson, my wife, and Jane Taylor for encouraging me to continue with this project at a particularly crucial time.

Discussions with James Fulcher of Leicester University, who shared my interest in the three countries, and Jochen Clasen, a Loughborough colleague, who has carried out a major comparative study of British and German social security, provided much-needed inspiration as the book began to take shape. James and Jochen were also kind enough to read the first draft and offer a number of helpful and critical comments.

Arthur Gould,
Department of Social Sciences,
Loughborugh University,
August 1992

CHAPTER ONE
Introduction

Generalisations are often made by social scientists about a wide range of capitalist countries or industrial societies. It is assumed that they have certain important structural characteristics in common that distinguish them from non-capitalist or pre-industrial societies. The three I have chosen are all post-industrial capitalist societies. They are parliamentary democracies with constitutional monarchs. Each has a centralised, as opposed to a federal, system of government. From the point of view of historical and political interest, each has an economy and a welfare system which at different times has been regarded as a model for others to envy and emulate.

Britain[1] was the first industrial nation and, in spite of its economic decline, remains a member of the rich G7 group of countries. For many years after the Second World War its 'welfare state' was seen as the most advanced in the world. During the 1960s Sweden was held to be a country which had managed to achieve both a thriving capitalist economy and an impressive system of state welfare. By the end of the 1970s, it was to Japan that many were looking for the secrets of success. Not only was its economy marvelled at but there were those who argued that even in social terms, Japan was 'Number One' (Vogel 1979).

The similarities, in my view, make comparison worthwhile but so do the contrasts. Sweden has a tiny, dispersed population, while Japan and Britain are large, densely populated countries. For both Britain and Sweden, economic success was firmly based on a richness in natural resources. Japan had no such advantage. Britain's economic pre-eminence has passed into history but the economic miracles of Sweden and Japan are late-twentieth-century phenomena. Sweden and Britain share a Northern European Protestant culture while

Japan is Oriental and Confucian. But what makes the contrast really fascinating is the politics of the three countries. At one extreme we have a country which since 1932 has been almost exclusively governed by social democrats; at the other, we have one which is consistently conservative; while in the middle, one in which two principal political parties have for many decades vied for office.

Ultimately, however, the justification for comparison will not come from some pre-determined ranking of criteria but from the results. Britain and Sweden have already been compared to good effect by Heclo and, together with the United States, by Furniss and Tilton (Furniss and Tilton 1977; Heclo 1974). T.J.Pempel has written a fascinating justification for comparing Sweden and Japan, regarding them as two countries which have been, albeit in different ways, adept at managing capitalism (Pempel 1990). Another study has examined the role of élites in the political systems of Sweden, Japan and the United States (Verba *et al.* 1987). As far as I am aware nobody has attempted to use the combination of Japan, Britain and Sweden, exclusively, for any kind of comparison.

Some of the justifications for doing so have already been alluded to. Another is the fact that they can be said to represent each of Esping-Andersen's 'three worlds of welfare capitalism'. Esping-Andersen, using various criteria, has ranked a number of countries according to their *decommodification* scores. By 'decommodification' he means the degree to which 'citizens can freely, and without potential loss of job, income or general welfare, opt out of work when they themselves consider it necessary' (Esping-Andersen 1990: p. 23). Those with the highest scores he describes as *social democratic*, those with medium scores, *corporatist-statist*, and those with the least, *liberal*. Sweden came into the first category, Japan into the second and Britain into the third (Esping-Andersen 1990: p. 52). It is not possible here to consider Esping-Andersen's typology or scoring methods in depth. My purpose in referring to his categories is simply to point out that by the criteria of one eminent comparativist's work, Japan, Britain and Sweden can be said to be representative of three different types of welfare system. However, it is appropriate to say at this point that the evidence presented in this book would suggest that Japanese citizens are much more dependent on the labour market than Esping-Andersen's decommodification score implies. Moreover, changes that have taken place in Britain in the 1980s, and in Sweden more recently, would seem to lend support to the argument that *recommodification* is a more appropriate description of the process that is currently taking place in European welfare systems.

THE WELFARE STATE, STATE WELFARE AND WELFARE SYSTEMS

A word perhaps needs to be said from the outset to justify the term *welfare system*. To begin with, a term is needed which enables one to categorise the phenomena under discussion. The *welfare state* is a term which should properly be reserved for those countries which are committed to a policy of full employment and in which the state is responsible for the provision of a comprehensive range of universalistic welfare benefits and services. Few would apply the term to Japan, least of all the Japanese themselves, and it is doubtful whether it can now be applied to Britain. Only Sweden, of our three countries, can still be said to meet the requisite criteria, and that may not be for much longer. *State welfare* is clearly too narrow a term when dealing with voluntary, occupational, informal and private welfare. *Welfare system* is, however, a term which would seem to cover the different welfare mixes which the three countries enjoy. Welfare system also has the advantage of being politically neutral. So many of the typologies which are applied to different welfare systems are value-laden. Titmuss's 'institutional' category, Furniss and Tilton's 'social welfare state', Esping-Andersen's 'social democratic régime' are all regarded as the best of the three they each place on offer. There would be nothing to gain in this study by saying from the outset which of the three presented here is the best buy. The general aim is rather to show how welfare systems have developed, how and why they are changing and what we can learn from an examination of the relationship between them and the capitalist societies of which they are a part.

More specifically, it will be argued that the crisis of the European welfare state has resulted in a drift towards welfare pluralism. It will be suggested that this drift is to be explained by the transition from *Fordist* to *post-Fordist* capitalism, which itself is often linked to the impact that Japan has had on the global economy. If Western economies, in certain respects, have become more like those of Japan, then it would seem likely that changes that have taken place in European welfare systems can be explained by a similar process.

In conclusion, it will be argued that while European welfare systems have come to resemble more closely the structure and function of the Japanese welfare system, so Japan's rapidly ageing population will inevitably lead to increases in welfare expenditure, suggesting the development of a *new convergence*. This argument will be developed below and the chapter will conclude with the presentation of a

3

selection of relevant international statistics and an outline of the rest of the book.

THE CRISIS OF THE WELFARE STATE

My own attempt to say something about the crisis of the welfare state in relation to Japan, Britain and Sweden was published in two papers a decade ago (Gould 1981 and 1982). Various writers had criticised the way in which Western-style welfare states had developed. In some publications these were simplified by distinguishing between conservative and radical critiques (Wilensky 1975; Furniss and Tilton 1977). The disillusion with the post-war welfare consensus was shared by academics and politicians from a variety of ideological and theoretical perspectives and reflected a growing concern amongst voters in many countries. While the disillusion, to an extent, preceded the Arab–Israeli conflict of 1973, it is clear in retrospect that it was fuelled by the economic factors which followed that event. What is also clear is that the dissatisfaction was widespread and grew throughout the 1970s.

There were social democrats who felt that social policies had not done enough to reduce social inequalities. Poverty, supposedly abolished by social security reforms, was 'rediscovered'. Unemployment levels were beginning to grow. Neo-Marxists felt that welfare reforms did little to advance the power base of socialism and the working class. Rather they reinforced the strength of capitalism by ameliorating its excesses. In consequence teachers, doctors and social workers were regarded as agents of social control, managing and manipulating a subservient mass. Ivan Illich reflected these concerns in a different way by suggesting that far from being mere agents of capital, welfare bureaucrats and professionals had created industries which served their own rather than their clients' interests. These same concerns were mirrored on the right of the political spectrum where traditional conservatives were concerned about the progressiveness of many reforms and what they regarded as the consequent lack of discipline. They, like their more liberal counterparts who were worried about the distorting effect that growing public services were having on advanced economies, blamed economic and social problems on creeping socialism and the vested interests of those employed in the public sector.

It seemed to me that a common theme of many of these critiques was the extent to which salaried middle class (SMC) people benefited from welfare provision both as consumers and producers of welfare. While some argued about whether state welfare in Britain had benefited the working class or the ruling class, much of the empirical evidence seemed to point to members of the SMC as the principle beneficiaries of welfare state expansion. State education subsidies benefited the sons and daughters of middle-class families; middle-class people seemed to benefit disproportionately from health care provision; housing subsidies, tax allowances on pensions, income-related benefits, occupational welfare – all seemed to reflect inequalities of the hierarchical division of labour rather than reduce them. Or at least, that seemed to be the logic implicit in the various published critiques on offer at the time.

If this were so then it seemed that a more significant case could be made for suggesting that the SMC was a new class that had managed to appropriate a higher degree of economic and political power than existing studies of class had shown. Instead of seeing the SMC as either the servant of capital or as undergoing proletarianisation, or both, there was a case for arguing that it had somehow advanced its own interests very successfully while appearing to lack the cohesion that was attributed to capital and labour. In the paper on Britain (Gould 1981) it was suggested that the politics of the post-war Keynesian, corporatist consensus had provided the SMC with a very firm power base. It was further suggested that the evidence of the early 1980s indicated that while the Conservative Party seemed to have realised this to an extent, the Labour Party had not.

The concept of the SMC was then extended to the literature on Sweden and Japan. It seemed to fit the Swedish model very well. The liberal corporatism of Sweden, which ironically seemed to give the labour movement such influence, also benefited the SMC. The vast state apparatus in Sweden had provided 25 per cent of the work-force with well-paid, secure jobs, while the historical compromise between the working class and the SMC had resulted in considerable state welfare benefits for the SMC in terms of pensions, child care, parental leave, education, health care and housing.

In Japan, however, the very weakness of organised labour and the left opposition parties resulted in those in middle-class occupations depending more on the private than the public sector for employment and on employers as much as the state for welfare benefits. State welfare was too residual to provide extensive middle-class benefits, and occupational welfare, while it favoured higher income groups, emphasised a dependence upon the employer.

It was as if a society which contained a strong labour movement and a healthy private economy created the ideal conditions for the growth and power of the SMC. The trade unions provided the industrial muscle; the SMC managed the state apparatus by representing both employer and employee organisations. This gave the propertied class little option but to accede to the demands made on it, whereas a society with a fragmented working class and a weak labour movement, like Japan's, gave the SMC no alternative power base. As a result, the SMC in Japan remained dependent upon the paternalism of the propertied class.

The starting-point of this book, then, is one of scepticism. The post-war European welfare state was of undoubted benefit to millions of people who had previously suffered tremendous hardship from the uneven development of capitalism. But the professional and class interests of a growing welfare bureaucracy led to seemingly inexorable increases in public expenditure, declining rates of profit, and a fiscal crisis (Bacon and Eltis 1976; Glyn and Sutcliffe 1972; O'Connor 1973). The control of this expansion became a source of concern not only for those who could be said to represent the interests of capital, but also, increasingly, for affluent working- and middle-class voters who no longer accepted that a large public sector was in their interests.

TOWARDS WELFARE PLURALISM

In the early decades of the European welfare state, it appeared that countries like Britain and Sweden had created more just societies, with fewer social problems and a more egalitarian distribution of income and opportunity. As a result, the Japanese government, in the early 1970s, began to experience considerable pressure to go down the same road. The oil crisis of 1973 and the subsequent recession convinced the Japanese authorities that the welfare state had become a disadvantage to the competitiveness of other advanced capitalist countries. They began to claim that Japan had no need for a welfare state, since it had a *welfare society* of its own. What state welfare provided elsewhere, it was argued, was provided in Japan by the family, employers, the voluntary and the private sectors. This unique welfare mix, it was said, had resulted in one of the lowest infant mortality rates in the world, high age expectancy, a very effective education system and fewer social problems than could be found in the West.

Meanwhile, this same truth was beginning to dawn on Europeans. The more affluent elements of the working class were coming to resent the burden of taxation to finance a welfare state from which there seemed to be few marginal gains for them. Employers, coping with recession and the threat of increased competition from the countries of the Pacific Rim, such as Japan, wanted a reduction in the size of public sectors. Growing sections of the middle class, particularly those employed in the private sector, were also demanding that welfare spending be reduced.

A number of writers have already documented the way in which many European countries have begun to move in the direction of welfare pluralism. Morris and his colleagues have shown how during the 1980s:

- increases in public expenditure were curtailed
- fees for public services were increased
- eligibility for benefits was tightened up
- privatisation of many public services occurred
- government became a *producer* rather than a *provider* of services in the move towards a mixed economy of welfare
- means–testing increased (Morris 1988)

Johnson has noted:

> In most . . . welfare states . . . policies of retrenchment have been introduced, and although the rhetoric of retrenchment has exceeded its practical application, a change of emphasis has undoubtedly occurred. This change in emphasis finds its expression in welfare pluralism: a reduction or reversal of the state's dominance in welfare provision and an increase in the role of the informal, voluntary and commercial sectors. (Johnson 1987)

What I want to suggest is that these moves towards welfare pluralism in the West were a response to a logic of events which in an important way was linked with the success and structure of the Japanese economy.

THE JAPANISATION OF WELFARE

The phenomenal rates of economic growth in the 1960s followed by a rapid recovery from the 1970s recession had transformed Japan into a world superpower. Its dominance in world markets for cars, electronics and information technology forced world business and political leaders to examine seriously the assumptions and structures upon which their own economies were based.

Two clear differences emerged between the economies of Europe and that of Japan – one at the macro level and the other at the micro level, each linked to the other. First, Japan did not have a large public sector and as a consequence taxation rates were low. Although the state financed welfare benefits and services to a degree, it had nothing like the universalistic, comprehensive commitment favoured by the concept of the welfare state. The state had not come to be regarded as responsible for high standards of welfare for all. Second, large Japanese firms made a clear distinction between their core work-force and a peripheral work-force. The core work-force had lifetime employment, belonged to company unions, lived in company housing and received company welfare. The peripheral work-force, consisting disproportionately of women, 'retired' older workers and immigrants, had no such benefits. They could be laid off easily, had few company benefits and were non-unionised. Many of them were employed in the small subsidiary firms whose task it was to supply the large firms.

In contrast, many European governments had become responsible for the welfare of all their citizens. Powerful national trade unions in Europe had pressed firms and governments to extend employment rights to all workers. In competition with countries like Japan, therefore, the Europeans faced considerable extra costs, and just as importantly lacked the flexibility of the Japanese. The Japanese state was not hampered by enormous public responsibiliites. Japanese parents had to save for their children's higher education. The family had to take care of elderly relatives. The Japanese firm had a core work-force which saw its interests as inextricably bound up with a career in the company. With no fears for job security, there was a willingness to undertake any task, anywhere, without the need to resort to restrictive practices. Moreover, Japanese workers had been through a schooling aimed at producing diligent and obedient workers.

The only way in which European governments and employers could meet this powerful challenge was to ditch and dilute some of their responsibilities and undergo a process of *Japanisation* (Murray 1989a). In the 1960s the Japanese were mocked as imitators. The 1980s were therefore something of an irony. If the concept of *Japanisation* could be applied to developments in Western economies, then surely it can be used to describe parallel developments in European welfare systems. It would seem more than a coincidence that, at a time when the economic success of Japan was stimulating major changes in multi-national enterprises and competitor economies, a welfare mix should be adopted throughout Europe which de-emphasised the role of the state.

British governments throughout the 1980s were committed to rolling back the frontiers of the state in terms of welfare, while at the same time the role of the state in terms of the discipline and control of the work-force increased. By the end of the decade, trade unions, local authorities and welfare bureaucrats and professionals had all been seriously weakened. Universal welfare benefits had been devalued, targeting and means-testing had increased, and voluntary and private welfare promoted. On training schemes for young people, meeting the needs of employers for a docile work-force had become the dominating theme of training programmes. In schools meanwhile, a national curriculum, based upon the three Rs, a nationalist sense of history and frequent testing, imposed a new disciplinary régime to replace the permissive pluralism of the past. Parallels with all these developments, as will be seen from Part One, were previously to be found in Japan.

Moreover, not only did Japanese firms move into the UK economy with their no-strike deals and work practices, but British firms began to emulate them, often with the active cooperation of British trade unions which, faced with mass unemployment and restrictive legislation, must have felt that they had no alternative. Robin Murray described the transition from a Fordist to a post-Fordist economy in the following way:

> The Japanese job-for-life and corporate welfare system provides security. For the firm it secures an asset. Continuous training, payment by seniority, a breakdown of job demarcations, are all part of the Japanese core wage relation. The EETPU's lead in embracing private pension schemes, BUPA, internal flexibility, union-organised training and single company unions are all consistent with this path of post-Fordist industrial relations. (Murray 1989a: p. 46)

At the beginning of the 1970s the British authorities were looking at the Swedish system for ideas. Twenty years later, Japan had become the model. With many of Britain's economic partners in Europe headed in the same direction, it was only a matter of time before the Swedes followed suit. And sure enough, the difficulties faced by the Swedish economy by the end of the 1980s began to force the Social Democratic Party to abandon its policy of full employment and state-dominated welfare provision. Like the British Labour Party before it, the social democrats found themselves paving the way for a government of the right committed to privatisation and extensive cuts in public expenditure and taxation.

A NEW CONVERGENCE

Convergence theorists of the 1960s seemed to imply that all industrial societies, by virtue of their use of similar technologies, were developing similar social structures. In social policy terms this was taken to mean that all societies were moving towards an *institutional* welfare state (Mishra 1977: p. 38). This is clearly no longer, if it ever was, the case. On the contrary, it may be that what we are now witnessing is the development of a new convergence towards a welfare pluralism in which the state continues to play an important role. This convergence is the consequence of the dynamics of post-Fordist capitalism.

If welfare pluralism represents a sort of Japanisation of European welfare systems, it has to be recognised that Japan, during the 1980s, has not – like a model in a life class waiting for others to catch its likeness – stood still. A neglected but important factor in the Japanese state's low commitment to welfare provision has been demographic. In the 1970s the proportion of the population above the age of 65 was very low – less than 10 per cent. That percentage is set to rise to a figure identical to that of Sweden and Britain by 2020. At that time it is likely that all three countries will have elderly populations of about 20 per cent. By then, the Japanese authorities will have had to rethink their position on state welfare. The demands of the elderly for pensions, health care and social services will be too great for the family, volunteers and the firm to cope with.

Western capitalism will have learnt that the principles of the welfare state were too costly and involved too great a transfer of political and economic power to the middle and working classes. Japanese capitalism, however, will have learnt that there is a sort of remorseless logic about the state needing to take on more responsibilities for the welfare of its citizens. The gap between European welfare and Japanese welfare might have been enormous in 1970, but by the year 2020 the differences will be less marked.

The above has been a simplification of the main argument of this book, but in the chapters that follow, I hope to justify the argument in greater detail. But first it would be useful to examine those statistics, derived largely from international sources, which will enable readers to start off with a global picture of our three welfare systems.

INTERNATIONAL STATISTICS

The Organisation for Economic Cooperation and Development (OECD), the International Labour Office (ILO) and the United Nations (UN) collect data which enables us to make comparisons between Japan, the UK and Sweden over time. These have been supplemented where necessary with figures from national sources, but it is not possible to be as sure that these are as comparable as those drawn from the international agencies.

It can be seen from Table 1.1 that the public sector in Japan is much smaller than that of the UK and Sweden. The table concerns final consumption and excludes transfer payments such as social insurance. All three countries indicate an expansion of the public sector during the 1970s and a slight decline during the 1980s.

Japan, however, experienced greater economic growth rates during this time, as can be seen from the figures in Table 1.2 which indicate that the *per capita* GDP differences have narrowed, with Japan overtaking the UK for second place.

The ILO publishes data on the costs of social security every few years (Table 1.3) but recently these have fallen badly out of date. An attempt has therefore been made to use national sources to give some idea of more recent trends. As can be imagined, terms like *social security* and *social services* mean different things in different countries, but the ILO has gone to considerable lengths to ensure comparability. Social security here refers to public social insurance schemes, health care and social services, and social assistance. In

Table 1.1 Government final consumption expenditure as a percentage of gross domestic product (GDP)

	1970	1980	1989
Japan	7.4	9.8	9.3
UK	17.5	21.2	19.4
Sweden	21.6	29.0	26.2

Source: Adapted from OECD, *National Accounts 1960–1989*

Table 1.2 GDP *per capita* in US$ PPP (at purchasing power parity)

	1970	1984
Japan	3,169	12,419
UK	3,563	11,068
Sweden	4,976	15,434

Table 1.3 Social security expenditure as a percentage of GDP

	1970[1]	1980[1]	1983[1]	1990[2]	
Japan	5.3	10.8	12.0	14.0	(1988)
UK	13.7	17.3	20.5	20.5	(1990)
Sweden	18.6	31.9	33.3	35.2	(1989)

[1] *Source:* ILO, *The cost of social security 1981–3*
[2] *Source for Japan:* Adapted from *Japan Statistical Yearbook 1990*
Source for UK: Adapted from *UK National Accounts 1991*, HMSO
Source for Sweden: SCB *Statistisk Årsbok för Sverige 1992*

many countries, people's right to health care depends on social insurance contributions, but although British health care is financed from general taxation, it is still included.

The figures in the last column may, for Japan and Britain, exaggerate the true percentages by a small amount. It can be seen that the Japanese are now approaching the point reached by the UK and Sweden around 1970. What is significant about the Japanese figures is that they are rising at a faster rate than the expansion of over-65s in the population. This group constituted only 7 per cent of the population in 1970 but will rise from less than 12 per cent in 1990 to over 20 per cent by 2020. It is therefore likely that the percentage of GDP devoted to social security by 2020 will be in excess of 20 per cent. The British and Swedish figures have now levelled out, but are unlikely to be substantially reduced because their populations too are ageing, albeit at a much slower rate.

ILO figures also show the distribution of different types of benefit which, when related to GDP, suggest that the Japanese in 1983 devoted less than a tenth of 1 per cent to family allowances, while the percentages for both Britain and Sweden were 1.5 per cent. Similarly, only 1.3 per cent of GDP was being spent on social assistance and social services in Japan in 1983, while in the UK the figure was 4.5 per cent and for the Swedes 5.6 per cent. The vast bulk of social security expenditure for each country (around 65 per cent) was devoted to social insurance including pensions and health care (ILO 1988).

For both the UK and Sweden, health care is dominated by public provision - around 90 per cent – whereas in Japan public provision constitutes only 70 per cent of the total. But the percentages of GDP devoted to health care as a whole are not so different for the UK and Japan. Sweden is a considerably greater spender than the other two in this area (Table 1.4). In real terms the Japanese have overtaken the British in terms of *per capita* GDP devoted to health care, but Sweden devotes more than twice as much to each citizen than Britain and almost twice as much as Japan (OECD 1987). These broad differences, however, conceal greater differences in terms of what the resources are actually devoted to. The Swedish health care system employed nearly 8 per cent of the work-force in the early 1980s, the British over 5 per cent (each reflecting a similar percentage

Table 1.4 Total expenditure on health as a percentage of GDP

	1970	1980	1984[1]
Japan	4.6	6.4	6.6
UK	4.5	5.8	5.9
Sweden	7.2	9.5	9.4

Sources: OECD (1985), *Measuring Health Care 1960–83*
[1] OECD (1987), *Financing and Delivering Health Care*

Table 1.5 Infant mortality and life expectancy

	Japan		UK		Sweden	
Infant deaths per 1,000 live births	5.5	('85)	9.5	('86)	5.9	('86)
Life expectancy at birth[1]: males	74.8	('84)	71.3	('82)	73.5	('82)
females	80.7	('84)	77.3	('82)	79.6	('82)

Sources: OECD (1987), *Financing and Delivering Health Care*
[1] *World Health Organisation Statistics, 1987/8*

of the GDP devoted to health care as illustrated in Table 1.4). The Japanese, however, employed less than 3 per cent (OECD 1987). The Swedes had more doctors per 1,000 of the population in the early 1980s than did the British and the Japanese (2.4, 1.4, 1.3 respectively), but Japanese doctors were paid around twice as much in real terms as their European counterparts (OECD 1987).

In spite of the greater amount devoted to health care in Sweden, it is the Japanese who dominate the league tables in important indices of health (Table 1.5). The very low infant mortality figures for Japan have to be qualified by saying that it is likely that they are slightly exaggerated. The Japanese figures have for many years shown a much larger ratio of late foetal deaths to early natal deaths. This is due to the Japanese use of a different definition of what constitutes an early natal death compared with many other countries (WHO 1978). None the less, if we take peri-natal infant mortality as the more precise measure, Sweden comes only marginally ahead of the Japanese. Unless Japanese high abortion rates influence these figures further (see chapter 3) it would seem that Japanese people are remarkably healthy compared with a country like Sweden which is considerably less polluted and congested, and which is the second highest health care spender in the world.

The proportions of GDP spent on education reflect a similar pattern to the health expenditure figures (see Table 1.6). Each of the three countries seems to have increased expenditure in the 1970s and tailed off in the 1980s. In the mid-1980s over 2.5 per cent of the Swedish population was enrolled in tertiary education, 2.0 per cent of the Japanese and only 1.5 per cent of the British (UNESCO 1988). It is likely that the British have at last woken up to the need for a mass system of higher education, with the result that the gap referred to above may begin to close somewhat.

Another gap that is likely to close is the proportion of elderly people in each population. This factor more than any other will

Table 1.6 Education expenditure as a percentage of GDP

	1970	1980	1985	
Japan	3.9	5.8	5.1	
UK	5.3	5.8	5.2	('84)
Sweden	6.2	9.5	7.6	('86)

Source: UNESCO Statistical Yearbook

Table 1.7   Selected population characteristics

	Percentage of the population above the age of 65[1]			Total population (millions)	Pop'n density per km²
	1980	*2010*	*2030*	*1988*	*1988*
Japan	9.0	18.6	20.0	122.6[2]	325[2]
UK	14.8	14.6	19.2	57.1[2]	233[2]
Sweden	16.2	17.5	21.7	8.5[3]	19[3]

Sources: [1] OECD (1987), *Finance and Delivery of Health Care*
     [2] *Social Trends*, HMSO, 1991
     [3] SCB *Statistisk Årsbok 1990*

have a major impact on Japan. As can be seen from Table 1.7, in 1980 only 9 per cent of the Japanese population was above the age of 65, much lower than the European figures. But by the year 2030, all three will be in a very similar position, with similar implications for the welfare costs of pensions, health care and social services. It is clear also from Table 1.7 that our three countries are very different in terms of population size and density. One would expect from this to find that it would be relatively easy for the Swedes to cope with social problems which are likely to be more severe in countries with the urban congestion of Britain and Japan.

Many of the above figures show that the growth in social expenditure in Britain and Sweden has slowed to a halt. In these two countries cuts are having to be made in some areas in order to pay for the higher costs of unemployment and the continuing, albeit modest, growth in the elderly population. In the future Sweden, like Britain in the 1980s, will be looking for ways to privatise some aspects of welfare or place a greater reliance on informal and voluntary welfare. In Japan too the government would very much like to keep the lid on public expenditure as a whole and social expenditure in particular. Unfortunately for Japan, it now faces a rapid increase in the elderly population and the state will not be able to avoid the consequences.

THE PLAN OF THIS BOOK

This book has been written in three parts, one for each country. Since the main thesis is that the welfare systems of Britain and Sweden are moving closer to the Japanese model, Japan is the starting-point. Britain follows, since the abandonment of the welfare state and the adoption of a more pluralistic system began there in the late 1970s. The Swedish section comes last because of Sweden's reluctance to depart from the principles upon which its welfare state was built.

Within each part there will be four chapters. The first will select those important factors – economic, political and social – which have contributed to the development of each welfare system. The second chapter will outline the existing structure of social security, health care and social services. It will discuss how these developed prior to the 1970s and what major changes have taken place in the last twenty years in particular. The third chapter will do much the same thing for education and employment services. The fourth chapter will examine different accounts of the nature and development of the three welfare systems and offer the author's own account based upon the material presented in the previous three. Although there are no strict cut-off points in terms of time, the period under consideration is roughly 1973–1992, thus making it possible to take the results of the recent central government elections in Sweden and Britain into account.

In a concluding chapter the findings of this study will be related to the wider literature on comparative social policy. This will be done through a commentary on the twelve theses, presented by Pierson in *Beyond the Welfare State*, which summarise the basic theoretical positions advanced in comparative social policy over the last decade or so (Pierson 1991: chs 1–4).

PART ONE
Japan

CHAPTER TWO

Economic, political and social context

It is impossible to make sense of welfare systems in isolation. Some background is necessary to understand the context in which social policies function and change. Obviously some selection has to be made, but it is the aim of this chapter, chapter 6 and chapter 10, to provide the reader with significant facts and features without which it is felt that welfare developments in Japan, Britain and Sweden would make little sense. The structure in each of these background chapters is similar, with some attention being given initially to the nature of industrialisation in each country and post-1945 economic and political developments. Brief accounts of the nature of the different labour movements and of political processes are also given. These are followed by attempts to mention some of the salient features of each country's cultural characteristics and social divisions, concluding with references to important demographic changes.

INDUSTRIALISATION AND THE IMPACT OF WAR

When, in the middle of the nineteenth century, the USA forced Japan to open up its borders to trade with the industrialised countries of the West, Japan had been a highly sophisticated society for centuries. The humiliation of having to accept the strength and authority of an alien power simply because it was technologically, economically and militarily superior had a profound impact. This traumatic event led to a determination amongst members of the Japanese ruling class that the country would have to modernise in order to compete with and achieve comparable status with other capitalist powers. Barrington Moore's thesis that Japan was a country in which

19

industrialisation was precipitated by an upper-class revolution is very relevant here, since it helps us to understand many of the characteristics of Japan's subsequent development, as well as the generally right-wing environment in which Japanese politics operates (Moore 1973).

Determined to catch up with the West, the country set about emulating the successful features of other social systems. Germany in particular seemed to offer the sort of model which the Japanese wanted to copy – hierarchical, militaristic, technologically advanced and economically successful. The social problems which economic development brought in its wake did little to encourage Japanese governments to develop appropriate systems of welfare. In the early years of the twentieth century attempts to form trade unions and socialist parties were ruthlessly put down, thus preventing any serious articulation of working-class needs. Only with the rice riots following the First World War did Japan begin to introduce, albeit reluctantly, measures of state welfare and an extension of suffrage to the male population. At the same time, however, the Peace Preservation Law of 1926 added 'new layers of control over political activity' (Steinhoff 1989: p. 173). Although this piece of legislation was intended to be used against communists and those dedicated to the overthrow of capitalism, it was applied to those on the left generally.

Militarisation in the inter-war years, the invasion of China and other countries in the Far East, brought Japan into open conflict with Western powers. By the end of the Second World War, Japan suffered its second humiliation at the hands of the Americans. The Occupation which followed saw a determination on the part of the Americans to introduce a range of liberal reforms aimed at reducing the militaristic and nationalistic aspects of Japanese society. The powerful private industrial groups which had formed a significant part of Japan's military efforts, the Zaibatsu, were broken up; trade unions were made legal; schools became co-educational, teachers were re-educated, and the curriculum democratised. Japan became a multi-party parliamentary democracy, with a two-chamber parliament. The independence of local authorities was guaranteed. The head of state, the emperor, was divested of his supposed divinity.

POST-1945 ECONOMIC DEVELOPMENT

From that period a number of important state welfare measures were enacted and socialist governments were elected for the first time. The

Occupation by the Americans had brought much-needed democratic reforms, many of which became firmly established. Events were to change with the outbreak of the Korean War when Japan became an indispensable ally to the American and UN troops. The USA had already begun to lose its enthusiasm for progressive reform and developed a more tolerant view of the conservative forces in Japanese society. The country became a base for the war effort and a major provider of goods and services for the military. The boost to the economy was enormous. The Korean War was Japan's springboard to economic regeneration. From a country notorious for its cheap imitations in the early decades after the war, Japan became first a major competitor with Western capitalist countries in the fields of shipbuilding, cars and electronics and subsequently a major world economic power with a GNP second only to that of the United States.

During the 1950s and 1960s growth rates averaged around 10 per cent (Tasker 1987: p. 47) and dropped to around 3 to 5 per cent after 1973 and the first oil crisis (Soeda 1991). The economy remained strong and adaptable, however. Japan has little in the way of natural resources and it was expected that the oil price increases in 1973 would strike a severe blow to its economic development. In the event, Japan began to expand its overseas activities, establishing firms in Britain and many other Western countries, while buying up considerable amounts of property in the USA itself.

THE SUCCESS OF THE JAPANESE ECONOMY

Tasker (1987: ch. 3) has explained the success of the Japanese economy in terms of its framework of low taxation and low interest rates and a high propensity for saving and capital formation. He suggested that shareholder interests and short-term profits were of less importance to companies than stable long-term growth and an increase in market dominance. In these aims companies were aided by shareholders earning a low return on their capital and employees not making excessive wage demands. While to a degree it can be argued that shareholders and employees accept such strategies as part of the corporate consensus, their acceptance can also be explained by degrees of manipulation and force. Shareholders who object to company policy at annual general meetings are dealt with by the Japanese mafia, the Yakuza (*ibid.*: pp. 88–9); while employees who refuse to accept the cosy deals of enterprise unions and management are also severely dealt with by both (Kamata 1983).

Others argue that it is illegitimate to 'equate hierarchy with exploitation and domination' (Dore 1987). Dore sees Japanese capitalism as having taken a quite different form from the market-dominated capitalisms of the West. Largely as a consequence of its late development, the state has taken a dominant role in the economy, and large companies have taken a more communal attitude towards their employees. The result is a paternalism in which it is felt that national and corporate goals take precedence over short-term, narrow self-interest. At the national level, this means that a norm is agreed for pay rises, which keeps inflation low in spite of full employment. At the level of the firm, security and stability become more important than the prospect of higher wages elsewhere. Employers can invest in training without the fear of their workers being poached; employees accept flexible work patterns without the need to defend job demarcations based on craft and skill. Dore argues that the mutual commitment of employers and employees, of management and worker, leads to a greater degree of motivation and efficiency than do labour relations based upon narrow, market criteria (Dore 1987).

Japanese economic success can then be attributed in part to the status and security enjoyed by workers as lifetime employees. To the extent that it exists and is genuine, lifetime employment does seem to lead to a mutual commitment. Employers are reluctant to make workers redundant except in the most severe economic conditions. Employees are willing to cooperate with management to achieve the firm's goals. There are said to be hierarchical differences between status groups within the firm but not sharp divisions between manual and non-manual workers. This cohesion is advanced by the existence of extensive programmes of enterprise welfare (see chapter 3) supported by and negotiated with enterprise trade unions. However, estimates of lifetime employment suggest that less than 30 per cent of the work-force (Drucker 1978: p. 571; Tasker 1987: p. 109) enjoy this status. Moreover, those who do not enjoy lifetime employment are not only likely to work for small and family businesses for much lower rewards and welfare benefits, but they are also less likely to have a trade union to protect their interests.

TRADE UNIONS IN JAPAN

Japan remains a country in which employees are poorly organised. While 80 per cent of government employees and nearly 70 per cent of employees in large firms were members of trade unions in 1975

(Stevens 1988: p. 105), only a third of all workers belonged to trade unions. Since that time unionisation has dropped from 33.2 per cent in 1977 to 27.6 per cent in 1987 (Ohta 1988: p. 638). Over two-thirds of employees, then, are neither employed for life nor unionised.

Until recently trade unions in Japan affiliated either to the Sohyo or the Domei confederations. The former represented those who were members of nationally based trade unions while the latter represented those who were members of enterprise trade unions. Sohyo was strongly associated with the Japan Socialist Party while Domei had strong links with the Democratic Socialist Party. The two have now amalgamated in a single confederation, Rengo (Eccleston 1989: p. 260). Since 80 per cent of all trade unions are enterprise unions (Shirai 1984: p. 308), Rengo clearly speaks mainly for them.

While it may be correct to emphasise the loyalty which workers owe to their firms as the basis for labour discipline in Japan, one might equally argue that it is due to the low level of unionisation, the fragmentation of trade-union organisation, and the dominance of enterprise trade unions.

THE POLITICAL SCENE

After an initial post-war flirtation with social democracy, the Japanese have consistently elected the conservative Liberal Democratic Party (LDP) to office. The other parties have never been in a position to form a government even through an alliance. The left opposition is divided between the Japan Socialist Party, the Democratic Socialist Party and the Japan Communist Party. The Buddhist Clean Government Party, Komeito, occupying the centre ground, accounts for only a small percentage of the vote in national elections. None of these parties comes remotely near to forming a government in its own right and even an alliance between any of them seems a dim possibility (see Table 2.1 below).

While the LDP has clearly far more support than any other party, its strength is also aided by advantages of varying degrees of corruption. Rural support for the LDP is to a large extent due to extensive rice subsidies. The LDP's refusal to revise electoral boundaries as the population has shifted from the country to the cities means that its true support in terms of parliamentary seats is exaggerated (Steinhoff 1989). Moreover, the factional structure of the LDP seems to have resulted in a number of financial scandals.

Table 2.1 The popular vote for House of Representatives elections 1960–86

	1960	1976	1980	1986
Parties of the right				
LDP	57.6	41.8	47.9	49.4
NLC★	–	4.2	3.0	1.8
Total	57.6	46.0	50.9	51.2
Parties of the left				
JSP	27.6	20.7	19.3	17.2
DSP	8.8	6.3	6.6	6.4
JCP	2.9	10.4	9.8	8.8
Total	39.3	37.4	35.7	32.4
Komeito	–	10.9	9.0	9.4
Total opposition	39.3	48.3	44.7	41.8

★New Liberal Club
Source: Adapted from Baerwald 1986

A characteristic of Japanese political parties which is difficult for a foreign observer to understand concerns this existence of factions within the parties. Whereas groups within political parties in the West are formed for reasons of policy and ideology, in Japan it would seem that the factions are more a matter of personal loyalty. As will be seen in the section on culture below, group orientation is said to be an important feature of Japanese life. Political factions seem to be a channel for fund-raising and the dispensing of favours, so much so that they also become vehicles for widespread corruption. In the wake of the Lockheed scandal in the 1970s, the prime minister resigned his official post, but was widely recognised for years as being the leader of the LDP's most important faction and therefore the most powerful figure within the party. Similar scandals in the 1980s, which resulted in the resignations of a number of ministers, did not prevent the LDP from being elected in 1990. Indeed it was reported at the time that the success of the LDP was because of the financial favours it dispensed and in spite of public recognition of the extent of bribery and corruption. Tasker has stated that even the Yakuza 'has access to some of Japan's leading politicians' (Tasker 1987: p. 91). In 1992 the opposition parties refused to cooperate over the national budget because of further allegations of financial corruption.

It is also important to note that the development of social welfare programmes has never been a priority for the LDP. 'Production First' was the motto of the post-war decades. At that moment in time when it appeared that the government had at last recognised that the Japanese people deserved an emphasis upon their social welfare, the 1973 oil crisis provided first an excuse to hold back and, subsequently, reasons for refusing to go down the path of extensive state welfare provision. As commentators in Western countries began to talk more and more of their welfare states as a burden, so there seemed to be good cause for avoiding the same fate. Instead the official Japanese line claimed that Japan did not need to emulate the West on matters of welfare. Its own unique culture and institutions qualified Japan to call itself a welfare society, since much of what was provided in the West by the state was, in Japan, provided by the family, the community and the firm.

BUSINESS, BUREAUCRACY AND GOVERNMENT

The neglect of social issues by government should not be taken to signify a distaste for state intervention as such. The Japanese state is built on corporatist rather than laissez-faire assumptions. But the style of corporatism preferred is one which relegates trade unions to a minor role. It would seem that there are only a few advisory committees on which representatives of the work-force sit, but a much larger number on which employers are represented.

Business interests then are very much part of the policy-making process. In particular, the close cooperation between business leaders and the bureaucrats of the Ministry of International Trade and Industry (MITI) is often cited as a very successful example of state direction of a capitalist economy. The bureaucrats in the Japanese state, especially those in MITI, are seen as the cream of the country's intelligentsia. Their views on the present state and future direction of the economy are respected both by politicians and employers. In place of European tri-partism, you have here a 'triad' of senior civil servants, ministers and business leaders in which

> The businessmen have influence over the politicians, the politicians control the bureaucracy and the bureaucrats keep the businessmen in line. It's a natural system of checks and balances.
>
> (Quoted in Fukushima 1989: p. 255)

The links between the three are not of a formal kind only. A large proportion of LDP members of parliament are ex-bureaucrats. Many senior bureaucrats are appointed to the boards of large companies when they retire. Bureaucracy and big business seek to recruit the most able graduates of Tokyo University, although in the view of some, the most able of the graduates will prefer the prestige of a career in the civil service to one in industry or commerce, in spite of the much lower material reward (Dore 1987). Dore also suggests that as a result of Japan's late economic development, many Japanese firms were established on bureaucratic principles and that this is one of the reasons why seniority, educational level and incremental wage increases are such an important feature of large companies in Japan.

While the views of bureaucrats on economic and industrial matters would seem to be highly regarded, this ought not to be taken to mean that their views on other matters are equally acceptable. Those in the Ministry of Health and Welfare have not been listened to to the same extent when they have advocated that Japan, like the West, ought to extend social policy programmes. They were successful to a degree in the 1970s but their 'efforts to rationalize the National Health Insurance system' have been resisted by LDP governments (Campbell 1989).

CULTURAL CHARACTERISTICS

Confucian values are often referred to when an attempt is being made to explain the essential differences between the Japanese approach to social organisation and the European. Dore seems to have in mind notions of fairness and equity, of a benevolent paternalism and familism, of a respect for authority, of good government and management, when he describes how Confucianism has been interpreted in Japan. Traditions and structures based upon such values are not easy to emulate but they do enable us to understand why political and managerial authority is more acceptable to the Japanese than in Britain, say, with its traditions of confrontation based on sectional and class interests. In Japan there is a greater sense of identity within social organisations, a genuine paternalism amongst employers, which is not always the same as authoritarianism, and a greater willingness on the part of employees to trust, accept and cooperate with authority.

Loyalty and obedience to one's group was discussed extensively by Benedict as far back as 1946 (Benedict 1946), but her observations have been echoed by more recent writers. Herman Kahn picked up similar ideas when making his prophecy of a Japanese super-state (Kahn 1971). Linked with notions of loyalty and obedience, group identity becomes a powerful force for socialisation. Nakane has described the difference between Western and Japanese culture in terms of the individual's identity in the former being a matter of *attribute* and in the latter a matter of *frame*. Attribute is said to emphasise the fact that as a student, an electrician, a manager one has much in common with other students, electricians and managers. Frame implies that the social organisation to which an individual belongs is of greater importance. A student is therefore first and foremost a member of a group, a school, a university; an electrician, a member of a work-group and a firm; a manager, a member of a different work-group, perhaps, but the same firm. The groups, families, institutions, organisations of which one is part are said to provide the basis for identity and loyalty (Nakane 1973).

These strong bonds of frame within a hierarchical setting form the basis for the argument that, in Japan, state welfare provision is hardly necessary since the individual is cared for and supported by his or her frame or group. The family cares for elderly people and the firm cares for its employees. Many trade unions also fall into this pattern, since they too are based upon the enterprise. A Japanese worker is more likely, therefore, to belong to a union whose identity is bound up with the fortunes of the firm than to a national union in which solidarity would derive from members in different firms having an overriding loyalty to each other.

Within each frame hierarchical distinctions become important. Within the family, women are subordinate to men, younger members subordinate to their elders. Within the firm there are clear distinctions to be found on the basis of sex, educational attainment and age. Moreover, organisations are also clearly ranked, so that one is aware of where one's school, university or firm fits in the appropriate league table.

Now these distinctions of frame, attribute and hierarchy cannot be said to be absolutes. Western societies can hardly be said to be unconcerned with hierarchy and rank. Employees in the West who attach more importance to the companies they work for than the national trade unions to which they belong clearly exist. Nevertheless there are good historical, structural and cultural reasons for accepting the basic distinctions between Western and Japanese orientations to social organisation made by Nakane and others.

It is not surprising to find that many commentators also have something to say about the sexist nature of Japanese society but also about Japanese hostility to other national and ethnic groups. If many Japanese see themselves as members of a superior nation, it follows that other peoples, nations and races are inferior. Strong group identity is bound to result in strong out-group hostility. Various writers have commented upon the difficulties that foreign visitors face in trying to get on social terms with the Japanese, the impossibility of acceptance by Korean immigrants and their descendants. What lends support to these assertions is the existence within the society of a pariah group, the Burakumin, who, though physiologically identical to the Japanese, are regarded as inferior, untouchable and on no account to be associated with – certainly not to be married into.

SOCIAL DIVISIONS

There is a tendency in much writing on Japan to explain social divisions in terms of culture – as acceptable aspects of social traditions which are basically functional rather than sources of conflict and instability – rather than the other way round. To others it seems to make much more sense to argue that the emphasis on cultural traditions of subordination and loyalty is a way of deflecting both participants and observers from discussing the power relationships that exist within the society (Dale 1986).

Rob Stevens has argued that the distinctions of age and sex within the family serve to legitimate the same distinctions operating within the firm. Family socialisation serves to justify employment status.

> There is little reason to doubt the general findings of a number of
> bourgeois studies that the Japanese working class sees the world
> primarily in terms of rank rather than class. It is widely documented
> that sex, age, education, and the size of the firm they are employed in
> are the uppermost considerations in workers' minds.
>
> (Stevens 1988: p. 105)

The distinctions of age, gender and education learnt within the family serve to reinforce the distinctions made between employees within and between firms. Whether the absence of working-class consciousness and solidarity is 'false' or not is not important here. What is of significance is that people find themselves embedded in a social structure that leads them to perceive the world in terms of finely graded hierarchical differences. Whether or not such structures have been consciously manipulated by employers or a 'ruling class' is also of little importance at the moment. I simply want to emphasise that the structures of Japanese society certainly seem to make the task of employers a lot easier.

It has already been shown that the labour 'movement' in Japan is weak. Socialist parties and trade unions are organised in a fragmented way. The predominance of enterprise-based unions rather than nationally based ones reinforces the identity of workers with the firms they work for. Lifetime manual employees, who constitute what Stevens describes as the labour aristocracy, make up little more than 12 per cent of manual workers. This 'aristocracy' is composed largely of young and middle-aged males. The rest of the manual work-force consists of full-time males and a large reserve army of temporary and part-time workers which is predominantly female, elderly and from minority groups.

Women are expected to 'retire' from full-time work when they get married or reach the age of 30. Their cash earnings per hour are about 50 per cent those of male employees. Their chances of promotion and training are significantly less than those of men and few can expect to reach leadership positions. Only 3 per cent of members of both chambers of parliament are women and few achieve cabinet rank.

Men are expected to 'retire' when they reach the age of 55, years before many of them are entitled to a pension. As a result they have to find further employment. Even if the employment they find is with the same firm which has employed them throughout their lives, their position becomes that of temporary workers who lose all of the status and seniority rights they previously enjoyed. Amongst those who are casual labourers there will be many who are either from Japan's small 'immigrant' community of Koreans or the Burakumin, Japan's outcaste group. Koreans amount to less than a million of the total population. The Buraku are officially estimated to consist of 'a million people living in grossly inadequate housing, earning very low incomes and experiencing very high rates of unemployment' (Eccleston 1989: p. 165). The international Minority Rights Group put the figure at 2 million in 1974 (De Vos 1974: p. 4) and argued that together with other groups

> a full four per cent of Japan's residents, or about 4,500,000 persons, suffer considerable discrimination, most as degraded minorities. This figure might be as high as five or sixteen per cent if we accept the

more liberal estimates of minority populations advanced by the leaders of minority group movements and would rise above ten per cent were we to broaden our implicit concept of the minority group.

(*Ibid.*: p. 4)

The picture of a homogeneous population enjoying meritocratic opportunities would seem to be justified only if one looks at the strictly Japanese male work-force. Income inequalities would seem to be similar to those in many European countries, not so wide as those in the USA but wider than those in Scandinavian countries. But the fact that unemployment benefit and social assistance are more restrictive than in the West, and minimum wage legislation is ignored, means that a 'wider range of jobs – jobs yielding a lower added-value at market valuations – are viable and on offer' (Dore 1987).

To argue that there are significant numbers of people in Japan who suffer from discrimination and inequality on the basis of occupational position, gender and minority status is to say no more than is said of most capitalist societies. However, the peculiarities of the Japanese system demonstrate that these disadvantages can be structured in such a way that social conflict is minimised.

Social divisions exist but do not seem to be interpreted or acted upon in the same way as in European countries. Ninety per cent of the population habitually describe themselves as middle-class in surveys. There is an acceptance of authority, of one's place in the home and in the hierarchy, which is not characteristic of more class-based, class-conflictual systems. While there may be a danger in exaggerating how pervasive, deep and lasting it is, few would deny that Japanese firms do create a greater sense of identity and commitment amongst their work-forces. Class cleavage is not so great and hierarchical differences have strong legitimacy in terms of fairness and equity. There is an egalitarianism which derives from enjoying a status as part of the firm, and even part of a common national purpose. There is the security that derives from a set of rules and procedures which bind employer and employee alike, and a sense of there being meritocratic opportunities in education and work.

It is possible to interpret this in terms of manipulation and false consciousness – the existence of punitive measures by the state and employers in the past would lend some justification to such a view. But it is not easy to dismiss a more consensual interpretation – that a significant majority of Japanese people consciously endorse a system of creative conservatism which has given many an enviable period of economic growth and social well-being.

What is certainly true is Dore's view that in Japan we can see a different form of capitalism which seems to inspire a greater sense of consensus and commitment and a higher degree of economic efficiency, than in many other countries characterised by a mixture of laissez-faire individualism on the one hand and social democratic notions of equality on the other (Dore 1987).

DEMOGRAPHIC FEATURES

Before we turn to examine the nature of the Japanese welfare system in some detail, some consideration must be given to important characteristics of the Japanese population, since some of the differences here between our three countries have important implications both for social problems and social polices.

Large parts of Japan are sparsely populated simply because the regions are mountainous. Its large (120 million) population is densely concentrated in particular urban areas. One third of the population inhabits 1 per cent of the land area (Tasker 1987: p. 73). This becomes an important consideration when one considers the quality of life of Japanese people. Land is at a premium. Housing of European dimensions is therefore extremely costly. Another consequence of population density is the comparative rarity of decent recreational facilities, be they public parks or sports facilities. Bennett and Levine (Patrick 1976: p. 452) remarked on the poor quality of housing in the early 1970s, claiming that Japan, in comparison with other Western capitalist societies, had the lowest number of rooms per person, the smallest size rooms, and the least number of houses without flush toilets. A decade later, an article refers to half the houses still not having flush toilets and reports that 'a third of all the houses in Tokyo at the end of the 1970s averaged only 3.5 square metres' (Dean 1986). A similar picture is presented by Tasker, who goes on to say that Tokyo has 'one twentieth of the park space per resident of Washington, one fifteenth that of London' (Tasker 1987: p. 75). Clearly neither space for housing nor for recreational purposes have been priorities for the Japanese authorities.

Of as great significance as density when it comes to social policy implications is the ageing of the Japanese population. Until recently, the Japanese government could claim that part of the reason for low state welfare expenditure was because the percentage of people above the age of 65 was low by European standards. In 1970 it was only

7 per cent (Ogawa 1982: p. 17), half that of Sweden and the UK. By the year 2000 it is expected to be 15 per cent and by 2020, 21 per cent, one of the highest in the world (Ogawa 1982: p. 19). Given that the elderly are the biggest consumers of welfare in the West, accounting for half the expenditure on social security, social services and health care, the implications for Japan are enormous. The tradition of families (i.e. daughters-in-law) looking after the elderly will find it very difficult to survive, especially as it is also likely that more women will join the labour market for jobs.

The ageing of the Japanese population is due to a decline in birth and death rates which has occurred in many other industrialised countries but nowhere more rapidly than Japan. The ratio of productive workers to the over-65s will decline from 7:1 in 1980 to 2.5:1 by the year 2015 (*Economist* 1983: p. 88). The higher percentage of elderly people inevitably means fewer productive workers to maintain themselves, their children and the aged. This situation will be even more serious given the official figures on life expectancy.

The Japanese authorities claim that on average Japanese men can now expect to live to 74.8 years and women until 80.4 compared with 50.1 and 54 respectively in 1947 (Tasker 1987: p. 125). These figures are the highest in the world. Given the pressure of life, the poor living conditions of many, the unremitting work-load of employees, the environmental pollution that the country has experienced in the post-war years of the economic miracle, these figures are quite remarkable, even if one does accept the likely benefits of a fish diet.

Even more difficult to imagine is the extremely low infant mortality rate. The most recent figures show that Japan has now surpassed the Scandinavian countries with 5.5 infant deaths per 1000 live births (WHO 1988). Reservations about low infant mortality rates in Japan have already been referred to (see chapter 1). Suffice to say that together with those for life expectancy they are used to justify the argument that the Japanese do not need the extensive state welfare programmes of the West since the social and cultural conditions they already enjoy obviously produce a very healthy population.

CONCLUSION

Japan's industrial revolution was engineered from the top. Political, business, administrative and militaristic élites consciously engineered modern Japanese society along nationalistic and authoritarian lines.

The militaristic ambitions were quelled by the outcome of the Pacific War in 1945, but the single-minded pursuit of economic success soon took their place. The results, not surprisingly, have been a source of considerable speculation in the West. It is clear that the Japanese deliberately set out to copy practices in the West which served the ruling élite's aims and interests. It is also apparent that whatever was copied was adapted to the idiosyncrasies of Japanese society itself, whether it was the German medical system or American business methods. So successful were these 'innovations' that it now became the turn of the West to emulate Japan. It is obvious that in so far as Japan's success has been due to Confucianism, Oriental family forms and cultural peculiarities which have taken centuries to develop, there was little profit in Western business, political and administrative leaders trying to transplant them. But certain features of Japanese society would not have gone unnoticed.

Socialist opposition parties are weak and divided. Strong independent trade unionism has not been allowed to develop, with the result that unionisation is low, the labour movement is fragmented and many unions are single-company unions which often share management's view of their members' interests. The privileges enjoyed by those who have lifetime employment ensure that the interests of the labour aristocracy are quite different from those of temporary and part-time workers. Conservative governments have employed many dubious practices to gain and retain political power. In making major decisions of policy they strive to achieve a corporatist consensus which involves business organisations and the state bureaucracy but which excludes trade unions. Moreover, the exercise of political power has always made economic and production objectives paramount. Social objectives are rarely treated as a priority. There is nothing here which cannot be transplanted to other capitalist societies.

It is difficult to deny that this successful form of capitalism has begun to have an effect on other societies. How much is a matter of argument. Dore has argued for a number of years that the late development effect in Japan has produced a prototype which other developing countries will follow, in preference to the model offered by Anglo-Saxon laissez-faire traditions on the one hand and continental corporatism on the other. More recently, he has argued strongly that in terms of industrialisation, and large, technological economic organisations, the British are going down the same path as the Japanese. He went further when he argued that 'Britain, too, might be moving towards a community model of the firm with

33

reduced mobility, more internally structured promotion systems and consequently more careful checking of ability potentials for recruitment purposes' (Dore 1987: p. 207). And, a little later: 'looking at Japan, as Japan is, can help us to see Britain, as Britain might be becoming' (Dore 1987: p. 210). What is more debatable is whether what Dore and others have argued in terms of the Japanese economy applies equally to its welfare system.

CHAPTER THREE

Health, social security and social services

INTRODUCTION

It has already been shown how Japan has developed economically to become one of the world's leading nations. Yet powerful forces in Japanese society have prevented Japan from expanding its state welfare to the same extent as many Western European states. This has been the result partly of a conservative political tradition which has resisted what it sees as a welfare burden that might jeopardise economic success. It is also because the development of the Japanese labour movement has been deliberately curtailed at crucial points in its history and as a result is too fragmented to challenge this tradition. These two factors are linked by a culture, emphasising duty, obligation, hierarchy and group solidarity, which has promoted alternatives to state welfare such as a reliance upon family care and enterprise welfare. But of crucial importance also is the fact that the proportion of elderly people – the largest consumers of welfare services and benefits – in Japan has, hitherto, been very small.

WELFARE DEVELOPMENTS PRIOR TO 1973

State welfare in Japan only really began to develop in the years between the two World Wars. After the Meiji restoration in 1868 relief regulations for the poor were established in 1874. A Factory Act passed in 1911 and a Popular Life Insurance Law in 1916. But it was only in response to the rice riots of 1918 that the government introduced the first genuine social security measure, the Health Insurance Act of 1922. This was, however, accompanied by a legislation to 'regulate extremist movements', the Peace Preservation Law of 1926, which made it possible for left-wing organisations to be banned. With a minimal scheme to help the unemployed in 1935, the establishment of a Ministry of Welfare in 1938, and pensions insurance legislation in 1941, it could be said that Japan had begun to lay the foundations of state welfare before 1945.

After the American Occupation a number of measures were enacted to promote the idea that the state had wider responsibilities in the field of welfare. These included the Workmen's Accident Compensation Law which was passed in 1947, the Unemployment Insurance Law of 1947, and a measure to provide means-tested social assistance, the Livelihood Protection Law of 1950. In subsequent years legislation was introduced which ensured that the mass of the population was covered by some form of health and pensions insurance. Casual labourers, organised in new trade unions, fought for a health insurance scheme in the 1950s which resulted in a Health Insurance Scheme for Day Labourers in 1953 (Takahashi 1973: p. 452). Subsequently the National Health Insurance Law of 1958 and the National Pensions Law of 1959 were passed. Eligibility for social assistance was widened and a range of social services established. In 1972, child allowances were introduced for the first time, but for the second and subsequent children only (Foreign Press Centre 1988).

By the early 1970s Japan had a social security system which covered virtually the whole population, but the benefits were considered by many to be very low. Pressure from civil servants in the Ministry of Health and Welfare, pressure groups and political parties insisted that after years of unprecedented economic growth people were entitled to a European-style welfare state. Although the LDP continued to be the party of government throughout the decade, it found its electoral support dwindling. Support for the socialist parties increased in general elections but was most marked in urban local authorities where the left was able to form a majority. These municipalities and prefectures were now able to introduce policies at a local level as a direct challenge to the reluctance of central government to act in social matters (Tabata 1991).

As already mentioned (Table 1.3), public expenditure on social security doubled between 1970 and 1980. Unfortunately the decision by the government to make 1973 the 'first year of welfare' coincided with the Arab–Israeli war, the oil crisis and the subsequent world-wide recession. Economic growth in Japan slowed down from an average of 10 per cent in the 1960s to between 3 and 5 per cent in the latter part of the 1970s (Soeda 1991). Reluctant to raise taxation or social insurance contributions, the government borrowed to finance increased social expenditure and government deficits began to mount.

By the end of the 1970s, the political climate began to change. The electoral fortunes of the LDP revived and the socialist threat diminished. The pressures for a European-style welfare state receded. Many Japanese workers and their unions had never been fully convinced that such an institution was necessary anyway. Happy with the existing state and company benefits to which they were entitled, they were not convinced by the idea that their taxes and contributions should pay for the benefits of those less fortunate or perhaps less deserving than themselves. The government felt able to produce a new seven-year plan in which the idea of a welfare state was abandoned and that of a 'Japanese-type welfare society' was introduced that would be equipped with 'a proper system of public welfare built on the basis of self-help efforts of individuals and co-operation within families and communities' (quoted in Tabata 1991). As Tabata went on to argue, 'the plan was clearly bent on cutting down benefits and reducing the role of the public social security system' (*ibid.*: p. 17).

But as can be seen from the more detailed account below, the government was not embarked on a new course. In abandoning the idea of a welfare state in favour of welfare pluralism, the government was merely reverting to the pattern that had already been established in Japan prior to 1973.

SOCIAL SECURITY

It has been argued that, by 1973, state welfare in Japan was fairly extensive but that by European standards the benefits and services remained minimal. Moreover the coverage and benefits of the social security system varied considerably, depending upon a person's occupational status. The state had required firms of a certain size to provide contributory pension and health schemes for employees. Employers and employees had to contribute a similar percentage of the employee's income with the state making a contribution as well. The funds of the Employees' Pension Insurance (EPI) scheme were administered either by employers or groups of employers or by government agencies, depending upon the size of the employing establishment. Mutual Aid Associations (MAA) administered separate schemes for central and local government employees. Both the EPI and the MAA schemes provided earnings-related pensions to their members. Apart from some small schemes for specific occupational groups, the remainder of the population were covered by a residual flat-rate National Pension Insurance (NPI) scheme administered by local authorities. It is clear that benefits from these different schemes varied a great deal. Those employed by large companies, which contributed more to their employees' schemes than the minimum laid down by the state, received very good benefits. Schemes for civil servants and local government officers were also fairly generous. Those in small companies received lesser benefits, while those in the national schemes were the most disadvantaged. It is therefore important to examine a little more closely the main differences between the principal schemes.

Pensions insurance

The proportion of those individuals contributing to the different schemes can be illustrated by more recent figures for the 1980s, outlined in Table 3.1. Because the EPI schemes have not yet matured, the proportion of those contributing at the time is lower than those who are actually benefiting from the schemes. It can be seen from the table that the proportion of contributors to EPI in 1980 was just over 40 per cent but that by 1986 this had risen to 46 per cent. EPI beneficiaries were only 16 per cent of the total of all beneficiaries in

Table 3.1   The structure of Japanese old-age pension schemes

Schemes	1980 [1]		1986 [2]	
	% contr's	% bene's	% contr's	% bene's
EPI society- and government-managed	42	16	46	27
MAA schemes for state employees	8	9	9	13
NPI schemes managed by local authorities	47	73	43	57
Other	2	1	2	2

Sources: [1] Noguchi 1986
[2] Foreign Press Centre 1988

1980 but amounted to more than a quarter six years later. During the same period NPI beneficiaries fell from 73 per cent to 57 per cent. It is clear that although the majority of those retiring are still receiving only an NPI pension, a growing proportion are receiving an earnings-related benefit.

In the early 1970s, Fisher had claimed that the income replacement levels of these schemes had failed to keep pace with economic growth and inflation. Moreover, full-time workers in large firms had the added advantage of an allowance which on retirement at the age of 55 gave the beneficiary a lump sum equivalent to one month's salary for every year worked. The disparity between those EPI contributors who received earnings-related pensions as well as retirement allowances and the rest of the population meant that talk of unifying the EPI and NPI schemes was bound to pose severe difficulties. Yet social security advisers and civil servants in the Ministry of Health and Welfare felt that there was little hope of providing decent pensions for the lower paid as long as the two systems remained separate.

The other complicating feature of these different pension schemes was that the retirement ages were also different. EPI members in the private sector were entitled to receive their pensions at the age of 60 but retired at 55, state employees retired at 60, and those in NPI had to wait until they were 65 for their pensions.

The government was faced in the 1970s with three main problems: the adequacy of pension levels, the different retirement ages of the various schemes, and the lack of any kind of redistributive mechanism to prevent NPI from falling into deficit. Over the next decade each of these problems was tackled, initially by a government willing to increase social expenditure, but subsequently, in the 1980s, by a government fearful of the financial consequences of an ageing population. In 1973 a decision was taken to raise pensions annually at the same rate as the rate of inflation. Moreover both EPI and NPI pensions were almost doubled, thus giving those few who had made the maximum contributions a pension equivalent to 60 per cent of an average employee's earnings. These earnings, however, excluded bonuses of around 30 per cent, so that the real, gross income replacement level of EPI was just over 40 per cent – a considerable improvement on what had gone before, however, and a reform of some expense to the treasury (Tabata 1991: p. 13).

On the question of different retirement ages some progress was also made. In 1979 legislation was passed which raised the age at which public employees could receive their pensions from 55 to 60. The following year the age of entitlement for men in the EPI schemes was to be raised from 60 to 65 over a fifteen-year period. Such a reform would have meant less cash going out to pensions and extra contributions coming into the system. The political hostility this has generated seems to have delayed the reform somewhat (Tabata 1991: p. 25).

But the major change in the system was the introduction in 1985 of an old-age, disability and survivor's pension for all which was to form the basis of both EPI and NPI. The distinction between the two was to be the earnings-related element which remained part of the EPI scheme only. The new basic pension would in the future be funded by all contributors and thus be assured of a more secure financial basis (Ministry of Health and Welfare 1985). At the same time benefits were reduced and contributions increased in order to prepare for the ageing society and equalise the burden between the generations (Tabata 1991: pp. 23–4). For EPI contributions now had to be made over 40 years rather than the original 25.[2] Of particular importance was the fact that wives for the first time were allowed a pension in their own right even though they might not have contributed to any scheme. Previously full-time housewives and divorcees had had no right to a separate pension and were dependent upon their husbands' and ex-husbands' pensions. Widows had been entitled to half their husband's pension on his death but not to a pension in their own right when he was alive (Foreign Press Centre 1988). Another important change in 1982 made it possible for non-nationals to participate in NPI (Ministry of Health and Welfare 1985).

It is important to note that the basic pension is still dependent upon a minimum contributions record of 25 years and is reduced proportionately if these have not been paid. In 1987 the basic pension amounted to ¥52,000 (£208 approx.) a month for a single adult. The average monthly pension for a married couple where the husband received a pension under both EPI and the Basic NPI pension and the wife received only the latter was ¥185,000 (£740) a month, compared with ¥104,000 (£416) for a couple on NPI only.

In addition to the state regulated schemes, there are employers who offer their staff additional pensions as well as the retirement allowances already referred to. Whereas over 70 per cent of large companies give their permanent staff an additional pension and a retirement allowance, less than 30 per cent of companies employing between 30 and 99 people do so. Figures are not available for companies employing less than 30. But it is not simply the size of the company that is important but the age that one graduated from the education system – after junior high school, senior high school or university. The retirement allowances for university graduates are roughly twice that of junior high-school leavers (Foreign Press Centre 1988).

It is also interesting to note that the government is now trying to encourage employees in large companies to opt out of EPI into private and occupational schemes, in the belief that this will aid capital accumulation in the future. There is a real worry that as the population ages, savings reserves will dwindle. By 2020 it is thought that Japan will have become a net debtor in the world economy with consequences for increased unemployment and the costs that that will entail. It is these wider economic worries that lie behind the need to reform and rationalise the pensions system.[3]

It can be seen from the above that although pension benefits overall have grown, and a greater degree of equity now exists with the introduction of the basic pension, the government in the 1980s has raised the pension age for some schemes in order to ensure that there will be greater contributions to cover the increased costs of old-age pensions in the future. What is also clear is the enormous importance of becoming a lifetime employee with a large firm. Not only is your company likely to increase its contributions to your EPI pension, but also the retirement allowance will depend very much on the company you work for and when you left the education system. Since relatively few women become lifetime employees, it is also important which sex you are.

Health insurance

Health insurance schemes which covered virtually the entire population in 1971 also included a scheme for employees working in establishments of more than five persons – Employees Health Insurance (EHI). Those working for small firms contributed to government-managed schemes, those in larger firms contributed towards 1400 society-managed schemes. Government employees were in separate schemes while the rest of the population was covered by National Health Insurance (NHI) administered by the local authorities. In Table 3.2 the different schemes are listed, together with the percentage of contributors in each. The figures relate to 1985 rather than the early 1970s but they give some idea of the relative importance of each scheme today.

As with EPI, large private employers topped up their EHI schemes more generously than could smaller employers (Takahashi 1973: p. 459, Fisher 1973: p. 34, Foreign Press Centre 1988; p. 36). State employees were quite well covered, but those in NHI, still almost

Table 3.2 The structure of Japanese health
insurance schemes

Schemes	1985 % insured
EHI Society-managed and government-managed } schemes for state employees	35
	7
NHI schemes managed by local authorities	57
Other	1

Source: Foreign Press Centre 1988

60 per cent, even in the 1980s, received inferior benefits. Prior to
1973 those in EHI had to pay nothing towards their own medical
expenses, but they had to pay 50 per cent of their dependants' health
bills, while those in NHI had to pay 50 per cent of the bills
for their dependants and for themselves. EHI beneficiaries qualified
for a cash sickness benefit (of 60 per cent of earnings for up to six
months according to Takahashi 1973: p. 461) but not those in NHI
(Lee 1987: p. 254). Takahashi reported that in none of the schemes
were the medical expenses of pregnant women covered since they
were not ill (Takahashi 1973: p. 458).

The principal problem posed by this system was that increasingly
the NHI scheme was in deficit because it consisted of those on the
lowest incomes and those who had the highest health risks. It must be
remembered that on reaching the age of 55, many members of EHI
would leave secure employment and thus become eligible only for the
NHI scheme. NHI has always had to provide disproportionately for
the needs of the elderly. Without an element of subsidy, NHI was
always in financial difficulty, which Ministry of Welfare officials could
see, as could various government commissions. Government action was
limited by the fact that both large employers and their employees were
very attached to a system which preserved particular advantages for
their labour forces – their lifetime employees (Fisher 1973: p. 34).

Nevertheless, Fisher remarked at the end of his description of
Japanese social security in 1973 that: 'It would seem that Japan is
on the threshold of a significant improvement of its social security
system' (Fisher 1973: p. 38). Free health care was granted to
the elderly above the age of 70 from 1973. Some socialist local
authorities had already introduced such measures independently

of central government and they proved extremely popular. The government was forced to go down the same road. Local authorities had been able to take such a measure precisely because they had a responsibility for the administration of NHI and the vast majority of elderly people were part of the NHI system. In the same year the proportion of medical bills which had to be paid for by NHI members and their dependants was reduced from 50 per cent to 30 per cent. The same reduction was made to the contribution made by EHI members to the medical bills of their dependants (Lee 1987: p. 254; Collick 1988: p. 215).

For the rest of the decade public expenditure on health care continued to increase, leading to considerable government concern. Elderly people, particularly those from low income groups, had taken expensive advantage of free medical care to get hospital places. The cost to NHI funds was great and a shortage of medical staff and facilities made meeting the demand very difficult (Foreign Press Centre 1988: p. 40). Amongst other things what this meant was that, offered the choice of being looked after free at the state's expense, many old people and/or their families had seized upon the opportunity to have free care whether their need was medical or not. This clearly showed that a need existed which families simply could not meet.

Although it was difficult to go back on the popular principle that the elderly should receive free health care, such an Act was passed in 1982 which introduced nominal charges for the over-70s. This was deemed sufficient to deter unnecessary use while falling a long way short of meeting the total costs. The significance of these growing costs is illustrated by the fact that, whereas in 1974 the proportion of the national medical care costs devoted to the elderly amounted to 12 per cent of the total, ten years later the figure was 24 per cent (Powell and Anesaki 1990: p. 97).

Another cost-saving measure was introduced in 1983. Whereas EHI contributors in the past had not been expected to make a contribution to the costs of their own medical care, from 1983 onwards they were expected to pay 10 per cent with the possibility that at a later date a further 10 per cent would be expected. Extra charges were also brought in for 'special treatment and medication' (Collick 1988: p. 230).

Collick regarded these measures, and those introduced after 1978 for pensions, as a levelling down for social security benefits even if they did introduce a greater element of fairness. The abolition of free medical care for the aged marked, he said, 'the beginning of a period of serious decline in the provision of publicly insured health care' (Collick 1988: p. 230).

Whereas the hope in 1973 had been to emulate the West, by the 1980s, saddled with commitments already entered into and the need for benefit rises in line with inflation, the Japanese authorities were concerned that all efforts should be made to keep the future growth of social security expenditure under strict control.

Other social security benefits

Some effort has gone into ensuring that Japan has a sound system of health and pensions insurance. But less attention has been given to other areas of income maintenance. Children's allowances, which were not introduced until 1972, are not paid for the first child. For the second child they amounted to a mere ¥2,500 (£10) a month in 1987 and ¥5,000 (£20) a month for the third and subsequent children. They were also only payable to those whose annual incomes were under ¥4 million (£16,000) (Foreign Press Centre 1988: p. 33).

Takahashi reported that nearly 21 million employees (out of a work-force of 58 million) were covered by the Unemployment Insurance Act of 1947. This scheme gave benefits which amounted to 60 per cent of income. Those employed for less than 5 years received benefit for only 3 months while those who had been employed for 20 years qualified for 10 months' benefit. Since the majority of employees in these schemes were rarely unemployed the scheme was in surplus (Takahashi 1973: p. 465).

Casual day labourers were organised in a separate scheme – only 320,000 of them in 1970 – and small employing establishments ran schemes for only 770,000 workers. Both benefits and duration of benefits were inferior in these schemes and, of course, the contributors were more vulnerable to unemployment.

Social assistance

Means-tested social assistance was introduced for the first time in 1946. Four years later the Livelihood Protection Act of 1950 widened its scope, and created a right of appeal. With the rest of the cash benefit system in its infancy it is not surprising that social assistance should have constituted around 50 per cent of the total social security budget in the decade after the war. The establishment of other income maintenance programmes inevitably reduced the importance of Livelihood Protection. However, an important concern in the

1960s, as with the rest of social security, was that the value of the benefit was being eroded in comparison with the increased prosperity which economic growth was bringing to the rest of the population. Soeda suggests that the Ministry of Finance tended to see poverty in absolute terms and could see little justification for increasing the value of Livelihood Protection. The Ministry of Health and Welfare bureaucrats, on the other hand, argued from their international experience that poverty was relative and that the poor had a right to a rising standard of living like others (Soeda 1991).

Between 1965 and 1973 Livelihood Protection was about 52 per cent of the average consumption expenditure of the lowest income quintile (Soeda 1991). Collick, using similar figures, claimed that by the 1970s, benefits were similar to those prevailing in Europe (Collick 1988: p. 211). Lee, however, emphasised that average consumer expenditure understated income since the Japanese are considerable savers. Nevertheless, he confirmed that the percentages referred to above had grown from 38 per cent in 1960 to 55 per cent in 1975 and 67 per cent in 1985 (Lee 1987). Soeda's figures for 1974–83 suggest an average of about 62 per cent (Soeda 1991: p. 51). The value of Livelihood Protection would seem to have improved relative to income in Japan by about 10 per cent in 1974. This was the same time as there were improvements in pensions and health benefits. It is clear also that the benefit must have kept pace with the years of high inflation (around 20 per cent) in the mid-1970s (Soeda 1991: p. 48).

If the value of the benefit has been maintained and can be compared with European levels, the same cannot be said for the numbers dependent on Livelihood Protection. Lee put the figure at about 1 per cent of the population in the mid-1980s. He also suggested that the numbers in receipt of Livelihood Protection was a third of those defined by the Ministry of Welfare as being in poverty (Lee 1987: pp. 251–3). Soeda has shown that the recipients of Livelihood Protection fell from 1.6 per cent of the population in 1966 to 1.24 per cent in 1973, but estimated that only one quarter of those eligible were in receipt of the benefit. None of those who have written on social assistance in Japan have suggested that the low numbers of recipients is attributable to a lack of need. On the contrary, it is assumed that many simply do not claim. This in turn is explained partly by people's lack of knowledge about their entitlement to benefit and partly by a deep sense of stigma concerning dependence upon the state.

That such a degree of stigma should exist should not itself be explained by simply resorting to Japanese 'culture' and 'traditions'.

Soeda describes a massive media campaign in 1980, just at the time when government was looking for ways to reduce public expenditure, which talked about alarming increases in fraudulent claims. It was even suggested that organised crime was benefiting from such fraud by the Ministry of Health and Welfare. In the event, the only clear evidence of fraud amounted to less than 1 per cent of total claims (Soeda 1991: pp. 60–2). Moreover, as we have seen, the percentage of recipients of social assistance in Japan is extremely low when compared with the percentages in Sweden and Britain of between 4 and 9 per cent. This illustration seems to show that no matter how low the number of beneficiaries of social assistance in a society, they still serve well as scapegoats for its ills.

MEDICAL CARE

Leichter, describing medical care in Japan prior to 1973, emphasised the way in which it had been influenced by German medical care in the nineteenth century and subsequently by the US Occupation after the Second World War. It is a system too that still makes use of traditional medical practices. Given the added complexity of the various health insurance schemes, then it is clear that the Japanese system is a lot more complex than the British and Swedish, dominated as they are by monopolistic state provision.

What has emerged in recent decades is a system which is pre-dominantly public in terms of expenditure, but largely private in the sense that most hospitals and clinics are privately owned (Steslicke 1988: p. 45). Moreover the state regulation of health insurance schemes and the joint interest that the state and insurance societies have in containing medical expenditure, means that major policy decisions are a consequence of bargaining between the Ministry of Health and Welfare, insurance societies and the medical profession, represented by the Japan Medical Association. The JMA is a powerful body, determined to protect the interests and autonomy of its members, and one which in the 1960s and 1970s showed itself to be prepared to go as far as demonstrations and mass resignations in negotiations with government over remuneration issues (Leichter 1979: p. 260).

There are those who doubt whether the resulting arrangement of 'loose and uncontrolled set of facilities and services' can be said to be a system at all (Powell and Anesaki 1990: p. 98). Powell and Anesaki claim that government preoccupation with finance and costs has been to the detriment of service delivery. They assert that there is little coordination and 'no centralised body with responsibility for planning and management' (Powell and Anesaki 1990: p. 98). The Ministry of Health and Welfare has a department responsible for policy matters and it is clear that it is able to influence the medical care activities of the prefectures and municipalities through both finance and legislation. But while the ministry might be able to promote new initiatives in the public sector, it cannot easily enforce the compliance of a largely private medical profession. Attempts made to encourage maternity and child health services in the 1960s and public health centres in the 1980s did not prove successful. The quality of the services was often high, as it is for public-sector hospitals generally, but the private sector inhibited their expansion. Powell and Anesaki show that public-sector hospitals tend to be much better staffed in terms of the number and quality of their nurses. In the private sector fewer nurses are employed and fewer of them have professional training (Powell and Anesaki 1990: p. 220). This is important when one considers that national and local government hospitals amount to less than 20 per cent of the total number of hospitals and provide only 35 per cent of hospital beds (Powell and Anesaki 1990: pp. 154–6). Moreover, it is envisaged that over the next ten years central government will divest itself of 30 per cent of the hospitals under its control. When it comes to the clinics which provide primary care, over 90 per cent of them are in the private sector (Leichter 1979) and there is little coordination between these and the hospitals.

The advanced nature of Japan's medical care 'system' is not doubted and is illustrated by various indicators. The proportion of deaths due to illnesses such as polio and tuberculosis has diminished enormously while the proportion associated with the stresses of modern life and old age have increased – cancer, heart disease, cerebrovascular problems, liver cirrhosis. With the decline in infant mortality and death rates generally, and the consequent ageing of the Japanese population, the problems faced by the health care system have changed in nature and financially. While good health indicators may be seen as the result of non-medical factors such as economic prosperity and diet, they do suggest also that the Japanese health care system performs well for a large section of the population.

Although many commentators would agree that Japan has established standards of medical care similar to those of Western countries, there remain features which are peculiar to Japan and are not easy to understand or interpret. They also illustrate why it is important when looking at other countries to go beyond general statements about national health services to examine how those services actually operate. I shall deal with four in particular: over-prescription, the care of the elderly, the care of the mentally ill and the abortion rate.

One of the principal ways in which Japanese doctors can increase their income is through their right to prescribe, dispense and sell drugs and medicines. Not only do the doctors insist upon this right but their patients have come to expect a visit to the doctor to result in prescribed pills and potions, so much so that Steslicke observes that 'over-utilisation of medicine has been a serious health hazard as well as a financial problem to consumers' (Steslicke 1988: p. 46). The latter problem is one which has seriously concerned the Ministry of Health and Welfare in its attempts to keep costs down.

Over-utilisation of hospital beds is another problem faced by the system. Japanese statistics show that compared with other countries patients are hospitalised for lengthy periods of time. Many of these patients are elderly. Although this indicator has been used to suggest that medical care in Japan is in some way superior (Nakagawa 1979), it is more generally recognised that passive hospitalisation is far from being a good thing either for the patient or for the efficient utilisation of hospital resources. As the proportion of elderly people in the population increased, and their care in the home became a problem, so the children of old people who became ill were more than happy, after 1973, to take advantage of free or subsidised hospital beds, particularly in the light of a shortage of adequate homes for the elderly provided by the social welfare authorities. It would seem as though in many ways, hospitals provide the modern equivalent of the old Japanese practice of 'leaving granny on the mountain to die'. Although Japan can boast about the numbers of doctors and clinics, and the amount of high-tech equipment used in its medical system, there is a serious shortage of nurses.

It is therefore not surprising to discover large numbers of elderly people packed in a small room with little space between the beds, in a hospital or clinic where the numbers of carers are totally inadequate to cope with the problem (Lawrence 1985: p. 687). Lawrence suggests that there is an over-reliance in Japan on institutionalised care. Lock attributes this to an emphasis upon the biological process of ageing as opposed to seeing it in social terms. The elderly sick are therefore the victims either of over-medication or of over-hospitalisation (Lock 1984: pp. 133–4). Instead of receiving care and rehabilitation, they are stuck in bed and left there. This is in part a consequence of doctors wishing to keep their patients and their profits; partly a refusal to see the need for any care which is neither family nor medically based; and partly a refusal to expand social services sufficiently (see below). Kiefer interprets the situation in cultural terms as well, implying that passivity in the elderly is encouraged (Kiefer 1988: p. 104). She writes: 'people stay in hospital because little effort is made to get them up and out.' She goes on to argue that Japan should look towards Sweden and the UK where medical dependency of the elderly is minimised. Another interpretation does suggest itself. In a society where people are expected to look after themselves and not to rely on social services for support, it is possibly easier to define a condition as medical, confine a person to bed and *care* for them there. As the proportion of elderly people in Japan increases, the expense and inefficiency of this policy will no doubt become apparent.

Another human condition with which Japanese society apparently finds it difficult to come to terms is mental illness, which continues to be regarded as a source of shame. It is therefore not surprising to find that it is comparatively easy for families, in agreement with the director of a mental institution, to have their mentally ill relatives committed compulsorily. Over 70 per cent of mental institutions are privately run and are inadequately supervised. Inmates receive little in the way of medical or any other kind of care. Like the institutionalised elderly, they are expected to be passive. Unacceptable behaviour can lead to solitary confinement. A British television documentary claimed that inmates were often violently treated by staff, sometimes fatally. Fires had resulted in those in solitary confinement being burnt alive. While it could be argued that similar cases of abuse of the mentally ill takes place in other countries, it must make a difference that 250,000 receive compulsory 'treatment' in Japan compared with only 7000 in the UK. Moreover, in many of the Japanese cases, the patient is not strictly ill, but simply deviant or beyond familial control (*Viewpoint* 1987). Having got rid of the problem, many Japanese families are reluctant to take the mentally ill back, particularly if they are women (Kargl 1988). This is explained by Sumama, who says that there is a tendency

> towards fear of disapproval of neighbours especially if they and family members believe the disease to be a peculiar one. *Courage is needed* to receive medical care under these conditions [my italics]. If the diagnosis should prove to be a mental disease, the family and other relatives will be labelled and discriminated against in matters relating to marriage, business and school entrance. (Sumama 1978: p. 476)

Lastly I want to mention another curious phenomenon connected with medical care. It is clear from a number of sources that Japan has had a law on abortion for many years which can be regarded as 'liberal' only in the sense that there is a lot of it. The original Eugenics Law of 1940 was similar in its racial purity aims to that of German eugenics policy in the 1930s. It was far from liberal and was in no way intended primarily to benefit women. Ironically, the US Occupation authorities introduced a revision to the law in 1948 which gave women the right to abortions on economic grounds. Four years later a new Eugenic Protection Law justified abortion on a number of grounds: the mother's mental illness or mentally disturbed character; either partner suffering from hereditary sexual disease, deformity or disturbance; economic or psychological reasons detrimental to the mother; or where the pregnancy is likely to have resulted from violence or compulsion.

While some of these conditions are fought for in the West by the liberally-minded and while many of their consequences might indeed have been of enormous benefit to Japanese women, the policy in Japan does have some sinister overtones. During the post-war years Japan acquired the reputation of being an abortion paradise. Abortion has been used in a widespread way as a form of contraception simply because Japanese men have been reluctant to consider alternatives. Kuroda has also suggested that limiting births in this way was, in the post-war years, the easiest way of avoiding poverty for many families (Kuroda 1978: p. 454). Certainly the economic reasons for abortion stated in the legislation include the need to keep people from claiming social assistance. Abortion has also been promoted as a way of preventing the birth of handicapped children:

> Family planning clinics have been receiving increased government funding since 1977. A stated objective of these clinics is to provide genetic counselling and screening services. In a detailed analysis of the range of services provided by Japan's family planning clinics Koga concludes that genetic screening is their primary function. The names of community action groups associated with the clinics would seem to confirm Koga's assertion: 'The Let's Not Bear Unhappy Children Group' or 'The Let's Bear Strong and Healthy Children Group' – 'Unhappy' here being a euphemism for handicapped.
>
> (Buckley 1988: p. 214)

The numbers involved are quite enormous. During the 1950s abortions amounted to 2 million a year at a time when the total population was about 90 million. Buckley, writing in 1988, claimed that government statistics suggested an annual rate of 600–700,000 abortions (Buckley 1988: p. 215). Coleman claimed that the official abortion rate in Japan in 1975 was 25 for every 1000 women, compared with 20 for Sweden and 11 for England and Wales. Moreover he quoted an authoritative source who estimated that the unofficial rate in 1975 was three times the official one (Coleman 1983: pp. 3–4). Not only would this represent the highest rate in the world; it would mean that in that year abortions outnumbered live births. It would also mean that on average each Japanese woman would undergo two abortions.

While Japan's policy on abortion may have given some women the right to choose, it would seem that this is an unanticipated consequence rather than the principal aim. The principal reasons behind the high rate of abortions in Japan would seem to be the difficulties the Japanese male has in dealing with contraception; difficulties in being poor and obtaining social assistance; and the difficulties Japanese society has in dealing with physical and mental impairment.

SOCIAL SERVICES

Most accounts of Japanese social services, both in terms of social work services and residential provision, suggest that the system was primitive indeed prior to 1973. It did not seem to have begun to develop in spite of six major pieces of legislation in the early 1960s concerning, amongst others, the mentally disordered, the elderly and children (Lee 1987: p. 249). Although 80 per cent financed by central government, service delivery takes place in local authority Public Welfare Offices at the municipal level – which also have reponsibility for the administration of Livelihood Protection (see pp. 44–5 above) – and through voluntary Councils of Social Welfare, which are linked to a national association.

Social workers themselves are few in number – only 15,000 in 1984 (Asano and Saito 1988) – and difficult to define. Although there are many schools of social work within higher education, graduates rarely go into social work as such. While some may work in residential settings, place the elderly into homes and organise the home help service, most are employed by the Public Welfare Offices to administer Livelihood Protection (Asano and Saito 1988: p. 146). The importance of professional social work is, however, slowly being recognised. A law to license social and care workers came into force in 1987 and the first professionals to take their examinations did so in 1989.

In place of social workers, the Japanese have relied upon a system of volunteers – *Minsei In*. Collick described how their forerunners, *Homen In*, had been created as a system of social control to check up on the reasons for the the rice riots in the 1920s (Collick 1988). By the outbreak of the Second World War, however, they had developed a clear welfare function and numbered 100,000. The *Minsei In* grew from 134,000 in 1971 to 178,000 in 1986. Surprisingly, given the predominance of women in other areas of social welfare, the majority of *Minsei In* are males, although the proportion declined from 68 per cent in 1971 to 58 per cent in 1986 (Toyoda 1988). If the percentage of women is increasing, so is the average age. In 1974 71 per cent were between the ages of 50 and 70 with 7 per cent above the age of 70. By 1986, 83 per cent were between 50 and 70 with 6 per cent over 70.

The role that *Minsei In* perform is very like that of ordinary social workers. They visit elderly and handicapped people and advise them upon help and benefits they may be able to get. They will help place those in need into homes and institutions. They can arrange for a home help to visit or help someone with an application for social assistance. *Minsei In* receive a small salary, but have no professional training or qualification.

The home help service begun in 1962 expanded from 250 home helps in that year to 25,000 in 1987 (Toyoda 1990). Kitazawa, who put the figure lower at 20,000, claimed that this represented 14 home helps per 100,000 of the population compared with 300 per 100,000 in the UK (Kitazawa 1986: p. 59). Prior to 1982, home helps were restricted to those on social assistance, at no charge. In 1982 it was agreed that anyone who felt they needed a home help could apply for one, but charges were introduced. The fees rose with income and are thought to discourage many of those who need the service (Toyoda 1990). Another consequence of the charges has been that relatives do not want home helps spending time chatting to the old people. Home helps complain that the job therefore becomes a matter of doing routine tasks only. This they say neglects the need of old people to communicate with others, something they need to do for their general welfare but particularly so that the helpers can discover what their real needs are.

Community-based services for the elderly have also expanded from 366 in 1970 to 5294 in 1984. These provide various counselling, rehabilitative and recreational services in urban and rural areas.

Facilities to provide short-stay services for the elderly have only 28,000 places. Long-term stay nursing homes rose from 1014 in 1970 to 2722 in 1984, providing beds for 190,000. However, Asano says that this represents only 1.5 per cent of the over-65s and is very low in comparison with Western countries (Asano and Saito 1988: pp. 140–1). Kitazawa claims that many of these facilities 'have no rehabilitative programs and are seen as places where the elderly are merely abandoned to die' (Kitazawa 1986: p. 58).

Toyoda puts the above into perspective when she reports research which claims that only 14 per cent of home carers receive an attendance allowance. Only 12 per cent of elderly people receive a visit from a nurse; 7 per cent get a home help; 6 per cent a short-stay service. Other services are said to reach less than 5 per cent of old people (Toyoda 1990). Considerably more Japanese families say they need these services – between 30 per cent and 40 per cent say they need an attendance allowance, visits from doctors and nurses, and short-stay facilities; 19 per cent say they need a home help. Ogasawa considers that even these figures are probably underestimates of need because people simply do not know about them (Toyoda 1990).

For a society which claims to have a tradition of respecting the elderly, it does not seem that either medical or social facilities exist in sufficient quantity or quality to provide for this group. The pressure for improvements on both counts is bound to increase as the numbers of elderly people in Japan rises.

CONCLUSION

In this chapter we have seen some evidence of a system which traditionally has relied less on state welfare than Britain or Sweden. Provision by the state has been complemented by the existence of private medical care; the topping-up of state-regulated social security schemes by company benefits; and an army of volunteers has taken the place of professional social workers. This system had already been established prior to the 1970s, but was seen by many to be inadequate for a society which had experienced such high rates of economic growth. Pressure on the LDP government in 1973 resulted in a new departure, an attempt to emulate the European welfare state. Benefits were raised and index-linked social services expanded, and the elderly given free medical care. Even Livelihood Protection benefits were raised.

However, it did not take much to convince the Japanese authorities that this was not the road for them. A series of cost-
cutting measures were introduced throughout the 1980s. Although
international economic problems of the 1970s still meant that
Japan had growth rates much higher than its competitors, they
were considered to be sufficiently low to justify concern about
rising social expenditure, especially in the light of demographic
projections predicting a rapid increase in the proportion of elderly
people in the population. The Europeans were clearly beginning to
have trouble with their ever-expanding welfare states, and business
and conservative political leaders in Japan were obviously happier
with their alternative 'Japanese-type welfare society'.

It is not difficult to see why. Japanese people had not yet come
to expect much in the way of state support. Their expectations had
not been aroused in the same way as had those of the British people
during the Second World War, or maintained with such pride as
they had been in the post-war years in Sweden. The various social
security schemes did not create a sense of social solidarity. On the
contrary, their very differences made it possible to play one group off
against another. The national schemes could only be improved by
a redistribution from the employees' schemes. Since those in large
companies were satisfied with the scale of their welfare benefits, there
was little reason to fight and pay for the benefits of others.

Japanese society has not come to expect a great deal in terms of
health and welfare services for its weaker members. A high degree of
stigma clearly attaches to claimants for Livelihood Protection and the
mentally ill. Nor are the elderly infirm treated with 'care'; rather, their
numbers are 'managed' with insufficient resources, space and staff.

The social divisions reinforced by various welfare schemes, the
discipline and self-reliance expected of people, and the stigma attached
to those who fail to measure up to these qualities, would seem to
accord much better with the needs of the first post-Fordist society
than the principles of universalism and equality favoured by advocates
of the institutional welfare state. In the next chapter we shall see how
these divisions and qualities are reproduced in the fields of education
and employment.

CHAPTER FOUR
Education and employment

INTRODUCTION

We have already seen that benefits from the health care and social security systems in Japan vary considerably and that services and benefits for disadvantaged groups are seriously underdeveloped. An individual's welfare is much more dependent upon market position than in countries with highly developed welfare benefits and services. In the Japanese labour market, one's position is likely to vary according to one's age, gender and educational qualifications. It is seen to be of particular importance that young males achieve permanent employee status in as large and as prestigious a work organisation as possible if they are to gain a good income, a high degree of job security, and advantageous health and social security benefits as well as the perks of enterprise welfare. While the socio-economic status of parents is an important factor in determining the future life-styles and prospects of their children, the Japanese education system in the post-war years has been said to have been one of the most meritocratic among advanced capitalist societies. It has been argued that it was precisely because the system was seen to be a relatively fair one and because the rewards at the end were of such crucial importance that young Japanese were so motivated to do well at school. In this chapter the focus will be upon the Japanese education and employment systems and the changing relationship between them.

THE EDUCATION SYSTEM

It would be simplistic to argue that it is only the future prospect of occupational advantage that has motivated young Japanese to value education. There is much in Japanese history and culture to suggest that education has long been a valued and important part of the social system. Confucian values of scholarship and perseverance are often referred to by those trying to account for the respect which parents, teachers and children alike seem to have for education:

> The creation of a strong group spirit . . . is a key to the whole of modern Japan. It derives from the organisation of late feudal times and before that from ancient Confucian concepts. Much the same could be said of the diligence and perseverance of the Japanese and of their pride in perfection in their work.
>
> (Reischauer quoted in Duke 1986: p. xix).

Of more recent historical origin is the fact that it became clear to the Japanese authorities in the nineteenth century that if the country was to be able to compete with the West then it would have to attach a high priority to the development of its human resources. In the absence of indigenous raw materials, the education of the whole nation took on particular importance.

It is clear from many accounts that the achievements of the education system were considerable even before the American Occupation of 1945, but it is to the structure that has evolved since that time that we must turn to appreciate the present situation. The Americans were concerned to introduce significant changes in Japanese education for a number of reasons. It was important to ensure that teachers were trained and re-trained to accept a more democratic and egalitarian approach to schooling if the nationalistic approach of the pre-war years was to be eradicated. Similarly it was important to change the curriculum taught in schools to reflect the new democratic spirit. Lastly, the Americans sought to create comprehensive, co-educational elementary and secondary schools to break down some of the more rigid class and gender barriers of the previous system.

The public–private mix of education

The result of the changes introduced by the Occupation was a structure which provided for free compulsory education for all those between the ages of 6 and 15. Elementary school was to last for six years, followed by three years at junior high school.

Three further years could be spent voluntarily in senior high schools before going on to further and higher education. In the 1980s about 25 per cent of school-leavers were going on to university to study for academic degrees; 10 per cent to junior colleges to gain qualifications in fine arts, domestic science and the semi-professions; and 13 per cent to special training colleges to pursue vocational courses. While the compulsory years remain largely state-provided, the rest of the system has increasingly become a mix of public and private provision.

Pre-school education, for example, is provided by kindergartens, 75 per cent of which are in the private sector (Simmons 1990). Of the senior high schools, 28 per cent are private. When it comes to universities, a distinction is made between the national ones, those funded by the prefectures and private universities. National universities provide for only 20 per cent of undergraduates; local authorities less than half that figure; while private universities cater for the majority of students. Most junior colleges are also private, as are the special training schools whose numbers have tripled since the mid-1970s.

What is interesting about the public–private mix is that private has not always meant 'best' or even the 'most prestigious'. The best universities until recently certainly were the national ones. During the latter part of the 1960s the government granted university charters to a wide range of private insitutions that had neither the resources nor the research capacity to call themselves universities in any accepted sense. Their staff–student ratios could be as low as 1:120. The attraction for parents was that they could claim that their children were benefiting from university education, while the value for the government was that the provision was at minimal cost to the public purse. It was as if the authorities in Japan had made a neat distinction between the needs of the economy to exploit the best in human resources wherever they might be found, and the demands from parents for social status for their children. What the latter received could depend upon the unequal distribution of parental incomes and was of no concern to the state. If the quality was low, it only mattered to those concerned. The national universities, on the other hand, had to provide places on a more meritocratic basis and were properly funded. It was the national universities that had the best resources, appropriate research facilities and the highest status. More recently, however, the competition for the best undergraduate recruits has resulted in the private sector often being preferred to some of the national institutions. Some private universities not only recruit from favoured prep schools, but these in turn give preference to particular private kindergartens.

The superiority that state universities were able to claim used to be generally true of the public senior high schools as well, but increasingly parents are buying senior high-school education and even junior high-school education for their children because of the likelihood of such education leading on to the more prestigious further and higher education institutions. Whereas in the 1960s the state senior high schools were the ones that sent most children to Tokyo University, by the 1980s the best private schools claimed that role (Simmons 1990: p. 78). The competition amongst schools to recruit the brightest pupils is intensified by

> the publicity given to the annual rankings [of senior high-school examination results] by the media and the widespread interest taken in them by the Japanese public. The result of this is that the educational efficiency or otherwise of the senior high schools has very high visibility in Japan.
> (Lynn 1988: p. 50)

This development has to be seen in the light of the characteristics of the examination system. In the last year of junior high schools, children take examinations to gain entry into particular senior high schools. In the last year of the senior schools, similar examinations are taken for entrance into universities and colleges. It is said that these significant hurdles help to create strong ties between teachers, parents and pupils since they cooperate with each other to beat the system. Increasingly, however, much of the formal instruction to get through the examinations takes places in cramming schools. Large numbers of children attend *juku* crammers to study for the senior high-school exams and *yobiku* for university entrance.

Japanese children not only spend more hours at school during the day, and more days at school during the year, than their counterparts in the West, but they are then sent to *juku* and *yobiku* in the evenings to undergo even more intensive examination preparation. As a result, 98 per cent of them stay on after the compulsory years and over 50 per cent enter tertiary education. It is ironic that when young people in Japan finally get to university, the pressure comes off. Employers are more concerned with what university you have been to and the extra-curricular activities you have been involved in than with the class of degree you receive.

Staffing and resources

It has already been mentioned that many private Japanese universities have poor facilities and adverse staff–student ratios. This is because many of them need to keep costs down in order to be profitable. But it would seem to be a characteristic of state schools also that they are not particularly well equipped nor well staffed in quantitative terms. Teachers are paid well and can feel that their occupational status ranks much more highly than in many Western countries (White 1987: p. 84), but the same emphasis has not been placed upon buildings and equipment. Primary schools have staff–student ratios of 1:40 and the nation of high tech does not boast many computers in the classroom. Spartan is how school buildings and decor are often described. Auxiliary workers are not employed in profusion. The children themselves are involved in the serving of school meals and in the cleaning of their schools. This would all seem to suggest a system in which mass education is given a high priority but where the emphasis is upon the human capacities involved rather than the material resources. Even where the Japanese state has been committed to a public service, it has not been prepared to lavish resources upon it. Moreover, it has let the private sector play a major role in provision.

Equality and Japanese education

Much of the educational motivation of pupils and their parents in the post-war years has been attributed to their perception that education is a route to better employment prospects and that the examination system is a meritocratic one. This may have been in part due to the importance placed on education by governments which saw education as contributing significantly to national economic success. While social expenditure might have lagged behind other countries in terms of the percentage of GNP devoted to it, education expenditure in Japan has long been proportionally similar to those of Western governments (see Table 1.6).

Another factor in the egalitarian nature of Japanese schooling seems to have been the influence of teachers themselves and their professional association – the socialist Japan Teachers' Union (JTU). It is often said of Japanese teachers and schools that they regard all children as educable. There is little sense of children as being born more or less intelligent and therefore more or less worthy of instruction. Instead, all pupils are assumed to be capable of reaching high standards of literacy, numeracy and other skills (Cummings 1980). The national curriculum is also thought to aid this process. Central government has laid down what it is expected that all children of certain ages, regardless of background and gender, should be taught. This nationalist egalitarian aim of government seems to be combined with the socialist egalitarian aims of the teachers to create an atmosphere in which the vast majority of children strive to learn and achieve.

It has been suggested that although the American education system may result in an impressive élite of Nobel prize-winners, the Japanese system produces a better performance by average and below-average pupils (Kerr quoted in Duke 1986). This is in part due to the collective nature of competition in schools. The pupil is part of a small group within the class and has to learn loyalty to both. The individual must perform and behave well not for personal reasons alone, but for the honour and reputation of the collective. Each group will have a leader; not one who stands out and dominates, but one who will enable the group to function effectively. Individualism is frowned upon. 'The nail that sticks out gets knocked down.'

> The leader . . . must learn not to get too far ahead of the group.
> He must listen carefully to his group and act compatibly with the
> general will of his group. He must patiently endeavour to persuade
> members of his group, often through lengthy discussions, to
> support a certain action. As leader his responsibility is primarily to
> harmonize the group attitude by forging a general consensus through
> reconciling various opinions into a resolution. A sense of fairness
> must prevail. Through this process, the loyalty of each child to the
> group is strengthened and leadership, Japanese-style, is developed.
> (Duke 1986: pp. 29–30)

The quality of educational outcomes of this system can be demonstrated in a number of ways. Literacy rates of 98 per cent are achieved (Duke 1986: p. 60). In international tests of maths and science, Japanese children have not only achieved the highest scores, but the spread of ability has also been wider than that of children from other countries (Simmons 1990: p. 70). The high standard is not simply a reflection of the excellent scores of a small élite but the high standards of average and below-average pupils. Lynn argued that Japanese children, on average, were three years ahead of their Western counterparts (Lynn 1988: p. 17). The meritocratic nature of state education in Japan is illustrated by Table 4.1, which shows that differential chances of getting to prestigious national universities for children whose parents' incomes were in the highest quintile were not that enormous when compared with those whose parents' incomes were in the lower quintiles. The differences were much greater when it came to access to universities in the private sector, where parental incomes would seem to have been a major factor.

The inequalities generated by this system have assumed greater significance since the mid-1970s. As more and more parents have

Table 4.1 The percentage distribution of university
students by family income and type of university, 1974

	Lowest quintile	2	3	4	Highest quintile
National universities	14.4	11.2	16.0	24.3	34.1
Private universities	6.1	6.5	11.6	21.2	54.6

Source: Pempel 1978: p. 151

sought to circumvent the egalitarian impact of the state system by purchasing advantages for their children, the motivation of those whose parents cannot afford the advantages of better secondary education, better *juku* and *yobiku*, may have begun to wane. The strength of the Japanese system for many years has been that an expanding economy and a state education system gave many young people an equal opportunity to become unequal, and gave schools and teachers, in turn, enormous legitimacy and respect. Many commentators are now worried that the expansion and significance of the private sector may well be undermine that legitimacy and respect (Amano 1989: p. 134).

Inequalities of gender and ethnicity

The equality of opportunity referred to in so much of the literature on Japanese education tends to take for granted that the subject under discussion is an ethnically homogeneous male population. Rarely is reference made to inequalities of gender and ethnicity. When these are examined, it is clear that discrimination against women and minority groups is certainly no better than in other capitalist societies but may be of a more deep-rooted nature.

It is often said, for example, that the Japanese employment system acts as a clear institutional barrier for women which in turn influences their educational opportunities (Edwards 1988; Fujita 1987; Kawashima 1987). What is the point of paying for your daughter to attend a four-year university degree course when there is no likelihood of her getting a good full-time job for life? Better and cheaper to send her to a junior college or a special training school where she can learn something useful. In 1983, according to Fujimura-Fanselow, 39 per cent of male school-leavers and 32 per cent of female school-leavers entered colleges and universities. Two years earlier, 90 per cent of the students in two-year colleges were women, but only 22 per cent of those enrolled on four-year university courses. Women made up between 7 and 8 per cent of undergraduates at prestigious universities like Tokyo, Kyoto and Keio. Junior colleges are often preferred for young women because they are (a) more likely to be single-sex institutions and (b) more likely to exist within travelling distance of the parental home (Fujimura-Fanselow 1989). If, as is likely, Japanese employers will want to make greater use of the female work-force in the future, attitudes and the institutional structures maintaining them may change, but little is likely to happen as a result of political goodwill.

Nor has political protest and affirmative action been of much use to the Buraku. Their pariah status is also guaranteed by the employment system. They continue to live in ghettoes, out of which it is difficult to break. Figures from the 1970s, quoted by Hawkins, showed that only 64 per cent of Buraku youngsters stayed on to high school, compared with 95 per cent of those in the population as a whole (Hawkins 1989). University entrance was said to be almost non-existent. In school there were significant problems of absenteeism, high wastage and low performance. Buraku political pressure has brought about some policy changes. Nursery provision has expanded; more upper secondary schools have been built close to Buraku areas; and more in-service training for teachers has been provided. However, these improvements are thought unlikely to have improved the situation in the 1980s a great deal.

Japanese education certainly has its meritocratic achievements but for certain groups in Japanese society, ascriptive values still serve as major barriers to educational and occupational opportunity.

Problems

Commentators in the West have been extolling the virtues of Japanese education for some years. The subtitle of Richard Lynn's *Educational Achievment in Japan* is *Lessons for the West*. Lynn, writing for the right-wing think-tank Social Affairs Unit, clearly thought that the British government ought to adopt many of Japan's educational practices. The Japanese themselves have been more concerned about the negative consequences of their system. Economic growth has slowed down and with it has come a greater stability in job opportuniites. As the competition for jobs with top companies has become even more intense, so parents have turned more and more to the private sector and cramming schools, and the degree of competition to which young people have been subjected has increased immensely.

In the early 1980s there was a growing worry that the pressure was resulting in an increase in the number of suicides committed by young people having to face the 'examination hell'. Others, it was said, turned to violence, bullying and truancy. There was no doubt that such phenomena were increasing:

> Between 1979 and 1983, the reported incidence of violence in schools almost doubled and attacks on teachers quadrupled. In 1986, the Ministry of Education reported that 55% of the schools were experiencing outbreaks of bullying. At the same time, the Ministry reported that absenteeism caused by school-phobia among junior high school students had quadrupled over the previous decade. All of these official figures were accompanied by a deluge of media reports on specific cases; suicides by teenagers distraught over bullying, a teacher forced to defend himself with a knife when he was threatened by his students. (Schoppa 1990: p. 4).

In response the government, in 1984, set up an *ad hoc* commission to recommend reforms to the system. Far from attempting to counteract the problems cited above, it would seem that the government cynically used public concern to attack the educational establishment in much the same way that the Conservative government did in Britain after the 1987 election. The government hoped to introduce a number of neo-liberal and neo-conservative measures which would have had the effect of strengthening the influence of government, business leaders and parents on the running of the education system, while at the same time reducing the impact of teachers and the local authorities. Apart from the introduction of a requirement that the national flag and the national anthem be employed on important school occasions, few of the government's hoped-for reforms survived the committee's three-year-long deliberations. Schoppa, in his comparative study of educational reform in Britain and Japan, concluded that the government was defeated by a powerful alliance of the Ministry of Education bureaucrats and LDP members of the Diet (Schoppa 1990).

If many Japanese felt that the degree of competition for young people was becoming too intense, outside commentators compared the problems faced in Japan with those that occurred in American and English schools and considered that the latter were much more widespread and severe. Certainly, parental and media interest in the problems seemed to abate by the time the *ad hoc* commission was ready to make its recommendations. Be that as it may, if the problems are due in part to the decline in occupational opportunities, lower economic growth, and the determination by better-off parents to buy advantages for their children, it is difficult to see how the problems can be prevented from getting worse. It was the great merit of Japanese schools in the 1960s and 1970s that they had meritocratic elements which motivated students and legitimised not only the educational system but the employment system as well. As opportunity becomes more overtly a question of parental income, both motivation and legitimation may continue to decline and the problems outlined above continue to grow.

This would have far-reaching consequences for employers for other reasons. As Duke has pointed out, the Japanese education system has turned out loyal, literate, competent and diligent workers (Duke 1986). This is possibly why it is praised so avidly by Western commentators. Certainly, others have criticised the docility and dependence encouraged by Japanese schooling. Even some business leaders in Japan are said to question whether the emphasis on skills and discipline which has proved so successful in the twentieth century will be appropriate to the more creative demands of the twenty-first (Schoppa 1990: p. 28). It is not difficult to see, however, why the traditional qualities of loyalty to the group, hard work and discipline would have been nurtured and encouraged by the Japanese authorities, nor why their possible decline should cause anxiety in many walks of life. They may turn out to have less durability than earlier cultural analyses have imagined. The Japanese economy and the employment system may have created ideal conditions for the expression of age-old Japanese values, but economic change can make traditional structures and values difficult to maintain.

In order to understand why many of the features of Japanese education already mentioned should have been of such importance to prospective employees and their employers, we must now turn to a consideration of the benefits associated with different kinds of employment.

THE EMPLOYMENT SYSTEM AND COMPANY WELFARE

It has often been said of the education system that the motivation to work hard and accept authority had something to do not only with employment prospects but also an inner compulsion deriving from the nature of Japanese culture. The pressures and privations were accepted if not willingly then without resentment. Similar comments have been made about employment itself. Ronald Dore, while favourably commenting on Kamata's critique of the authoritarian and exploitative nature of employment in the Toyota car firm, insisted that it was not simply the compulsion of an external authority that made Japanese employees work so hard but an inner compulsion (Kamata 1983: p. xx). One may argue endlessly about the extent to which the Japanese worker is driven by an internalised work ethic or by coercive employment practices, but few would dispute the importance of Etzioni's third category of power, the remunerative. The person who succeeds in obtaining permanent employment with a large Japanese company will calculate the benefits in terms not only of wages but bonuses, retirement allowances, enterprise housing and welfare, as well as secure employment. None of these extras is peculiar to Japanese management practice, but they have been combined in such a way in Japan as to create a formidable set of reasons for being committed to one's employer.

The range of benefits

Abegglen was one of the first to describe the array of benefits which impinged upon the daily lives of employees in large companies: subsidised meals and accommodation, haircuts and baths, company shops, a medical centre, sports and recreation facilities:

> The worker is most likely to spend his holidays at the mountain or beach dormitory maintained by the company. . . . In short, nearly every detail of his life is interpenetrated by the company's facilities, guidance and assistance.   (Abegglen 1973: pp. 102–3)

He went on to describe how on marriage not only would there be an allowance from the company but also the likelihood of more generous housing in the form of married quarters:

> He will also receive financial aid in the event of illness, death or other misfortune. His income increases with marriage, of course, and will increase still more as children are born. His children may attend the company school.   (Abegglen 1973: p. 103).

Abegglen wrote the above about Japanese factories in 1956, but in his comments written about changes in the following two decades he gave the impression that the range of benefits had not altered to any great extent.

Dore's more recent comparison of Hitachi and English Electric provided a similar picture. He claimed that most young Japanese recruits could expect dormitory accommodation and 40 per cent of married couples some form of company housing. Whereas English Electric provided housing for a small minority of emergency cases, regarding housing as a personal matter, Hitachi assumed that its job was to provide housing for its workers. Similarly with other benefits. To English Electric fringe benefits were exactly what the term implied. They were of peripheral importance, whereas the general affairs department of Hitachi was 'positively entrepreneurial' in its approach to welfare provision. The firm boasted a large concert hall, an athletics stadium, a baseball stadium, gymnasium and other sports facilities. Social life was also firm-based. Departmental outings and social events for smaller groups such as sections and teams were encouraged and subsidised by the firm. Not only was the social life of employees considered to be important to the company but their moral welfare was also thought to be the firm's concern. A branch of the Ethical Society promoted ideals of serious-mindedness, clean living and honesty through articles in a magazine and weekend outings.

Dore showed how the firm also provided employees' families with allowances and gifts to mark all the important events and stages of life from the cradle to the grave; gifts to mark weddings, births and funerals. The education of employees' children was supported through educational loans, and the maintenance of a dormitory in Tokyo 'for those children of employees attending universities or cram schools preparing for university entrance' (Dore 1973: p. 209).

Perhaps the most important company social security benefit, however, was the lump sum provided on retirement. This would seem to be a considerable sum for those who have been with a company for many years – often equivalent to one month's salary for every year employed. It is received at the age of 55 but heralds the firm's break with its commitment to the employees' lifetime employment. Thereafter employees might be re-employed but on lower wages and without the benefits of seniority and security.

These various benefits are provided by most large and many medium-sized companies but are not a consequence of managerial whim to be conceded or curtailed at will. They are negotiated by enterprise unions: 'Company welfare is counted as part of the rights of employees to be guarded and extended' (Dore 1973: p. 208). And having been negotiated there is often very little discretion exercised by the company. Once it has undertaken to provide a particular benefit, rules, regulations and tariffs bind management to dispense benefits as and when the needs and circumstances arise. This sort of commitment by the employer results in a greater willingness by employees to identify with the firms they work for.

The loyalty and commitment of the workers is matched by a reciprocal obligation on the part of the employers to treat the employee as a member of the firm and not just as labour-power. This is underpinned by the phenomenon of permanent employment, which means that management will only lay people off if the firm itself is collapsing. In any other eventuality, enormous efforts are expected to be made to prevent redundancy.

The analogy that is often used to describe Japanese firms and the relationship that exists between management and worker is that of the family. Given the size of many large corporations, that analogy must often be insufficient and misleading. In many ways a more appropriate analogy might be that of the welfare state itself – albeit in miniature. The firm is an institution which guarantees to its members full employment, common leisure facilities, subsidised housing and a series of benefits from the cradle to the grave.

The scale and distribution of benefits

Dore's view of the scale of Hitachi's welfare provision was that it was much greater than the equivalent in the UK. Whereas large British firms might devote 2.5 per cent of labour costs, excluding sick pay, to welfare and recreational facilities, he argued, Hitachi devoted 8.5 per cent excluding sick pay (Dore 1973: p. 203). Cole showed that whereas social security contributions per employee in medium and large firms came to 6.1 per cent of total wages, voluntary welfare costs came to 7.8 per cent of total wage costs while the retirement allowance came to 5.1 per cent (Cole 1971). These proportions would not seem to be negligible and it would be understandable that enterprise unions would be concerned about anything which threatened the size of their members' occupational welfare packet.

The important point to be borne in mind is that it is workers in certain industries and larger companies who benefit from these arrangements. In 1973, welfare costs as a percentage of pay ranged from 9.1 per cent in the publishing industry to 22 per cent in mining (see Table 4.2). A much greater variation of expenditure on non-statutory welfare was found by Woodsworth when he looked at company size. Companies employing

Table 4.2   Welfare costs as
a percentage of pay, 1973

Communications	11.2
Publishing	9.1
Precision machinery	10.5
Metals	13.1
Transport	10.8
Mining	22.0
Textiles	14.6

Source: Adapted from
Woodsworth 1977

Table 4.3   An index of average monthly labour costs
per regular employee by company size, 1988

Number of company employees	Total labour costs	Retirement allowances	Statutory welfare	Non-statutory welfare
30–99	100	100	100	100
100–299	111	161	102	103
300–999	122	189	112	127
1000–4999	142	293	125	179
5000+	171	509	142	389

Source: Adapted from *Japan Statistical Yearbook* 1991

more than 5000 people were on average spending 40 per cent more per
employee on such benefits and services than companies employing less
than 500 (Woodsworth 1977). The more recent figures shown in Table
4.3, although not strictly comparable, suggest that if anything the gap
between small and large companies has grown. Retirement allowances
per employee are five times higher in the largest companies than in the
smallest, and non-statutory welfare is four times as high, whereas labour
costs in total are only 70 per cent greater.

A study by Stevens, using data from the early 1970s, illustrates the
overall picture above in more detail (Table 4.4). Whereas it was often
90 per cent of firms employing over 5000 people which provided
welfare and fringe benefits, the corresponding percentages for small
firms were invariably in single figures. Although small firms took
on the responsibility for housing a considerable proportion of their
employees, few of them could compete with the large companies
in the provision of hospitals and clinics. Their inability to provide
athletics grounds and mountain lodges would seem to have meant

Table 4.4 Availability of company welfare by firm size, 1973, in percentages

	Large firms (over 5000 employees)%	Small firms (30–99 employees)%
Housing		
Family	93.9	42.2
Unmarried	89.9	28.8
House buying incentive	96.5	28.2
Housing loan	93.9	10.8
Medical and health care		
Hospitals	31.3	2.2
Clinics	74.3	3.8
Family medical check-ups	37.4	1.1
Living support		
Barber shops, beauty salon	50.3	1.3
Purchasing facilities	70.2	4.1
Nurseries	12.0	0.8
Culture, sport, recreation		
Athletics grounds	84.5	5.0
Seaside, mountain lodges, ski resources	73.3	9.8
Rehabilitation facilities	95.6	9.4
Pleasure trips	64.3	91.5
Others		
Supplementary labour compensation insurance	93.6	23.8
Supplementary health insurance	98.8	14.8

Source: Adapted from Stevens 1988

Table 4.5 Average monthly labour costs
per regular employee as a percentage of total
labour costs 1975–88

	Retirement allowances	Statutory welfare	Non-statutory welfare
1975	3.1	6.1	3.0
1980	3.4	7.0	2.8
1988	4.2	7.9	2.7

Source: Adapted from *Japan Statistical
Yearbook* 1991

that they made up for the lack by providing pleasure trips, an area
in which the large firms did not feel it was as necessary to compete.

Although the figures in Table 4.4 are somewhat dated, it is possible
to say that there has been little change in the last fifteen years in terms
of the overall scale of company welfare, as can be seen from Table
4.5. As one would expect, with an ageing work-force, the percentage
of labour costs devoted to retirement allowances has grown. Whether
the slightly lower percentage devoted to non-statutory welfare and
the higher percentage devoted to statutory welfare represents a clear
trend for the future, it is not easy to say.

Enterprise welfare is, then, a significant factor in the budget of many
firms and more so in some industries and firms than others. Its very
size and significance means that employees and trade unions in large
firms negotiate for its maintenance and increase rather than pressurise
political parties and the government to provide more state welfare
for all. Conversely, those who work for small firms, day and casual
labourers, female workers and those outside the labour market lose out
by neither benefiting from the welfare provided by large employers nor
from the state. Enterprise welfare serves to attract young people to join
a company in the first place and acts as a reason for staying with the
company once employed. If you leave the company or lose your job,
you also lose your accommodation; you presumably have to repay any
low-interest loans; and you lose the right to top-ups for your health
insurance, old-age pension and retirement allowance.

PUBLIC EMPLOYMENT AND TRAINING SERVICES

As company welfare has contributed to the comparatively minor role
played by state welfare in Japan, so the propensity for employees to be

recruited, trained, promoted and re-deployed within a company has led to a a residual role for public employment and training services. The Ministry of Labour is responsible for a national network of employment agencies, and no job placement service can operate without the ministry's authorisation.

Public vocational training has also played a minor role in the Japanese labour market. Companies have preferred to recruit young workers and give them specific, on-the-job training. Moreover, there has not been the same degree of youth unemployment as in the West and therefore little need to provide the sort of youth training schemes to be found in Britain and Sweden. The Ministry of Labour does, however, finance a number of Vocational Training Centres. These would seem to bear a resemblance to what used to be called, in Britain, Government Training Centres and which are now referred to as Skill Centres. Like the GTCs the VTCs seemed to concentrate on traditional manual skills and became less relevant to labour market needs as information technology began to expand. It was the private sector which met much of the demand for initial training in a variety of occupations through Special Training Schools, which operate alongside other tertiary-sector educational institutions to provide young people with vocational training. The VTCs had a budget of less than £300 million in 1986 of which only £24 million was devoted to training schemes for redundant workers. In addition £22 million and £1 million respectively were spent on programmes for the handicapped and the elderly (Dore and Sako 1989: pp. 58–9). The total number of trainees who attended the various courses under Ministry of Labour schemes in 1984 was 330,000 (McCormick 1989: p. 141). McCormick's view of this provision was that it would probably be inadequate to meet future needs. He felt that large corporations were already reducing the numbers of 'core' employees and their training budgets and that this would probably mean a need for more than 'a residual role for the state in continuing adult education and training'.

A similar point was made some years ago by Inoue (Inoue 1979). Structural changes in the 1960s for the coal mining industry had led the government to implement a comprehensive range of measures to ease the problems which arose. Special help was given to find new jobs for the miners: removal allowances were given; training programmes with allowances were established; public works and redevelopment projects were created. It was clearly recognised that the adjustment expected of miners was made more difficult by the specialist nature of their occupations and by the problems redundant workers faced in a labour market where job mobility was on an intra- rather than inter-company basis.

Similar measures have been established to deal with the restructuring of industry and redundancy more generally. The 1977 Employment Stabilisation Fund pays grants to employers to retain and retrain workers while their businesses are converted from one activity to another. Similar grants can be paid to employers who, faced with a downturn in a business cycle, none the less keep workers on the payroll. Inoue clearly felt that while these measures were adequate for a country experiencing high rates of economic growth and minor recessions, they would not suffice if growth was low and recessions prolonged. Since he foresaw that the Japanese economy would experience the latter characteristics increasingly in the future, policies which encouraged the hoarding of labour would be counter-productive. He therefore felt that an effective set of labour market instruments needed to be in place and capable of adapting to the unforeseen demands of structural change.

CONCLUSION

In the decades since 1945, Japan has developed an education system and an employment system which have greatly contributed to its economic success. Schools have produced loyal, disciplined recruits for the country's work organisations. Students and employees have both been characterised by a group orientation and a commitment to work of a high standard. Economic growth and full employment have been achieved without massive public expenditure on educational establishments or public employment and training programmes.

Parents have been expected to take on much of the responsibility of financing kindergarten and post-school education and increasingly they are paying for junior and senior high-school education as well. The competition for one's children to get into good senior high schools, colleges and universities is so intense that parents also pay for their children to attend cramming schools. The national curriculum emphasises the acquisition of factual knowledge and the basic skills of literacy and numeracy. It ensures a high degree of standardisation throughout the country and in subjects like history a commitment to traditional values. It is hardly surprising that conservatives abroad have applauded such a system and ascribed much of Japan's economic success to the achievments of its educational institutions.

But Japan is not immune from the global economy even if it is a major driving force within it. Faced with competition from the Pacific Rim as well as Europe and America, it is increasingly confronted with the need for structural changes in its own economy. Until recently high rates of economic growth and a low proportion of elderly people in the population have enabled change to take place without too great a disruption of traditional values and institutions. The future may be very different. Affluence and privatisation may weaken the meritocratic emphasis of the education system and thereby its legitimacy. Moreover, faced with increased labour costs and competition, restructuring for large firms may not result in a simple redeployment of labour within the firm but give rise to redundancies. It will be the public sector that will increasingly have to bear the burden of such structural adjustment.

But all that is for the future. What Japan has achieved in the recent past is what has captured the admiration of a number of observers. It is to their evaluation of the Japanese welfare system that we now turn.

CHAPTER FIVE
Perspectives and evaluations

INTRODUCTION

'Japanese capitalism was and is nationalistic, paternalistic, and anti-individualistic' (Morishima 1982: p. 18). Perhaps Morishima could have added 'with authoritarian tendencies'. For the features which have distinguished Japanese capitalism from its counterparts in the West are not simply benevolent. Authoritarian societies are disciplined societies in which clear distinctions are made between the deserving and the undeserving; friends and enemies; leaders and followers; what is superior and what is inferior. Japan is less authoritarian than it was but strong elements remain. The position of women, pariah groups and immigrants is worse than in more liberal forms of capitalism; the rights of the individual are less secure. Moreover, the fragmentation of trade unions and of socialist parties has not been the result of historical accident but of systematic manipulation and repression throughout this century.

This picture of divisiveness has been reinforced through an examination of the welfare system – state, voluntary, occupational and familial – in which it has been shown that the national schemes for health and pensions insurance were inferior to those of the employees' schemes. Occupational welfare clearly benefited those in the more privileged sectors of the work-force; voluntary welfare and social services were shown to be inadequate; and family welfare were shown to be both inegalitarian and a disproportionate burden on women. Education, while relatively meritocratic in the past, is becoming increasingly less so, but schools continue to produce diligent, competitive workers through a socialisation process which emphasises groupism, loyalty and other traditional values.

In this chapter we shall examine the ways in which developments in Japanese welfare have been interpreted by different commentators. My argument will be that official conservative ideology backed by national ideologists has emphasised the positive features of the system to the neglect of the less attractive features; that foreign observers have to a large extent accepted a set of arguments couched in cultural terms. I shall then turn to the work of Peter Dale for an alternative interpretation of Japanese culture and its apologists and present a more critical assessment of the Japanese welfare system. This will place a greater emphasis upon the way in which, historically, the Japanese establishment has actively sought to prevent the rise of a unified labour movement. As a result the development of Japanese capitalism hitherto has not been hindered by the costs and commitments of extensive state welfare provision.

FROM WELFARE LAGGARD TO WELFARE SUPERPOWER

It was common practice to regard Japan as a welfare 'laggard' in the early 1970s. The country's economy had grown spectacularly in the previous two decades, but it was clear that in terms of state welfare expenditure Japan lagged behind advanced Western capitalist countries. A variety of pressures – not least the sense of international inferiority – led to major governmental decisions to increase welfare spending. 1973 was to have been the 'first year of welfare in Japan'. The subsequent international oil and economic crises changed all that. With the prospect of an ageing population and slower economic growth, conservative views on the prospective damage of the welfare burden led to a different tack. Lee claims that new slogans succeeded the 1973 one, such as 'reconsider welfare', 'welfare state disease' and finally 'Japanese-style welfare state' (Lee 1987: p. 251). Watanuki describes how the ultimate phrase used by various ministers around 1976 was 'Japanese-style welfare society' (Watanuki 1986: p. 264).

What was meant by this was clearly stated in a government public information sheet for foreign consumption, which explained that the reasons for Japan's seemingly low state welfare expenditure was due to four main factors: (a) the low proportion of elderly people in Japan; (b) the extensive provision of enterprise welfare; (c) generous tax benefits for private insurance policyholders; and (d) family solidarity (Ministry of Foreign Affairs 1978).

A more robust statement of this position was put forward by Nakagawa Yatsuhiro in an article published in 1979. He claimed that Japanese old age pensions and social assistance benefits had already surpassed those of England, the USA and West Germany. Moreover, the high life expectancy and low infant mortality rates showed that the Japanese were the healthiest people in the world. Statistics which showed that

> the average number of days of hospitalisation per year due to illness
> in Japan in 1974 was 34; this was four times the American figure
> of 8.3 days; 2.5 times the figure of 13 for Sweden and 13.1 days
> for England.   (Nakagawa 1979: p. 11)

indicated that Japanese hospitals and their comprehensive medical and therapeutic facilities were the 'best in the world'.

He also claimed that in terms of food and clothing, the Japanese were able to afford higher standards than those of their Western counterparts. In England most middle-class families could not 'provide their families with a decent supper' and in Europe and America 'people must make do with very little to eat'.

> One is told that for the American middle classes, beefsteak is
> something that can be enjoyed on the average only twice a month.
>   (Nakagawa 1979: p. 13)

He went on to say that Europeans and Americans were 'also distinguished by their plain and simple clothing'. Income after tax was on average 1.5 times that in the USA but when enterprise welfare benefits were added to Japanese earnings they were three times those of Americans. In terms of education and home ownership, the Japanese were also superior and if Japanese houses were small by Western standards this was because Japanese culture placed more priority on food and clothing than on shelter.

Japan was also a very egalitarian country. Gini coefficients showed that income distribution in Japan was not very different from that of Sweden. These high living and welfare standards for all had been achieved because of the Japanese willingness to work hard and the ambition and energy of Japanese workers. Even the elderly wanted to continue to work after retirement. Diligence and the high degree of cooperation between the state, business and people ensured a highly efficient society. It was Japanese efficiency which had made it possible to become a 'welfare superpower' without having to devote a crippling proportion of its GNP to social expenditure. Whereas other countries had found that 'high welfare' had meant a 'high burden' in terms of government expenditure and taxation, Japan had acheived 'high welfare' with a corresponding 'low burden' of taxation.

> Even heroic Sweden, that paragon among the welfare states of northern Europe, famous for its noble experiment of trying to build a socialist nation within the framework of a free economy, must clearly relinquish its crown in favour of Japan.   (Nakagawa 1979: p. 10)

Those Japanese intellectuals who could not see this had allowed themselves 'to be completely governed by uninformed preconceptions'.

> Many of the problems in this area of Japanese life are clearly the result of the conscious manipulation of data, carried out by so-called intellectuals whose actual credentials might fairly be categorised as little more than shop signs identifying them as 'vendors of imported merchandise', in this case, imported but badly shop-worn preconceptions about the relative status of Japan and the West.
> (Nakagawa 1979: p. 26).

I have dealt with Nakagawa's paper at length, not because I think it stands up to academic scrutiny – the comments on relative standards of living alone would destroy its credibility and be themselves evidence of 'manipulation of data' – but because so many of the elements of his argument were subsequently imported to the West.

JAPAN AS NUMBER ONE

Ezra Vogel was one of the first to observe Japan's superiority in areas other than the economic. In his renowned book, he argued that state welfare had to be seen in the context of generous enterprise welfare and traditional family welfare. Firms did not lay off their workers, thus preventing unemployment and its attendant costs. A reliance on *Minsei In* volunteers made publicly employed social workers unnecessary. Compared with the USA, Japan had little need for an army of welfare bureaucrats and professionals.

The Japanese, with their different system, he argued, had created a society where the old lived longer, where infant mortality was lower, where the streets were free of crime, where divorce and broken homes were fewer than in the West. In the UK, Sweden and the USA workers had lost their drive; not so in Japan. Moreover, there was no sizeable group

> that feels indignant out of a sense of entitlement or self-deprecatory out of a sense of inadequate achievement. Nor is there the deep social cleavage between taxpayers who object to supporting those who work

less and the recipients who object to the inadequacy of their payments, their uncertainty, and the spirit in which they are given.

(Vogel 1979: p. 201)

Richard Rose, the British political scientist, took up these themes in an article entitled 'Welfare: the lessons from Japan' (Rose 1985). It was Rose's view that the British should not look to small Scandinavian countries as a model. The population of Japan was six times that of Scandinavia and 'in reviewing the welfare of people it is impossible to ignore Japan'. He went on to argue that the Japanese had a different approach to welfare and as a result had created a different welfare mix. Japan showed that 'welfare in society need not depend upon welfare from the state'. Japanese social and economic indicators were extremely impressive – low infant mortality, high life expectancy, low unemployment, low inflation, generous retirement benefits and a high material standard of living. All this was achieved and perhaps even maintained by an unwillingness to rely on the state and a reluctance to pay taxes towards public welfare benefits. People preferred a system in which they provided their own social services to members of their families and in which employers rather than the state took on welfare responsibilities.

Yet Rose admitted in his article that Japanese society faced serious problems. The high price of land made decent housing difficult to afford. Industrial pollution had created major problems and attempts to control it would add to industry's costs and reduce its competitiveness. The ageing of the population and the decline in the numbers of elderly living with their children would mean increased costs for the state in terms of pensions and social services. Given his prognosis for the future, which seemed to suggest that Japan was doomed to face increased private and public expenditure to cope with its economic and social problems, it was difficult to know exactly what was the lesson we were supposed to be learning.

A subsequent set of papers in a book edited by Rose pursued the theme of a different welfare mix (Rose and Shiratori 1986). In one of them, Maruo argued that Japan was a society in which *gemeinschaft* principles operated, as opposed to the *gesellschaft* principles of the West (Maruo 1986). As a result of strong family and enterprise ties there was considerably less crime and divorce in Japan. However, while claiming that younger people wanted to live with their elderly parents and take care of them, she quoted statistics which suggested that whereas a quarter of the elderly in Sweden had home helps, and one tenth of those in the UK, in Japan the ratio was one to three hundred. The author went on to argue that Japan's welfare mix would remain distinct, but listed a range of factors which would necessitate increased state welfare expenditure in the future. There would be demographic pressures to increase expenditure on the elderly and political ones to reduce the differences between the major pension and health insurance schemes. Moreover economic pressures would lead to more older workers being forced to retire early to make way for younger (and cheaper) employees. Maruo predicted that state welfare would increase in Japan because the same factors, needs and demands operated in Japan as in other industrialised societies, but insisted that Japan would maintain its 'unique' welfare mix.

Using very similar arguments, Pinker, a prominent British social policy analyst, tried to explain the difference between welfare systems in the West and Japan in terms of culture. He felt that if we ignored cultural differences, then our understanding of Japan would be limited:

> In Japan we have a society in which the formal welfare arrangements closely reflect and complement the informal patterns of the tradition and culture.   (Pinker 1986: p. 127).

He felt that

> social psychological features help to explain some of the marked differences between British and Japanese notions of obligation and entitlement in social welfare.   (Pinker 1986: p. 123)

Given the collectivist and Fabian academic environment in which Pinker worked in Britain, this was an even-handed attempt to come to terms with a different system and not condemn it outright for failing to measure up to social democratic standards. It is clear that Pinker none the less found this approach difficult. He realised that inferior national health and pensions schemes were not conducive to redistribtion; that there was a 'relative indifference to the welfare of strangers'; that small companies could not provide the same range and quality of benefits as large ones; and that ethnic minorities and other groups suffered in consequence. Pinker could see clearly that in spite of being a major industrial power, Japan was 'seriously deficient in the provision of statutory social services' (Pinker 1986: p. 124). Yet he seemed to be convinced by cultural explanations that insisted that Japan had found a different way of solving the social problems associated with industrialisation.

THE MYTH OF JAPANESE UNIQUENESS

Many Western commentators were obviously trying to come to terms with a successful country from which it was felt there was something to learn. A reading of Peter Dale's *The Myth of Japanese Uniqueness* (1986) would suggest that they were falling for an official argument that Japan's culture was so different from that of the West that it should not be judged by Western standards.

While Dale was prepared to consider Japan unique in the sense that it had an individuality of its own, as had other societies, he was unhappy about accepting that it was somehow *uniquely* unique – so different that its ways, values and traditions were somehow incomprehensible to Westerners even if they had managed to grasp the language. He accused the *nihonjinron* tradition of scholarship of perpetuating myths about Japanese uniqueness that sought to mask some of the more obvious defects of Japanese society. When foreign observers criticised aspects of Japanese society, writers in this tradition were likely to respond by saying that, as outsiders, they had not understood that in Japan what might seem to be a defect by Western standards was in fact a peculiarly Japanese phenomenon. Dale cited the writer Suzuki who attempted to explain the decapitation of prisoners of war by insisting that it was not the swordsman 'but the sword that does the killing. He has no desire to do harm to anybody, but the enemy appears and makes himself the victim.' The example was an extreme one, but consider a similar piece of obfuscation by Chie Nakane:

> It is well-known that Japanese women are nearly always ranked as inferiors; this is not because their sex is considered inferior, but because women seldom hold higher social status(Quoted in Dale 1986: p. 32).

Dale described the *nihonjinron* as the work of self-appointed scholars whose job it was to articulate the 'soul of the Japanese essence'. Much of what was written in this field, if published in English, would, according to one commentator, become the 'butt of amazement and ridicule abroad'.

The work of Nakagawa, referred to above, would seem to have all the hallmarks of a piece of *nihonjinron*. Foreigners, he implied, could not really understand that what appeared to them as inadequate social welfare was really a peculiarly Japanese way of caring. The elderly liked to continue to work well after their retirement – it was not out of necessity because of their low pensions. Houses were not inadequate but reflected the low priority the Japanese placed upon the commodity. Nakagawa's work certainly conforms to another characteristic that Dale attributes to the *nihonjinron*:

> It deflects critical analysis of underlying power relationships by placing the emphasis on cultural structures as determinants of reality.
>
> (Dale 1986: p. 59).

Thus it is supposed to be the essence of Japaneseness that the Japanese see themselves as part of a group, institution or organisation. Western notions of individuality and individual rights then become alien. Loyalty and obligation are defined in terms of traditional values, thus obscuring the possibility that they might simply be ideological devices whereby individuals are subordinated to more powerful interests – women to men in the family; employees to employers in the firm; citizens to the state in politics.

Dale's interesting blend of Marx and Freud led him to conclude that the Japanese male's 'need' for the group was not just a chance cultural phenomenon, but the result of clear child-rearing practices which first indulged the male child's every whim but subsequently and suddenly abandoned him to his own devices. The consequence, Dale argued, was that what for many passed as Japanese uniqueness would in Western terms be described as a 'condition of infantility'. This is a controversial statement to make about a whole culture, and a study of social policy ought perhaps to be wary of accepting such a judgement too glibly. None the less Dale provides a useful perspective from which to analyse some of the work already referred to. He does not specifically deal with matters of social welfare but he does comment upon the way in which the *nihonjinron* tradition has influenced Western writers. He suggests that some of those who have seen Japan as Number One, not only in economic terms (which it undoubtedly is) but social terms as well, are perhaps nostalgic for an 'idealised world of nineteenth-century capitalism minus the encumbrance of bourgeois institutions and civil rights'. While on the one hand they might have been deceived by the 'arcadian dialect of uniqueness', their approbation might also belie their own 'secret sympathy' with the Japanese way (Dale 1986: p. 177).

A WELFARE MESS?

There have certainly been writers who have doubted the claims made for the Japanese welfare model. Drucker, writing as early as 1978, wondered whether the 'strengths' of lifetime employment and the seniority wage system could survive the consequences of an ageing work-force. Many of the features that had been held responsible for the success of the Japanese system would become liabilities as demographic changes took their toll. The future in Drucker's view would require commensurate changes in 'social structure, social policies and social values'. Far from thinking that the Japanese had a system to export, Drucker felt clearly that its major features would have to change (Drucker 1978).

By 1983 an anonymous Japanese observer was claiming that companies faced with rising salary costs were keeping workers on until a later retirement age of 60, but were either freezing wages at the age of 50 or even reversing the seniority principle. Neither lifetime employment nor a seniority wage system existed for many workers. The ageing of the work-force was eroding a system which others at the same time were claiming were features of some enduring set of cultural values. The government might have pinned its hopes on older workers continuing to support themselves into old age; on families taking care of their children; and of companies looking after their employees – but as time went on, each of these 'traditions' was being eroded. Faced with similar problems, Japan would find itself having to resort to the solutions the West had pioneered (Anon. 1983).

Watanuki mounted an even more scathing attack on the claims of a 'Japanese welfare society' when he insisted that the whole exercise had merely been a government ploy to keep state welfare expenditure down. There was no superior 'unitary' Japanese system, but 'a patched up system of discrete schemes with varied provision of benefits' (Watanuki 1986). Frightened by the increasing costs of welfare and the economic crisis in the mid-1970s, the government had sought to argue that Western welfare states were inefficient and that the Japanese had their own way of dealing with social problems. Neither the aims nor the means were peculiarly Japanese, according to Watanuki. The desire for low public expenditure and small government was no different from that traditionally espoused by conservatives in the West like Thatcher and Reagan. The rhetoric of communities providing was hollow when urban communities could hardly be said to exist. To claim that the family would provide when elderly people were increasingly living on their own was wishful thinking. He went on to argue that company welfare was hardly uniquely Japanese when firms in the USA had been providing occupational, medical and pension insurance schemes for years. Nor was family welfare Japanese. Rather it was an Asian phenomenon which was fast fading in Japan.

Far from thinking that the West could learn from Japan in the care of the elderly, Watanuki argued that

> The Swedish type of welfare state spends a great deal of money in building homes for the elderly and in employing a large number of public social workers to visit the elderly in their homes. In the British type of welfare state, greater effort is made by voluntary organisations

and workers to care for the elderly in their homes. The evidence shows that in Japan, too great a burden is placed on families to care for the aged and this has already surfaced in a higher suicide rate of persons over the age of 65 years which is higher than that of Sweden, and episodic reports of exhausted daughters, both natural and in-law, in caring for their parents. (Watanuki 1986)

Like the previous writer, Watanuki clearly thought that Japan, faced with a growing elderly population, had more to learn from the West than the other way round.

Other critics in the 1980s, Japanese and non-Japanese, have drawn attention to the inadequacies of Japanese welfare system. Takahashi has criticised the inadequacies of the personal social services, the fragmented pension system, and the over-reliance in health care on pharmaceuticals (Takahashi and Someya 1985). In his view, an emphasis on medical care and some aspects of social security in the past would have to be complemented by making personal social services a priority in the future. Takahashi was also critical of the way in which the welfare of non-nationals had been neglected. He argued that 'increased economic interdependence at the international level' meant that Japan could not afford to be indifferent to the welfare of immigrant workers (Takahashi and Someya 1985: p. 173). Dean, in an article entitled 'An economic miracle and a welfare mess', drew attention to the inequalities in benefits resulting from a system which claimed to be based upon the family and the firm rather than the state. The sick, elderly and the unemployed were paying the price of a 'failing tri-partite system' (Dean 1986).

Low unemployment figures have also been disputed by Takashima. Unemployment, he claimed, was based upon those officially registered as unemployed. The true figure, he claimed, was three times as great. Moreover, since the duration of benefit was only a few months for many of those claiming and since unemployment was not regarded as an adequate reason for claiming social assistance, many of those who had lost their jobs were forced to accept employment at extremely low rates of pay under conditions far worse than those they previously enjoyed. In a decent welfare system with effective legislation on minimum wages and adequate social benefits, he argued, it would not be possible to pretend that forced labour was employment (Takashima 1988).

SOCIAL DIVISION AND SOCIAL CONTROL

Any welfare system offers scope for differing interpretations as to what contribution it makes to general well-being and social stability.

Capitalist Welfare Systems

What is interesting about Japanese welfare is that it began to attract favourable attention around 1980, when ten years previously it had been universally considered to be inferior to the Western welfare state. What had happened in the meantime was that the latter had come to be considered as an expensive failure from a number of standpoints, particularly that of capital accumulation, whereas the Japanese system seemed to be a relatively cheap but effective way of ensuring social harmony without becoming too great a drain on economic resources. The emergence of this system had been neither an accident nor inevitable.

Garon's historical study of the relationship between the state, employers and labour demonstrates clearly a constant struggle to find a form of welfare provision which did not result in unacceptable economic and political concessions. There were those even before 1920 who considered the Western compromise to be too great a price to pay for industrial peace.

> What makes us proudest is that we have no labour problems on the order of the Western nations. This condition results from the true tranquillity and peace of our society. . . . Conflict currently plagues the societies of the West to a degree unimaginable to us. Take the workers of England. In an effort to increase wages, they have launched widespread strikes, oblivious to the Great War and the precarious fate of their nation. Or Germany and France, where socialist parties, based on workers, dare to engage in conduct and speech, harmful to the unity and tranquillity of their nations. American workers have also organised to resist capitalists, thereby precluding harmonious relations between the two groups. Lastly, the recent revolution in Russia, rests on an alliance of workers and soldiers. . . . Social policy in the West looks for cures to the 'labour disease' . . . which has already broken out. Social policy in our country aims at preventing the outbreak of this disease.   (Minoru Oka quoted in Garon 1987: p. 38)

The need to catch up with the West made it even more imperative not to give way to socialist demands and pressures.

Welfare and control have always gone hand in hand, but in Japan the forces of control have kept the upper hand. Concessions there have been, but as Garon shows, at the price of greatly increased control. It is ironic that the Home Ministry, in the early decades of this century, had a twin responsibility for social policy and policing. As the activities of the social and police bureaux within the ministry grew it was not unusual for 'liberally minded' bureaucrats to move office and repress the very groups that they had previously been trying to appease. The social bureaucrats in the 1920s often argued in favour of recognition for and cooperation with labour unions. Those who had travelled abroad had been impressed by both Bismarckian and British Liberal efforts to come to a compromise with labour. It is not surprising that the German influence was the stronger, but as Garon remarks, 'The Japanese Government refused to deal with workers as a corporate entity' (Garon 1987: p. 32).

After concessions in the 1920s concerning poor relief, health insurance and the right to vote, the Peace Preservation Law of 1926 was implemented with a vengeance by the judiciary. For the next twenty years Japanese authoritarianism sought its own compromise. The communists and socialists who were clearly antagonistic to capitalism were repressed in a violent manner, but accommodation was sought with what were regarded as the moderate, sensible, cooperative labour representatives. After the failure of military rule and the attempts to borrow ideas and practices from the Nazi Labour Front, the American Occupation strengthened the hands of the social bureaucrats in the post-war reconstruction. But again, the Japanese system found it impossible to cope with the emergence of strong trade unions and their political demands. Again, through a combination of social policy concessions, the cultivation of moderate unionists and the repression of the radicals, the Japanese state in alliance with employers forged an approach to labour and social issues distinct from the policies adopted in the West.

The result, a Japanese-style welfare system, may be judged deficient from a socialist or liberal viewpoint, but as far as capitalism is concerned, there is a case to be made for it. The discouragement and repression of national trade unions and socialist political parties had created divisions and prevented the rise of a national movement capable of making great demands of the state. This in turn prevented the rise of a large body of welfare bureaucrats and professionals within the state apparatus, claiming to mediate working-class needs and demands. The combination of these two factors – a national labour movement and a strong public salariat – has proved, in Britain and Sweden, to be expensive, inflationary and not particularly effective in terms of creating equality, ameliorating social problems, providing social stability or aiding capital accumulation. The Japanese authorities deliberately sought to avoid such a situation from the early years of this century and achieved it through a ruthless 'divide and rule' policy. Company welfare and enterprise unionism have focused the commitment and loyalty of large numbers of the labour aristocracy and the salaried middle class in the private sector on company and nationalistic goals, and have prevented the rise of welfare statism. But this does not make the Japanese welfare system unproblematic, simply more suited to the imperatives of Japanese capital.

Sugimoto has argued that those advocating that the West should learn from Japan

> fail to see a correlation between the success and failure of Japanese modernisation. While their books and articles mention such darker aspects as environmental pollution, sexual discrimination, the disparity between big and small business, poor housing and the pathological effects of frantic competition for entry into prestigious schools, negative phenomena are nevertheless treated as though they were isolated from the more positive aspects . . . any country attempting to fashion itself after Japan must be ready to accept both the strengths and weaknesses of the model. (Sugimoto 1986: p. 67)

To Sugimoto what seems to others to be a voluntary consensus is in reality authoritarian control:

> Groupism itself is an explicit ideology directly communicated by dominant to subordinate groups in an attempt to routinise the obedience of individuals to the so-called needs of the company, school or state. (Sugimoto 1986: p. 68)

CONCLUSION

The Japanese welfare system, then, has its admirers and critics inside and outside the country. Japan's brand of welfare pluralism has some strong points but, from a variety of standpoints, many weaknesses. Indicators of good health and educational performance are high. Costs have been kept down through a reliance on extra-state resources such as the family, the firm and volunteers. The avoidance of state monopolies in welfare provision has reduced the power of the public sector and prevented the proliferation of state programmes and exaggerated labour costs. There is no doubt, however, that there are many needs which go unmet in the Japanese system. The elderly, the mentally ill and the poor suffer serious neglect while young people's education increasingly depends upon the size of their parents' purse. While it is unlikely that the Japanese authorities will abandon a preference for a welfare mix in which provision by the state is characterised by a reluctance to become too involved, it is inevitable that costs for all welfare providers, including the state, will increase as the percentage of elderly people in Japan grows. Social security costs will mount, as will the costs of the labour-intense services of health care and social services.

The principle appeal of the Japanese welfare system to conservative observers in the West must surely lie in the fact that, in their view, a more favourable accommodation with labour has been reached than was achieved through the post-war welfare state consensus of both Britain and Sweden. However, in advocating the view that Western countries could do well to emulate Japan, they have probably underestimated the problems the Japanese system will face in the future.

But as we shall see in the next two sections on Britain and Sweden, there is one lesson that conservative governments in the West have learnt. The post-war welfare state contained the seeds of its own expansion and, faced with the competitiveness of post-Fordist Japan, could no longer be afforded. Such governments have been forced to adopt new techniques to control their citizens' welfare demands and expectations. In this they might well agree with Sugimoto that 'Japan may indeed be "Number One" in having engineered highly-developed techniques of material, bureaucratic and ideological manipulation' (Sugimoto 1986: p. 75).

PART TWO
Britain

CHAPTER SIX

Economic, political and social context

Britain was the first industrial nation. From being the superpower of the nineteenth century, its economic and political significance has declined as its competitors in Europe, Japan and the USA have taken larger shares of international markets and a greater part in global politics. The concept of 'the welfare state' had its origins in Britain and for a time it was a model for others to follow. Britain's decline in welfare terms can best be understood by looking at its relative economic decline and the attempts by various post-war governments to reverse that trend. Many of Britain's problems are rooted in its imperial past and its antiquated class structure. It struggles to be modern but seems to be held back by the accumulated deadweight of the past; its decaying infrastructure, its archaic political institutions and entrenched social attitudes. During the 1960s and 1970s governments of the left and the right experimented unsuccessfully with corporatism in an attempt to revive the British economy. More recently a series of Conservative governments have tried a different approach. The end result is a society in which the social priorities of the welfare state have given way to the dictates of a post-Fordist market economy.

FROM INDUSTRIALISATION TO THE SECOND WORLD WAR

It is tempting to conclude from the various accounts of Britain's economic decline that for over a century it has been managed incompetently by fools and knaves who had numerous opportunities to turn the economy around but failed. Usually, those who analyse the malaise can point to those periods where something positive could and should have been done. They more often than not conclude with a recipe for the future which if followed will drag the country out of its mire. The assumption that something can be done will not be made here. Instead, it will simply be assumed that a number of complex factors have led to the slow decline of a country which had its hour of greatness and has been overtaken by younger competitors with many advantages including hindsight. Japan and Sweden in particular, industrialising as they did towards the last quarter of the nineteenth century, were bound to be able to avoid some of the pitfalls the British stumbled into. It is not surprising that the British, having achieved so much with the ideas and institutions they had, should have found it difficult to abandon them.

An empire had been built up which seemed to give Britain unparalleled economic and political dominance in the world. It provided favourable markets for British exports and a source of cheap raw materials. It was the empire which gave British finance its international character. British businesses were based in various colonies, which were run by British administrators and defended by the British military. The British ruling class was educated in public schools, founded in the middle of the nineteenth century, whose task it was to educate those who would run the empire. The British and their empire were so strongly linked for such a long period of time that inevitably no major institution could fail to have been affected by the relationship.

Empires are relinquished reluctantly, usually long after they have ceased to be of value to the country of origin, and too long after they have become a military and financial liability. The British clung to their empire long after it had ceased to be of use to them. It gave them a distorted view of their strength and greatness; it justified a commitment to free trade and laissez-faire economics and blinded them to the benefits of protectionism and state intervention that their competitors were so quick to take advantage of (Eatwell 1982); it encouraged the development of a banking system which gave little priority to the parochial needs of domestic, industrial investment. Captive imperial markets have also been cited for the reluctance to invest in new technology in the first half of the century, since they cushioned British manufacturers from international competition.

Britain's relative economic decline is often said to have begun around 1870, but the empire itself was not finally abandoned until the 1960s. Almost a century of delusion prevented the British from seeing why it was that other countries were developing stronger, more sound economies. Since the 1960s various attempts have been made by successive governments to improve the performance of the British economy, but none so far has succeeded. It may be that having become a deprived region amongst advanced capitalist economies, the rot will continue.

The strength of the economy was also sapped by Britain's involvement in two world wars. Emerging on the victorious side would itself seem to have been a liability since victors expect something from the sacrifices they have made. Those defeated had no alternative but to examine where they had gone wrong and to set about putting it right. Britain emerged from the Second World War with enormous debts, the administrative and military responsibilities of a decaying empire, and an electorate demanding a set of social programmes to compensate for the sufferings endured in the recession of the 1930s and the privations of wartime.

POST-WAR ECONOMIC DEVELOPMENT

After the difficult years of reconstruction following the Second World War, Western countries as a whole enjoyed two decades of unprecedented growth. Jordan has shown how the comparative economic growth rates of countries before the 1930s recession seemed to change little in the post-war years. Japan remained above 6 per cent; France and Germany about 5 per cent; the USA about 4 per cent; while Britain remained below 3 per cent (Jordan 1982: p. 18). Jordan attributed much of Britain's low growth to the fact that manufacturing industry had used up its reservoir of cheap labour from the agricultural sector whereas its competitors still had something to draw on. In Germany, France, the USA and Japan, 'Workers from low paid agricultural occupations were still being absorbed in large numbers into new industries, as new industrialisation and urbanisation took place' (Jordan 1981: p. 24).

The management of the economy during the early period after the war was characterised by a commitment to full employment. Although unemployment remained below 500,000 for many years, the commitment was made difficult by the tendency for balance of payment problems and inflation to arise which required a deflationary response from government. 'Stop-go' policies made sustained growth and investment an unachievable target. Increasingly, from 1960, governments sought to organise economic – and to a degree social

– policy through collaboration with business and trade-union associations. This tri-partitism – which in the view of some, never quite became full-blown corporatism – was an attempt to overcome a particular set of problems. Full employment without a degree of wage restraint became inflationary. That restraint could be achieved through greater cooperation between government, employers and the unions. Poor industrial relations were also seen to be more of a problem in Britain than for some of its competitors. If strikes were to be avoided; if demarcation disputes were to be overcome; if rationalisation of production and new investment were to be effective; if long-term planning was to be successful – then government, management and unions would need to cooperate with these ends in view.

But what had worked so successfully in some European countries did not work so well in Britain. There was neither the institutional framework nor the degree of trust that enabled government and the two sides of industry in Austria, Germany and Sweden to cooperate. The unions were often blamed for the failure of incomes policies; the miners were seen as the cause of the downfall of the Heath government in 1974; and the demands by trade unions in the late 1970s for industrial democracy and a greater say in the country's and industry's management, together with their rejection of the then Labour government's pay norm, were seen by conservative elements as a threat to social stability.

The international crisis of 1973 had been followed by inflation and recession all over the world, including Japan, but in Britain there were additional problems. The net rate of profit in manufacturing industry in major European countries had been under half the rate of Japan for over a decade. In Britain the rate was almost half the European average. In 1975, when the Japanese rate had plummeted to 15 per cent, the European rate was less than 9 per cent and the British 2.4 per cent (Armstrong *et al.* 1991). Part of Britain's problem at the time was attributed to the growth of public-sector employment which had resulted in there being 'too many producers' (Bacon and Eltis 1976). Bacon and Eltis argued that the use of the public sector to create employment opportunities had caused the net take-home pay of manual workers to remain static for ten years. Moreover, the seeming failure to bring public expenditure under control and to reassure the financial markets on the value of sterling led to demands by the IMF for tough measures. Even before the 1979 General Election, there had been a reversal of post-war economic policies. The Keynesian commitment to full employment was allowed to slide. Public expenditure was cut and the growth of money supply restricted (Smith

1987). In a speech to the Labour Party Conference in 1976, the Prime Minister said:

> We used to think that you could just spend your way out of a recession, and increase employment by cutting taxes and boosting government spending. I tell you in all candour, that option no longer exists.

Public expenditure and taxation levels had grown during the war, which had itself contributed to a greater acceptance of state intervention in economic and social matters. The establishment of the welfare state in the aftermath of the war and its expansion during the affluent 1960s was maintained by that acceptance, and helped by economic growth. Public expenditure as a percentage of GNP rose from 36.1 per cent in 1951 to over 46.2 per cent in 1974 before declining a little to 45.6 per cent in 1979. Much of this expansion was due to social expenditure – including health, social security, housing and employment – which had risen as a percentage of GNP from 16.1 per cent in 1951 to 28.3 per cent in 1979 (Judge 1982: p. 28). Defence expenditure during the post-war decades also remained at a high 5 per cent compared with much lower percentages of other European countries. Although tax and social security contributions had obviously grown to finance this expenditure, it had always been possible to point out that many of Britain's economically more successful European competitors levied even higher tax rates and social security contributions. Using the same comparisons, it had been possible to suggest that a successful capitalist country needed a strong public sector.

While these arguments had made some sense in the past, they were becoming less relevant as all Western capitalist countries faced increasing competition from Japan and the rapidly industrialising nations of the Pacific Rim. Korea, Hong Kong, the Philippines and Singapore were all encroaching on Western markets. Their low labour costs, low public expenditure and low taxation created a new competetive threat which demanded a rethink by Western companies and governments.

Parallel with these developments there were the revolutionary implications of the new information technology to take on board. The institutions and politics that had emerged from an economy based upon mass production and assembly-line techniques were not appropriate to the new computer-based technology. The Japanese system, however, was coping well with these changes. It was in the forefront of technological change and soon had the highest number of robots *per capita* in the world. The organisational flexibility required by non-Japanese multi-national companies to compete with Japan was already beginning to emerge to meet the demands of the new global order by the end of the 1970s.

In Britain, private industry could see the need to respond. But a response from government was also necessary to bring about major adjustments in the whole political climate. This could hardly have come from a Labour government and a trade-union movement wedded to Fordism, Keynesianism and welfarism. Even amongst trade unionists like Jenkins and Sherman, who could see the employment implications of the new technology, the inclination was to view the situation in terms of an avoidance of the worst consequences for the unemployed and a desire to expand opportunities for all workers. For all the talk of flexibility and modernisation, they hoped for a new leisure society in which all shared the fruits of technological change. Those made unemployed would receive higher levels of benefit; the employed would have lengthy periods of leave and a shorter working week; there would be an expansion of leisure, health, welfare and educational opportunities. All of this, they argued, could be achieved through sound government policies, sensible collective bargaining and enlightened management (Jenkins and Sherman 1979: ch. 11). Such a stance, whatever one might think of its intrinsic and humane merits, was rooted in the politics and assumptions of the Euro-centred 1960s, rather than the global needs of the 1980s.

Economic policy was to change even more radically with the election of a Conservative government in 1979. Keynesianism was abandoned for monetarism; low inflation and not low unemployment became a major goal of policy; privatisation, liberalisation and deregulation were the order of the day. The old consensus had included the trade unions, the new consensus was between government and business. As the Japanese had put production first, so the British government made business and the economy an over-riding priority. The aim was to unshackle industry and commerce from unnecessary constraints. There was less concern about environmental pollution and health and safety measures. Profit and incentives were in, equality and vertical redistribution were out. Wider share and property ownership were encouraged, as were private education, pensions and health insurance schemes.

The end results were mixed. There were years in which growth had reached 4 per cent but the average rate for the decade was no different from that of the 1970s, 2.2 per cent (Johnson 1990). Productivity had increased. But total manufacturing output and investment rose by only 12 per cent and 11 per cent respectively throughout the whole period. More people might own their homes and a few shares but the ownership of marketable wealth, less the value of dwellings, indicated that a substantial redistribution to the wealthiest 25 per cent of the population had taken place (*Guardian* 1992). A new climate, more favourable to free enterprise, had been created by the middle of the decade but that was dented by the subsequent recession when unemployment began to climb again, large numbers of houses were repossessed because of mortgage defaults, and many businesses became bankrupt. Public and social expenditure as percentages of GDP remained well over 40 per cent for most of the decade, but came down to almost 38 per cent in 1989–90; public-sector employment was reduced by over 6 per cent, but much of this was due to privatisation. Central and local government employment was reduced by less than 2 per cent (Johnson 1990).

But if the economic gains and losses were mixed, there could be no doubt that the power and influence of groups and institutions in society that had been identified by the Conservatives as a threat to free enterprise had been weakened. Local authorities were much more restricted by central government; public employees had lost their political clout; and the Labour Party had learnt to extol the virtues of the market. Of even greater significance was the change in the role and status of trade unions.

TRADE UNIONS

Like their Japanese counterparts, British workers had faced considerable hostility from employers during the course of industrialisation. Trade unions established themselves with great difficulty. Workers with similar crafts and skills gradually combined in national organisations. Many of these had affiliated to one federation – the Trades Union Congress (TUC) – in 1868, and had helped to establish one political party in 1900 – the Labour Party – to represent the interests of working people in Parliament. At the end of the nineteenth century only 11 per cent of the labour force was unionised. By 1948 over 50 per cent of blue-collar workers and 30 per cent of white-collar workers were unionised. These percentages had grown by 1974 to 57.9 per cent and 39.4 per cent respectively – considerably more than in Japan, though much less than in Sweden. Trade unions experienced major conflicts with government and employers in the first half of the century which reinforced a mutual distrust and suspicion between them. With the onset of the Second World War, union leaders began to play a bigger role in government and policy-making which continued in the post-war years. Apart from anything else, full employment made the cooperation of trade unions indispensable.

During the 1960s and 1970s there were few government agencies or commissions that did not have trade unions represented on them in one form or another. Trade unions played an important role on the National Economic Development Board, the Industrial Training Boards, the Industrial Re-organisation Commission. The Manpower Services Commission, set up in 1974 on lines similar to the Swedish Labour Market Board, had strong union representation, as did the National Enterprise Board, set up in 1974 to act as a major planning agency for the development of British industry (Holland 1975). The price of trade-union cooperation seemed to get higher with each government elected. The Labour government passed a number of measures to give greater protection to employees – the Sex Discrimination Act, the Race Relations Act, a new Health and Safety Act and the Employment Protection Act itself. In addition, a Committee of Inquiry into Industrial Democracy recommended in 1977 that all major companies should have equal numbers of trade-union and shareholder representatives on their management boards. Although the Labour government had no intention of implementing such a measure, it was an indication of the strength and importance that trade unions had achieved in British economic and political life (Elliott 1978).

It was not surprising that trade unions in Britain should have wanted to extend their role in the decision-making process at government and company levels. But nor was it surprising that those more sympathetic to the needs of capitalism took the view that corporatism in Britain had become a kind of 'creeping socialism' or 'socialism by the back door'. Although in many respects the performance of the British economy during the 1970s was not that bad, it was clear that there were those who took the view that the power and influence of trade unions had become too great both on the factory floor and in the corridors of power and was, to a considerable extent, responsible for the continued weakness of the economy. Those who held this view clearly felt that the major economic and social decisions of the 1980s should be made with little regard for the trade-union movement.

There had already been government attempts to reform the unions. The Donovan Commission which reported in 1968 had been set up to recommend improvements to the structure of unions and their role in collective bargaining. Concern had often been expressed about the conduct of union elections and ballots, and the protection which the law gave to certain kinds of trade-union activity. Wildcat strikes seemed to present management with a significant problem in Britain, as did the need for one employer to negotiate with a number of different unions, each representing a different occupation or skill.

There was a view within the Conservative Party, amongst some employers and to an extent in the country at large, that the power of trade unions should be reduced. The Conservative government elected after 1979 felt that it had a mandate to do just that. The government's task was made that much easier by the growth of unemployment from just over 1 million in 1979 to over 3 million in 1982. Unemployment made employees less willing to take strike action and more fearful for their jobs. In this climate, the government enacted measures to limit strike action, and to regulate the internal affairs of unions including their elections and strike-ballot procedures. New rules were introduced which were intended to restrict the amount of money which trade unions could donate to the Labour Party. In addition to legislation, the government began systematically to exclude trade-union leaders from important policy discussions, commissions and committees in which they come to expect to play a part. Lastly, whenever a major industrial dispute occurred, the placatory, intermediary role played by previous governments was abandoned in favour of a tougher line in support of the employers. In the national strike called by the National Union of Mineworkers against the closure of coal pits, and when printers demonstrated against the use of new printing technology, the police, with full government backing, dealt severely with those involved. In many other ways the government sought to restrict or weaken trade-union activity in the public and the private sector.

In the 1970s the position of the trade unions in British society had borne an increasing resemblance to the powerful role of unions in Swedish society. By the end of the 1980s they had become cowed by unemployment, legislation, impotence and repression. They were easier prey for employers who wanted single-union agreements or no unions at all. As the hostile climate around 1960 in Japan had led to a decline in union membership, the same had begun to happen in the UK in the 1980s. In the 1970s over 57 per cent of manual workers had been unionised but by 1988 the figure had fallen to 46 per cent (Johnson 1990). As in Japan, moderate unionism was rewarded and militancy punished. The number of strikes was reduced by 75 per cent from 1980 to 1991, while the number of working days lost plummeted by over 90 per cent during the same period (*Guardian* 1992).

THE POLITICAL SCENE

Post-war British governments

The lower house of the British Parliament has traditionally been dominated by two major political parties. The simple majority system of producing constituency members of Parliament has made it very difficult for smaller parties to thrive. Prior to the First World War the Conservative Party had vied with the Liberal Party for office. Since that time the Labour Party has been the Conservatives' principal opponent. The alternation between parties is, however, not even. Between 1951 and 1964 the British electorate elected three Conservative governments. Since 1979 four have been elected in succession. Moreover, Conservative governments have never had to rely on a third party for parliamentary support, but the Labour Party has had only three periods of office, in 1945, 1964 and 1966, when it has had an outright parliamentary majority. It would seem, then, as if the electorate prefers long periods of Conservative rule punctuated by shorter periods of Labour government.

For a time during the 1980s this pattern was threatened by a fragmentation of the parliamentary left, not dissimilar to the one which has prevailed in Japan. In 1981 a breakaway group from the Labour Party, calling themselves the Social Democrats, achieved considerable electoral success. Its supporters were clearly disturbed by the socialist direction of the Labour Party and felt that a new party of the centre would make a greater appeal to the electorate. In an alliance with the Liberal Party in the election of 1983 they received 27 per cent of the votes compared with Labour's 28 per cent. But while Labour gained 209 seats in Parliament, the Alliance parties gained only 23. The British electoral system has always thrown up such anomalies. In the 1951 election the Conservatives had a majority of seats while Labour had more votes. In the 1980s, the Conservative 'landslide victories' were based on less than 45 per cent of the total votes cast. In a system of proportional representation few British governments would have been able to form majority administrations.

Without a system of proportional representation, support for the Alliance dwindled and after the 1987 election, a re-alliance resulted in a smaller Social Democratic Party and a larger Liberal Democratic Party. Electoral support for the Liberal Democrats, however, then declined to the pre-1981 position of around 15 per cent. This period of turmoil may not have resulted in the realignment of British politics which the Social Democrats had hoped for but it did result in a realignment within the Labour Party itself. By the end of the decade it had moved much closer to Conservative policy on taxation, the public sector, Europe and defence. The chief distinguishing feature between the two had become their attitudes towards the role of the state in a modern economy. Whereas the Conservatives continued to distrust interventionism, regarding civil servants as unfit to make judgements about planning and investment, the Labour Party felt that the only way to prevent the further erosion of Britain's manufacturing base was for the state to play a greater role in financial and industrial decisions.

Had the Conservatives maintained their laissez-faire stance under the leadership of Margaret Thatcher, the Labour Party might have won the General Election of 1992. As it was, the new administration under Prime Minister John Major took a much more pragmatic line than his predecessor on a whole range of issues including state intervention in the economy. The Labour Party's critique was defused and the Conservatives were given another mandate. What interventionism there may be in the future, however, is unlikely to reflect the corporatist tripartitism of the 1960s. While the new Secretary of State for Industry was an avowed interventionist, the last remaining body which gave trade unions a voice in economic and industrial policy – the National Economic Development Council – was abolished within weeks of the election.

The British political élite

If there seems to be a built-in tendency amongst the British electorate to prefer the Conservative Party to the Labour Party, that tendency has additional institutional support from the upper house of Parliament. The House of Lords is not an elected chamber. In spite of a number of life peers with a wide range of political allegiances who are 'appointed', the Lords consists of a built-in majority of hereditary peers who overwhelmingly vote Conservative. Government bills are, to be fair, often debated in a way that contributes something of value to the policy-making process and they may occasionally be rejected. But if an issue is of major importance to a Conservative government, the hereditary peers will attend in large numbers to help the measure through – and the opposite, in the case of a Labour government measure. This archaic aspect of the British political scene only serves to reflect the ingrained nature of a traditional class structure.

As hereditary peers continue to wield undue influence, so the British royal family is both more extensive and more costly than the constitutional monarchies of Sweden and Japan. The political and social significance of its members is out of all proportion to the actual amount of constitutional power that they are supposed to wield. They represent the apex of a class system based upon tradition and deference which helps to preserve an unconstructive nostalgia for imperial greatness, which is further reinforced by the British public-school system.

It remains the case that a clearly identified British political élite drawn disproportionately from public schools continues to dominate political life. Sixty to 80 per cent of senior military and diplomatic personnel, the higher reaches of the judiciary, the civil service, leading figures in commerce and other forms of public life are still drawn from a group of schools which caters for 3 per cent of the population (Reid 1989). It is this which gives the British ruling class its unique character. It is not difficult to see why the stability and continuity of political life should be seen to be conservative in more ways than one. Nor is it difficult to see how a set of institutions dominated by such people should be seen as the principal cause of Britain's slow abandonment of empire and imperial pretensions nor its inability to adapt to institutions of modernity. The significance of these important features of British political life may partly account for the failure of radical governments of both the left and the right to achieve what was expected of them.

Policy-making and consensus

Nor can a rational, professional approach to policy-making be pursued in institutions still dominated by a public-school tradition of 'amateurs and gentlemen' in contrast to the professional, meritocratic technocrats found in Sweden, France, Germany and Japan. Two American commentators on comparative welfare, Heclo and Ashford, have both pointed out, in different contexts, that the British system of public policy-making lacks important elements that its counterparts in Sweden, France and the USA have. Heclo argued that the Swedish approach to systematic, extensive investigation and consultation was totally different from the more *ad hoc* British system of setting up inquiries and commissions when it suited the government's convenience or public demand. He claimed that although British civil servants had played an important role in the making of social policy, the constitution operated in such a way as to 'obscure' that role. The British system refused to 'acknowledge the political contribution of adminstrators to policy' unlike the Swedish (Heclo 1974: p. 304). Ashford also pointed to the lack of a clear role in policy-making for administrators. Their ambiguous position was in sharp contrast to France and the USA where their policy-making role was acknowledged. The resulting conflict between politicians and the bureaucrats meant that 'in most other countries politicians developed a keen sense of how politics and administration interlock' (Ashford 1981: p. 19). Japan also learnt this lesson early on:

> Late modernizers, such as Japan, had to have powerful administrative agencies if they were to catch up with other industrial powers, and the more dynamic remnants of the Tokugawa bureaucracy became the agents of modernization. (Ashford 1981: p. 19)

Ashford also found the limited powers of backbench MPs and their committees difficult to understand when he compared them with the 'the wide ranging policy intervention found in the American Congress or the French National Assembly' (Ashford 1981: p. 50). He went on, though, to say that this presupposed 'a flexibility of partisan alignments and party loyalties on various choices and issues'. It would seem that the need for a 'neutral' civil service is a consequence of adversarial, alternating governments. Having to serve governments claiming to have completely different ideologies and policies, with the clear possibility that the opposition may indeed form a government, the political role of the civil service cannot be too partisan unless, as in the USA, you change the whole administration when there is a change of government. If the role of the administrators is strong and more partisan in Japan and Sweden, this may be largely due to the stability of the ruling governing party. But even in Britain the neutrality of civil servants is relative. The predominance of Conservative governments, institutions and personnel inevitably detracts from their impartiality.

But Ashford's criticism that too much policy-making is concentrated in the hands of ministers and a few senior civil servants is quite damning:

> Perhaps the greatest loss is that learning from past errors and experience depends on a remarkably small number of persons who in fact have very little time, and very little incentive, to make critiques and evaluations of policy effectiveness that are more pronounced in most other democratic political systems. The odd

result is that, in an age of mass politics, British government makes many crucial decisions with relatively little policy guidance.

(Ashford 1981: p. 16)

If Ashford could argue this position in 1981, how much more true must it appear ten years later. Although he described the British system of policy-making as complex, *ad hoc* and ramshackle, it none the less did sustain the consolidation and growth of the public sector with a high degree of consultation and consensus in the post-war years. Governments did seek civil service advice; quangos did exist which brought in outside business people, trade unionists, professionals and managers; professional associations and interest groups were consulted; investigating commissions representing the great and the good were set up and did produce research and reports which played an important part in the policy-making process.

However, recent Conservative governments, determined to carry out a radical New Right programme, decided to dispense with many of these procedures and institutional practices, relying instead on private think-tanks which followed a particular ideological line – the Adam Smith Institute, Omega and the Hillgate Group. The result has been a series of under-researched experiments which, whatever their philosophical merits, have proved administratively disastrous. A radicalism which ignores too many interests and institutions in a pluralist society is in danger of getting bogged down in the mire of its own errors. None the less, such an approach was deemed necessary to ensure the rightward move of British institutions.

The policy-making arena today is much more selective. Consultation exists, but it tends to be with those individuals and organisations closely identified with the government's aims and ideology; a form of corporatism remains but, as in Japan, it has become a corporatism of the right.

CULTURAL CHARACTERISTICS

The adherence to a laissez-faire individualism was an important part of Britain's transition to an industrial society. It defined the boundaries between the old aristocratic state and the new bourgeois capitalism. It informed every aspect of economic and social policy in the nineteenth century, and has been a constant theme in political life whenever state intervention, for any reason, has been proposed in the twentieth. In contrast to Sweden and Japan, where a strong interventionist role for the state is widely accepted, state intervention in Britain has always been the subject of controversy. In neither of those countries could one imagine a political leader saying 'there is no such thing as society'. The liberal state had the job of protecting individual rights and private property – and could be very coercive and partisan in its interpretation of that role – but for the state to take on the task of running an industry, or providing a service or benefit required special justification.

That justification often took the form of a related tradition – utilitarianism. This pragmatic approach to public affairs enabled its adherents, from the Victorian reformers to Keynes and Beveridge, to question the harsher consequences of a reliance on unfettered free enterprise and to propose practical solutions to social problems (George and Wilding 1976). Those who advocated an approach to public affairs did not do so in opposition to a system of free enterprise. Their arguments, on the contrary, were entirely supportive of a market economy. But, whereas the more ardent advocates of a liberal, laissez-faire approach saw few deficiencies in market mechanisms, those of an equally liberal but utilitarian persuasion took a more critical stance. It was conceded that markets did not always work well. Moreover, the adverse consequences to which they often gave rise created problems of public squalor, disease, environmental pollution, crime and social unrest, which were not only damaging to those involved but threatened the social stability that a capitalist economy required.

It is not difficult to see how this utilitarian approach to public administration would come to share some common ground with the reformist social democracy of the labour movement. While there might have been disagreement about the desirability of capitalist free enterprise, there was some agreement over its more damaging consequences and the need for government action to remedy them. Social democracy, however, went a step further than utilitarian reform in its advocacy of a greater degree of equality. Government action, it was claimed, was required not simply to counteract the negative features of capitalism but to promote better conditions and opportunities for the mass of working people. The desire here was to change the nature of capitalism and to create a better, more equal, more just society.

It is hardly surprising that out of these three traditions – laissez-faire individualism, utilitarianism and social democracy – a consensus emerged, not of a strong state, but of a pragmatic state. The state might be viewed with suspicion by laissez-faire liberals and socialists alike, but its mechanisms and institutions could be used to deal with specific social and economic problems. The result has been a sort of collectivism which has allowed the state apparatus to be used reluctantly rather than with enthusiasm, reactively rather than proactively. Japanese politicians of the right and Swedish politicians of the left have been able to work with a social acceptance of the strong state. In Britain, alternating governments of the right and left have had to contend with a social scepticism concerning the use of state power.

In consequence, while none would deny the capacity of the British state for coercion and control, few would decribe it as authoritarian. Traditionally Conservatives exhibited a concept of the public good which overrode their objection to state intervention; while the socialists and social democrats who made up the Labour Party could be fervent in their defence of individual rights. In social matters – from the provision of social security, the maintenance of roads and law and order, the defence of the realm and matters of environmental health – there were often areas of agreement. Indeed, in the post-war years of consensus, the existence of nationalised industries, intervention in private industry and the welfare state were accepted, to a degree, by all. But there has always been a tendency on the right to see state intervention as socialist, dangerous and threatening – with some justification, since there were always those within a Labour administration who, given the opportunity, would have used state power for socialist ends. Such a possibility has hardly existed in Japan, where the right has been able to use state power unambiguously to promote the interests of Japanese industry.

The reluctance of many of those on the right in Britain to get involved in industrial policy was not, however, simply a matter of laissez-faire individualism. Wiener has shown that although industry, applied science and technology were the foundation of British economic and political power in the nineteenth century, the very class of people most associated with engineering and manufacturing succumbed to a desire for a social status similar to that held by the aristocracy. They used their wealth to buy country houses and large estates. Their children were sent to the newly created public schools to learn how to be gentlemen and ladies. The curriculum of these schools preferred classics, history and literature to engineering; pure maths and science to applied maths and science. The established universities reflected the same bias. On graduation, the sons of the new bourgeoisie chose the professions of law and medicine, joined the military or the church, became civil servants or diplomats – rather than consider a life in industry. Indeed, industry and trade were associated with a sordid materialism that ill became those of status and wealth. The new bourgeoisie was absorbed by the old aristocracy and its values. This over-simplification of Wiener's thesis does none the less explain why British industry became so neglected. Industry was unloved and criticised both by those who derived their profits from it and by its socialist critics. A nostalgia for a Britain – or more precisely, an England – of rural tranquillity meant that industry failed to get the political, financial and institutional support that it found in countries like Germany, Japan and Sweden (Wiener 1981).

While the Thatcher governments of the 1980s sought to combat the decline of the industrial spirit through the promotion of a new spirit of entrepreneurialism, they sought to do so in an anti-interventionist style. It is only in a fourth term of office, under a new leader, that the Conservative government may be persuaded to give the more solid institutional support that industry requires.

SOCIAL DIVISIONS

Class

It is often said of Britain that it is a class-ridden society. This cannot mean that other capitalist countries do not display the same degrees of material inequality, but it does suggest that divisions in British society have been less open to meritocratic competition than many others. The lateness with which the British accepted the comprehensivation of secondary education and the idea of mass tertiary education is one indication of this, as is the whole preparatory/public-school tradition with its privileged access to the universities and other prestigious institutions.

Class has also been important in the past in the organisation of work. British companies have traditionally provided separate eating facilities for blue-collar workers, white-collar staff and executive personnel. Fringe benefits, health insurance and occupational pension schemes have tended to exclude the manual workers.

It is not surprising that blue-collar trade unions developed an antagonistic style in relation to employers. The employer provided work when he could at the lowest possible wage. There were few perks and benefits for ordinary employees. An employer, brought up in a laissez-faire tradition, was unlikely to feel any compunction about dismissing an employee or closing down a factory. In such an environment, British workers developed a strong tradition of class solidarity. There was considerable support for trade unions and the Labour Party.

Working-class solidarity has always posed a threat to other classes in capitalist societies. It has therefore been important for the threat to be countered or incorporated. The Conservative Party has traditionally been able to rely on a sizeable degree of support from working-class people in elections – more so than its Swedish counterpart, though less than the Japanese LDP. In the 1960s, sociological studies began to show an interest in 'affluent workers' who perhaps owned their own homes, belonged to a trade union for instrumental reasons only, and voted for whichever party seemed to promise them the best deal. This breakdown in class solidarity was associated with rising living standards and the decline of the old industries of the docks, mines, railways and steel, with their ties to occupational communities and loyalties.

More recently, the erosion of class identity has been the result of post-Fordist developments and political opportunism. Many firms in Britain have begun to adopt Japanese labour-management practices. A greater emphasis has been put on developing and maintaining a core labour force with skilled and semi-skilled workers being upgraded in terms of training and responsibility, with commensurate rewards in terms of security and fringe benefits. A corollary of this mode of organisation is to create a peripheral work-force of part-time and temporary workers with no security and no fringe benefits.

More affluent workers had begun to feel the impact of increasing rates of personal taxation in the 1970s to finance a growing public sector, a situation which they came to resent. It was to these kinds of people that the Conservative Party was able to appeal so successfully from 1979 onwards. Together with sections of the middle class, they formed what Wilensky has described as a 'middle mass'. Wilensky had hypothesised that 'The more the social distance between the middle mass and the poor, the greater the resistance to spending that appears to favour the poor' (Wilensky 1975: p. 57). The consequent welfare backlash predicted by Wilensky took a few more years to arrive in Britain.

Ethnicity

Wilensky had also argued that 'social heterogeneity and internal cleavages' would promote a welfare backlash. He had in mind at the time the particular case of the USA, where whites appeared increasingly reluctant to finance what they saw as black poverty. Heclo, in comparing Sweden with Britain, had considered both of them ethnically homogenous societies. But he was writing about policy developments which had taken place over the previous century. The big change to the ethnic composition of British society came with post-war economic growth, after the establishment of the welfare state. In the 1950s immigrants from the Caribbean began to come to Britain. This was considerably reduced by the passing of the Immigration Act of 1962. Towards the end of the 1960s and into the next decade, immigrants from the Indian sub-continent arrived and Asians who had lived in what had been the British colonies of East Africa. In one sense, given that the immigrants from the New Commonwealth and their descendants make up about 5 million people out of a population of 55 million, homogeneity might still be said to be a characteristic of British society. What has to be remembered, however, is that partly for reasons of job supply, partly because white Britons moved away from the areas in which blacks settled, and partly because the new minorities defensively chose to create their own communities, there is a concentration of ethnic minorites in many of Britain's cities. A city like Leicester, for example, has an Asian and Afro-Caribbean population of 30 per cent, while there are areas of Birmingham and London which are predominantly black.

The immigration factor has had a number of consequences for a society which had prided itself on its multi-racial empire and commonwealth. First, Britain discovered that it was racist to an unexpected degree. Asian, Caribbean and African soldiers might have died in two world wars for the old country but their kin were not expected to emigrate there. Certainly no advance provision or social planning preceded them. A number of investigations have conclusively demonstrated the existence not just of racial disadvantage but prejudice and discrimnation in the provision of employment, housing, education and social services. While most whites might not be racist in the same sense that the Nazis and segregationists in America were, the institutional racism of Britain has none the less been subtle and systematic.

Second, social problems have arisen because of the exclusion and hostility of the inappropriately named 'host' society. Blacks have suffered unemployment at twice the rate of whites. Working-class Caribbeans and Pakistanis have been relegated to the lowest paid jobs with the worst work conditions. In the early stages of immigration immigrants could not get council housing easily; later generations have found that they were entitled to accommodation only on inferior council estates.

Third, white society began to see the poor as 'black', poor areas as 'black areas', social problems as caused by 'blacks'. Welfare provision was seen as something which blacks were only too eager to take advantage of. It is surely not too fanciful to suggest that such perceptions in a society where empire had bequeathed strong notions of black inferiority, wickedness and idleness, might have contributed to a lessening of white support for the idea of a generously provided welfare state.

Gender

Gender differences are also very marked in Britain. While overt discrimination is not pronounced in education in terms of the numbers of young men and women staying on after 16, taking and passing examinations, and proceeding to post-school education, there is gender socialisation which directs males and females to different types of employment with different expectations as what their future employment patterns might be. The employment experience of women means that their work is more likely to be low in status, pay and promotion prospects. Their position in the labour market is likely to be segregated, thus facilitating indirect forms of discrimination. Fifty-five per cent of women are employed part time, but only 4 per cent of men (Millar and Glendinning 1989). Even after sixteen years of the Equal Pay Act being in operation women still receive only 75 per cent of men's pay. Almost 3 million low-earning women have

> no entitlement whatsoever to statutory sick pay, unemployment
> and invalidity benefits, maternity pay and, in the future, retirement
> pensions. (They are also very likely to be ineligible for occupational
> benefits in sickness, maternity and old age.)
> (Millar and Glendinning 1989: p. 365).

The poor provision of nursery facilities means that women remain disproportionately responsible for child-rearing. Women are more likely to have the responsibility for children in one-parent families, and are more likely to survive into old age without adequate pensions. They are, for these and other reasons, more likely to experience poverty. Towards the other end of the social scale, we find very few women on the boards of directors of major companies. The position of women in British society is typified by the small number of women in government and Parliament.

Government anti-discrimination measures

During the 1970s, a number of government measures were introduced to combat discrimination. The Equal Pay Act of 1970, the Sex Discrimination Act of 1975, the Employment Protection Act (which gave rights to maternity leave) of 1975, and the 1976 Race Relations Act, all gave public support to the idea of equality of treatment. Although those measures were not revoked in the 1980s, the financial and political support for them diminished considerably. In an interesting study of the operation of the Race Relations legislation, the Equal Pay Act and the Sex Discrimination Act, Gregory showed that very small percentages of the cases brought had been successful from the point of view of either ethnic minorities or women (Gregory 1987).

The rights and benefits of women and ethnic minorities in Britain would seem to be greater than those in Japan, but there can be little doubt that both groups have suffered from the wider socio-economic changes that have taken place in the last decade or so. As unemployment increased so blacks and women suffered disproportionately because they were more likely to be employed in the secondary labour market. The 1980s was also a decade in which what employment was created tended to be temporary and part-time. The increased duality of the post-Fordist labour market weakened some of the old class and status divisions but accentuated others, especially those of ethnicity and gender. Moreover, government policy was not only less inclined to strengthen measures to reduce discrimination and opportunity, but actually mocked those in local authorities who attempted to do so.

DEMOGRAPHIC CHANGE

Like Japan, Britain is densely populated and many of its 56 million people live in heavily crowded conurbations. The population soon after 1945 was around 48 million and is now 56 million. The latter figure, however, has been fairly stable for 20 years. According to Parry only West Germany has had a slower growth rate. From 1951 to 1980 the proportion of over-65s in the population grew from 10.8 per cent to 14.7 per cent of the population while the numbers of over-75s doubled. Parry estimated that with the decline in the birth rate and the stability of the elderly population the dependency ratio in Britain would not change a great deal until the turn of the century

(Parry 1986: pp. 210–11). The dependency ratio measured by the proportion of those under 15 added to those over 65 as a percentage of the total population was 72 per cent in 1971 and fell to 63 per cent by 1986. It is expected to rise again to 73 per cent by the year 2025 (Ball 1988: p. 183). As in Japan, a principal concern of governments and policy-makers in Britain has been the costs of the elderly into the twenty-first century and, in the short term, the rise in the number of over-75s. Falkingham has disputed the more pessimistic forecasts of costs of the elderly on the grounds that much of the evidence fails to take into account (a) other forms of dependency like unemployment, (b) the possibility of unemployment being reduced, thus increasing the numbers of providers, and (c) the growing numbers of women in the labourforce. While all of these factors lead her to suggest that policy-makers may be exaggerating the future costs of elderly care, the fact remains that the government has been influenced by projected trends and as a consequence has tried to reduce the future costs of the state earnings-related pension scheme (Falkingham 1989).

The household composition in Britain has also changed dramatically in the last twenty years. According to Wicks, divorces increased from 27,000 in 1961 to 158,000 in 1984 while one-parent families generally increased from 570,000 in 1971 to 890,000 in 1979–81 (Wicks 1987). By 1986 it was estimated that this latter figure had increased still further to over 1 million, of which it was estimated that 659,000 were living in or on the margins of poverty (Tintner 1989). The moral stance taken by the New Right towards the 'family' meant that the government was less willing to attend to the needs of this group than had been the case in the previous decade.

CONCLUSION

Prior to 1970 there was little in the British social structure that excited comparison with Japan. The experience of the recession in the 1930s and the Second World War had helped to create conditions favourable to the expansion of the public sector and state welfare programmes. The subsequent commitment by the two main political parties to full employment helped to sustain a powerful trade-union movement whose cooperation was sought in important aspects of economic and social policy during the 1960s and 1970s.

Underlying the post-war consensus, however, were a number of factors which constantly threatened the future of welfarism.

Britain's economic performance relative to other countries continued to decline. At the same time, the increased demands of the left and the trade unions, dissatisfied with the fruits of the years of corporatism, aggravated important elements of British society. Britain's conservative establishment had always been a powerful one. A disproportionate number of business, political, military, legal and administrative leaders shared the same public-school background and were hostile to what they saw as the socialist direction in which the country was moving. Moreover, the Conservative Party itself had always had a strong appeal for sizeable sections of the middle and working classes, amongst whom there was a growing element that wanted to 'roll back the frontiers of the state', emphasise the importance of the market economy and to return to 'Victorian values'.

The combination of these internal factors and the processes of globalisation and post-Fordism have brought about significant changes in Britain which suggest parallels with Japan. One of these is that increased international competition has created a climate in which production, the market and profit come first and social and environmental objectives a poor second. Another similarity is that in order to cope with the competition companies have had to become more flexible and in doing so have widened the distinction between their core and peripheral work-forces. The final similarity is that a continuous period of Conservative government has reinforced these trends with its own policies to weaken trade unions, local authorities and public-sector employees. The result is a society in which the post-war alliance between the working and salaried middle classes to create a welfare state based upon full employment has been broken. The politics of divisiveness and control have been necessary for capitalism in Britain to maintain its competitive edge. In the next few chapters we shall see how social policy has been affected by these trends.

113

CHAPTER SEVEN

Health, social security and social services

INTRODUCTION

While the post-war welfare reconstruction, based on the Beveridge Report and implemented by a Labour government with a large majority in Parliament, undoubtedly built upon programmes, policies and legislation established earlier in the century, it is difficult not to see the reforms of that period as a major watershed in British social policy. For the next thirty years successive governments sought to maintain a commitment to full employment and comprehensive state welfare. But with the stagflation of the 1970s, the commitment amongst supporters waned and the conviction of critics grew. Successive Conservative governments in the 1980s attempted by various means to reverse the growth in public and social expenditure, and to weaken those forces in society which were perceived as responsible both for the high level of state welfare and the consequent decline of the British economy – the trade unions, the Labour Party, local authorities and welfare bureaucrats and professionals. The rapid growth of unemployment between 1979 and 1982 helped this process, as did having a Prime Minister who had a vision of putting an end to 'socialism' and its attendant evils. While there is considerable argument as to how successful these governments were in achieving their aims, there is little doubt that the character and structure of the British welfare system changed during the 1980s and will continue to do so in the 1990s. The transition from Fordist welfare state to post-Fordist welfare pluralism is well under way.

THE RISE AND FALL OF THE BRITISH WELFARE STATE

A plan for the social reconstruction of Britain had been written by the civil servant and academic William Beveridge during the Second World War. With the declared aim of ridding British society of five major evils – idleness, squalor, disease, ignorance and want – the report proposed an extensive revision of economic and social policy. While it was primarily concerned with the details of social security, it was rooted in the assumptions that full employment needed to become a goal of government policy; that a national health service was required; and that educational opportunities needed to widen. Beveridge's principal aim, however, was to create a system of social security which would be adequate to meet all those circumstances likely to result in a loss of earnings.

The National Insurance Act of 1946 provided for flat-rate contributions and benefits for old-age pensions, sickness benefit and unemployment benefit. It was intended that these benefits would be high enough to make further assistance unnecessary. Those who for any reason did not qualify for these benefits would be entitled to apply for a lower, means-tested benefit under the 1948 National Assistance Act. In addition a system of family allowances was introduced in 1945 for second and subsequent children. This benefit was intended to ease the expense of financing a family and was payable to the mother. Maternity and death grants were also provided for.

The National Health Service Act of 1946 established a comprehensive service for the whole population, based upon medical need, free at the point of use, financed largely out of general taxation and in no way dependent on contributions. The Children Act of 1948 strengthened the powers of children's departments of local authorities to intervene to protect the welfare of young children. New powers were also granted to local authorities under the 1949 housing legislation.

It was generally felt for some years that this comprehensive range of measures had achieved a considerable reduction in social need. Only in the 1960s with the 'rediscovery of poverty' was the social security system felt to be in need of overhaul. With growing numbers of people dependent upon national assistance, and many of those in receipt of old-age pensions and unemployment benefit also having to top up with the means-tested benefit, the Social Security Act of 1966 was passed. This Act introduced the idea of earnings-related unemployment and sickness benefits. Contributions from employers and employees ceased to be flat-rate and became a percentage of earnings up to a given ceiling. The Act also brought changes to national assistance. The new benefit was called supplementary benefit, and rights to a comprehensive range of payments for special needs and exceptional circumstances were established After much public debate and various proposals for different schemes, the State Earnings-Related Pensions Scheme (SERPS) was introduced in 1975. While those with private and occupational pensions were entitled to opt out of SERPS, it provided the rest of the population with a pension for the future related to the size of their income. Moreover, contributions were credited to those – mainly women – who were unable to make contributions due to family responsibilities (Hill 1990).

Evidence of family poverty prompted the introduction of the family income supplement (FIS) in 1971. It had seemed ironic that the earnings of some families could be lower than benefit levels and therefore, potentially, a disincentive to work. FIS was calculated so that such families received a proportion of the difference between their earnings and the benefits they would have been entitled to. The resources devoted to family allowances, which had been of greater value to poorer families, and child tax allowances, which had benefited the more affluent, were combined into child benefit in 1975 and were extended to include the first child.

Help was also provided for those whose incomes were considered too low to be able to pay their rent. Those on supplementary benefit received a rent addition, while those whose earnings were too low claimed rent rebates and allowances from their local housing authorities.

In the 1970s, many of the above benefits were index-linked annually to price or wage increases, whichever was highest, to ensure that those receiving benefits did not fall behind the general prosperity of the rest of the population. The Labour government had succeeded in its aim to provide universal and insurance benefits above supplementary benefit levels, to increase the amount of resources devoted to social security, and to protect claimants against inflation (Barr and Coulter 1990).

Other areas of the welfare state were expanded and reorganised during this period. The Health Service was reorganised by the Conservatives in 1974 with the introduction of a new layer of authorities. Integrated social services departments had been created in 1970 following criticisms of fragmented, uncoordinated work by the health, children's and welfare departments of local authorities.

The local authorities themselves were subsequently restructured in 1974. Super-ministries had been created at central government level for Health and Social Security (DHSS), and the Environment (DoE). Public and social expenditure had grown, and employment in the public sector had increased tremendously. Social security was providing the basic income of a large proportion of households and was becoming increasingly complex.

There was general agreement by the end of the 1970s that the system needed to be simplified and streamlined, and the Supplementary Benefits Commission (SBC) produced a report in 1979 which recommended many changes. Those on the right, however, were more concerned with the overall cost of social security, which they argued was damaging to the economy. At the level of individual claimants they argued that benefits had become so high that many were better off out of work than when they were employed. Benefits, it was insisted, were a disincentive to work.

Until the middle of the 1970s, criticisms of state welfare provision had tended to result in the expansion of services and the improvement of benefits. Increasingly, however, ways were being sought to make benefits more selective and services more efficient. By the end of the decade a number of factors were conspiring to bring about a more fundamental review of the Beveridge welfare state. Continuing economic difficulties, the threat of inflation and growing unemployment were all leading to a climate which favoured a stricter control of public and welfare expenditure. The rest of this chapter will deal principally with the attempts by Conservative governments after the election of 1979 to create a new welfare system.

SOCIAL SECURITY

The overall cost of social security had not changed a great deal by end of the 1980s. It had risen to 9 per cent of GDP during the latter half of the 1970s, climbed to 11 per cent in the mid-1980s and come down to 9.7 per cent by 1989 (calculated from Barr and Coulter 1990: pp. 334–5). The failure of the Thatcher governments to reduce the cost of social security should not, however, diminish the importance of their policy changes. The rapid growth of unemployment in the first three years inevitably led to increased social security expenditure in terms of the overall expenditure on unemployment benefit and supplementary benefit. But these were complemented by reductions

117

in both the real value of many benefits and restrictions placed upon entitlement. From 1980 benefits rose annually in line with prices only. Since earnings rose at a higher rate, the position of claimants relative to the rest of the population worsened.

Worried about the future cost of SERPS which, like the Swedish ATP scheme, had been organised on a pay-as-you-go basis, the government considered its abolition, but in the end contented itself with reducing its value while at the same time encouraging more contributors to opt out and enter private pension schemes. Not only have the inducements to do this been costly (*Guardian* 1990) but the viability of the scheme will obviously be eroded if better-off groups no longer contribute (Hill 1990: p. 59). In 1975 29 per cent of pensioners were in receipt of occupational pensions; ten years later that figure had increased to 37 per cent. In the late 1970s, state pension payments amounted to over 50 per cent of all pension payments; by the end of the 1980s they had dropped 43 per cent (Barr and Coulter 1990). These trends had begun prior to 1979 but were certainly reinforced by subsequent government measures. They are an illustration of the way in which increases in occupational and private schemes make reductions in state schemes politically more feasible.

In 1980 a decision was taken to abolish the earnings-related element in unemployment benefit and sickness benefit. Two years later Statutory Sick Pay (SSP) was introduced which made the payment of sickness benefit for the first eight weeks of illness the reponsibility of employers. As a percentage of average male, blue-collar earnings the value of unemployment benefit declined from 18 per cent to 16 per cent between 1983 and 1988 (Barr and Coulter 1990: p. 296). National insurance contributions (NICs), however, increased from 6.5 per cent of earnings in 1979 to 9 per cent in 1983. Higher income earners were only having to pay these contributions up to a certain amount of their income while at the same time they were receiving considerable reductions in income tax. Lower-paid workers, however, were having to cope with large increases in Value Added Tax and NICs in return for minor income-tax reductions.

A unified housing benefit was introduced in 1983 to replace the anomaly of claimants getting help with their rent from either their social security offices or their local authorities. As with other changes recommended by the Supplementary Benefits Commission at the end of the 1970s, the government was determined to introduce them at no extra cost. While some gained from the new arrangements, therefore, others lost. Not only was more hardship created, but the administration of the new benefit proved cumbersome and complex for many years – a consequence of the reluctance of the government to consult with experts in the field when introducing its radical measures. The value of Housing Benefit too was eroded over successive years. It is perhaps worth mentioning that while Conservative policy generally aimed at reducing the value of benefits, targeting and means-testing often cost a lot more in administration. The overall cost of social security administration rose from 1.4 per cent of the total in 1979 to 2 per cent in 1989 (Barr and Coulter 1990: p. 285).

Child benefit was either raised very little or not at all for a number of years in the 1980s. By the end of the decade its value had been severely eroded. The government claimed that its preferred approach was to target needy families by replacing FIS with a new family credit scheme. While family credit was more generously conceived than FIS, there is little expectation that the take-up of the benefit will be greater than the 50 per cent take-up of its predecessor. The universal maternity and death benefits were abolished in 1986 and replaced with a means-tested equivalent.

While the government preferred to rely on means-testing – or 'targeting', as it preferred to call it – to maintain and improve insurance-based and universal benefits, it also wanted to reduce the value of means-tested benefits and discourage too great a reliance on them. Reducing the value of benefits was a relatively simple task. They were simply not raised in line with inflation and between 1982 and 1987 their value declined from 18 per cent to 16 per cent of adult, blue-collar, male earnings (Barr and Coulter 1990: p. 307). More difficult was the control of the additional payments that claimants applied for to pay for special needs or exceptional circumstances. The first attempt, in 1980, was to tighten up the rules governing the award of such payments since it was felt that leaving too much to the discretion of social security officials was a major cause of their take-up being too high or subject to abuse. The new system failed to halt the growth of these payments, which was hardly surprising given the growth of unemployment. The 1 million payments made in 1981 had become 4 million by 1987 (Becker and Silburn 1990: p. 25).

A new Social Security Act in 1986 approached the problem in a different way. Since neither discretion nor rules could keep the payments down, then the overall budget and the budgets of individual benefit offices would have to operate within strict limits. When the money ran out, the benefits would cease. In the original proposal for the reform, the government had said that it wanted to create a social security system 'that was consistent with [its] overall objectives for the economy' and which did not 'discourage self-reliance or stand in the way of individual provision and responsibility' (DHSS 1985) (almost a paraphrase of the Japanese government's seven-year social and economic plan of 1979 Tabata 1991: p. 16).[1] The name of supplementary benefit was changed to 'income support' but the basic benefit remained largely unaltered, although additional premiums were to be paid for disability, old age and to single-parent families. What did change were the additional payments which in 1986 had amounted to £334 million. The new legislation set up a cash-limited Social Fund of £201 million. Of this amount £60 million would be in the form of grants but the remainder would be in the form of loans which would have to be repaid out of the claimant's income support. The critics of this system, who included the government's own advisory council and the National Audit Office, said that the policy was not meeting need, that it was expensive to administer, and that the same requests for assistance were getting different responses in different areas, from different offices, within different offices, and at different times of the year – another example of the administrative consequences not being properly thought through. Others complained that between half a million and a million applications for assistance had been rejected in each year that the scheme had been in operation and that large numbers of people in desperate need were being forced to go to charities, friends and relatives and loan companies (Becker and Craig 1989: p. 14). But this was entirely in keeping with the government's policy of keeping expenditure down, while at the same time encouraging the voluntary, informal and private sectors.

Throughout the decade various measures were introduced to discourage or prevent the young unemployed from living on social assistance. Increasingly they were expected to participate in government training schemes. Unemployed adults were subjected to the same pressures. Those who were unemployed 'voluntarily' (who it was deemed had given up their job for no good reason) were denied benefit for six months. More stringent measures were introduced to ensure that claimants were 'actively seeking work'. Everything short of outright compulsion was used to make claiming difficult for many. By the end of the decade Digby was to describe the process as one which had led from the 'workhouse to workfare' (Digby 1989).

When all those on benefit and on low pay were taken into account Barr and Coulter concluded:

Whatever the poverty line used, the number of poor individuals in poor households has risen very substantially over the period for all groups. The number of individuals in poor households [living on or below supplementary benefit level] rose from 5.1 million to 6.1 million between 1974 and 1979, and to 9.4 million in 1985.

(Barr and Coulter 1990: p. 314)

MEDICAL CARE

The British National Health Service (NHS) was formed out of the pre-war local authority and voluntary hospitals. It remains unique amongst capitalist welfare systems in being financed out of general taxation and free at the point of use. Initially hospital and primary care were distinct services while public health continued as a local authority reponsibility. From 1974 all three parts of the system were brought closer together under a reorganised NHS. The new structure included three levels – regional, area and district health authorities (RHAs, AHAs and DHAs). From 1982, it was decided that the AHAs could be dispensed with.

Until the Conservative government's 1989 White Paper, *Working for Patients* (see below), the basic structure of the NHS had changed little. The British health care system was largely a public one with a small private sector. It had been dominated by the medical profession from its inception. Outside interests were represented at various levels, including local authority politicians and other representatives from the local community. In addition, bodies like the Community Health Councils had been set up to deal with dissatisfactions and grievances amongst users of the service, but few would deny the dominance of the medical profession within the NHS.

British medical care has not, compared with other countries, consumed a vast share of GDP (a modest 5 per cent as opposed to the 9 per cent of Sweden and the 10 per cent of the USA). Moreover, many health indicators suggest that its performance in the past has been reasonably good. While the governments of the 1980s wanted to privatise health as much as any other aspect of the public sector, they came to accept that while the costs of and demand for medical services grew, the NHS remained comparatively cheap, efficient and effective (Klein 1989: p. 237; Barr *et al.* 1989: p. 117). For this reason, and because of the public's particular attachment to it, Conservatives have had to declare that the 'NHS is safe in our hands' while harbouring the ideological urge to dismantle it. Only in the last few years have a set of proposals been put forward that may drastically change the whole structure.

Attempts at change

The above notwithstanding, the same concerns about spiralling costs, rising demands, professional dominance and accountability have preoccupied governments in Britain as much as in other advanced countries. Since there is no end to the demand for new treatments and new expensive technologies; since it is in the interests of medical personnel to exploit public anxieties about health care; and since there are other competing calls on the public purse, governments have had to tread very warily in trying to placate the consumers of medical services on the one hand without giving the professionals everything they have asked for, with the fiscal problems that that would entail on the other.

When the Conservative reorganisation of 1974 seemed to do little more than create a new and unnecessary layer of administrators, the search was on for a more efficient and accountable system. A start was made, however, in putting a greater emphasis on primary care, community services and preventive medicine. As a result each DHA has a community physician in overall charge of maternity and child welfare, rehabilitation services and health education. A third of all general practitioners (GPs or family doctors) now work in medical centres which offer a range of medical and paramedical services. Health education and preventive work in terms of the promotion of healthier diets, more exercise, and advice on excessive smoking and alcohol consumption are all much more familiar parts of primary care than they were a decade or so back. Another area of change has been a greater emphasis on administration and accountability. The Royal Commission set up by the Labour government, which reported in 1979, recommended the abolition of the AHAs, but it was the succeeding government which implemented the recommendation in 1982. This was followed a year later by proposals which resulted in greater central direction and a greater emphasis on monitoring performance and budgetary control.

Another problem which demanded attention in the 1970s was the inheritance of many old and inadequate hospitals and an inequitable geographical distribution of hospitals. The RAWP (Resource Allocation Working Party) formula built upon the planning exercises of the 1960s in order to ensure a more just distribution of resources. This has been a slow and difficult process since it often meant cutting resources in some areas, notably London and the South East of the country, in order to benefit others. Ironically, it is thought that most of the reforms currently being implemented by the government may undo what RAWP has achieved (Barr *et al.* 1989).

Class inequalities too have persisted in terms of people's health and the care and treatment they receive. The Black Report of 1979 (Townsend and Davidson 1982) documented these very clearly, but the recommendations which called for more resources to be devoted to medical care were hardly likely to appeal to an incoming government committed to public expenditure cuts.

The private sector and privatisation

In contrast to the Labour governments of the 1970s which were committed to the phasing out of pay beds (places in NHS hospitals taken up and paid for by private patients) and which abolished tax allowances for occupational health insurance schemes, the governments of the 1980s have been committed to private health in a variety of forms. Pay beds and tax exemptions for occupational schemes have been re-introduced and privatisation, in varying forms, has certainly had an impact. In 1979 there were 149 private hospitals with 6600 beds in the country, while 5 per cent of the population were covered by private health insurance. By 1988 there were 203 hospitals with 10,370 beds and 10 per cent of the population had private cover (Klein 1989: p. 214).

In Klein's view, much of this expansion remained in the field of repair surgery and in no way threatened the major functions of the NHS. Nor had the practice of putting out tenders of ancillary services, like cleaning and laundry work, undermined the service. Many of the successful bids anyway had been won by those already employed within the NHS. The one big area of expansion of the private sector had been in the field of the long-term nursing care of the elderly. The government had sought in the early 1980s to discourage local authority spending and to encourage the growth of private care. Unfortunately for the government, local authorities exploited a loophole in the regulations so that a large part of the costs of staying in such homes could be paid for by what has become the Department of Social Security (DSS). The result has been the most enormous explosion in the social security budget. Klein's view was that the consequences of this loophole, ironically, had brought long-term nursing care for the elderly to a wider section of the population than had previous provision by local authorities.

Moreover, the need to regulate the standards of these private homes had led to higher standards in the public sector as well. The costs and consequences of this particular example of privatisation could hardly have been intended (Klein 1989).

'Working for Patients'

It is not yet clear what the consequences of the most recent attempt to restructure the NHS will be. In 1989, the government embarked upon a new experiment, outlined in its White Paper, *Working for Patients*, which is supposed to bring about a greater degree of choice for patients, GPs and hospitals. Hospitals are allowed to opt out of NHS control and become self-governing. GPs, in certain circumstances, can become budget-holders and have greater autonomy over how they run their finance and practices. Services will have price tags so that GPs and hospitals may decide to go for the cheaper services on offer elsewhere either within the NHS or in the private sector. The intention is to create more competition, choice and efficiency. Worries about the reforms concern the degree to which they may result, over time, in an expansion of an affluent private sector and a residual public sector. There is concern too that GPs may avoid performing under-priced tasks and refuse patients who 'cost' their practices time and money with insufficient return from the DHAs. Such an eventuality would adversely affect those with chronic conditions, disproportionately the elderly and those in lower socio-economic groups. On the other hand there are those who believe that this is just the kind of shake-up the NHS needs, putting the emphasis on pluralism and regulation rather than monopoly provision (Klein 1989). What is clear is that market mechanisms and criteria are increasingly being used in a service which was originally designed to meet need.

Other trends

In line with other government reforms, local authority influence on the NHS has been reduced by taking away their representation on DHA management committees. There has already been a trend towards the Secretary of State favouring the appointment of business people to such committees to the disadvantage of other interests. It is clear too that, with the ending of national wage agreements, the public sector unions will have less negotiating power. Already, however, the changes envisaged in *Working for Patients* have been rushed into legislation with a lack of preparation. The failure to consult with the health professionals and bureaucrats may have resulted in the government's having a freer hand to do what it wants, but the unanticipated consequences of hasty implementation without adequate planning and experimentation might prove of more importance than the purity of the government's ideological intentions.

Although the growth of government health expenditure, in real and volume terms, increased during the 1980s, it did so at a slower rate than in the 1970s. Moreover, Le Grand, Winter and Woolley, using the Department of Health's own criterion of need, based largely on demographic changes, have argued that that growth in the 1980s barely matched the growth in need, while in the 1970s, need had been outstripped by growth (Le Grand *et al.* 1990: p. 100). In other words there was no real growth in the 1980s at all, simply a keeping pace with standards already set. Charges for prescriptions, dental examinations and eye tests also rose during the decade. Charges financed 2 per cent of total NHS expenditure in the year before the Thatcher government took office but 2.7 per cent nine years later, with every prospect of the percentage increasing still further (Le Grand *et al.* 1990).

SOCIAL SERVICES

The provision of statutory social services in Britain has traditionally been the responsibility of local authorities. In the post-war years this responsibility was shared by three local authority departments – the Children's Department, the Welfare Department and the Medical Department. During the early 1960s this mode of organisation was increasingly seen to be inadequate. Various reports drew attention to the fact that social services were operating in isolation from each other, in a fragmented way. Families with a number of needs would receive a multiplicity of visits from, amongst others, the child care officer, the welfare officer and the health visitor. Another criticism was that too great a distinction was being made between children who suffered problems of neglect and bad treatment and those whose behaviour made them difficult for their parents and social agencies to control. There was also a feeling that professional barriers between different types of social worker were artificial and that their counter-productive specialisms should give way to more generic work within a more unified organisational setting. These concerns came to be summarised in the Seebohm Report of 1968 and resulted in a complete reorganisation of social work services in the Social Services Act of 1970.

Until the 1970 Act, social services had remained the Cinderella of the welfare state. The Act itself upgraded them at a stroke. Social Services Departments (SSDs) within the counties and metropolitan boroughs took over many of the responsibilities of the old children's, welfare and health departments. They were run by a director who had to have social work qualifications (to prevent the new posts being 'monopolised' by ex-medical health officers) and became accountable to a single committee of councillors. Along with education, social services became significant players in the larger local authorities in terms of the number of people they employed and the budgets they managed.

With the movement towards reform, resources for more social workers, for different kinds of residential accommodation and for domiciliary services began to grow. Growth was considerable from 1965 until 1975 but even after that, with cuts in central government and local authority expenditure, social services continued to increase to respond to the needs of growing numbers of elderly people, and to provide for those groups who were being cared for less and less in large medical institutions, like the mentally ill and the mentally handicapped. New needs have surfaced as unemployment and poverty have grown. Child abuse has received considerable media and political attention and its high profile has made it difficult to reduce social work services too drastically. AIDS, and the problems of drug and alcohol misuse have also demanded some sort of input from social services.

By 1974 expenditure on social services had risen five-fold to consume 1 per cent of the UK's GDP. It has stayed at roughly that level ever since. The growth rate of the services under Labour governments in the late 1970s averaged 3.4 per cent while under the Conservatives during the 1980s, the average was 3.1 per cent (Evandrou *et al.* 1990: p. 217). Public expenditure reviews in the last decade have considered a lower growth rate of 2 per cent as sufficient to meet growing needs, and the general exhortations of government have been for local authorities to reduce expenditure. However, as Evandrou has pointed out, rhetoric has not been the only determinant of social services provision. The Department of Health and Social Security has itself encouraged greater community care and thereby channelled some funds to local authorities, and local authorities themselves have within their total budgets been prepared to protect their SSDs (Evandrou *et al.* 1990: pp. 223–4). Another way in which local authorities have maintained their commitment to particular services has been to introduce new charges or increase old ones. Charges accounted for 13–15 per cent of the budget in English SSDs but that varied tremendously from one service to another. Over 33 per cent of the cost of residential care and meals at home was met by charges, but less than 10 per cent of the cost of home helps and day care (Evandrou *et al.* 1990: p. 224).

However, these broad figures indicating that services have grown may be misleading. Personal social services are labour-intensive, which means that their costs are likely to rise higher than inflation generally. It has been suggested that needs have been seriously underestimated and that greater growth would have been required to meet them (Webb and Wistow 1987). It may be that social services have not been as savagely cut by central government policies as might have been expected, but there have been clear moves to alter the already mixed economy of welfare services in the direction of non-statutory provision.

The care of the elderly

Certainly targets set by the DHSS in the mid-1970s for the care of the elderly had not remotely been achieved a decade later. Instead of there being 12 home helps per 1000 of the elderly population, there were only 7 in 1987; and only 100 meals were provided for every 1000 elderly persons, instead of the target of 200. Moreover, expenditure on the elderly, which had grown by 6.8 per cent in 1974–79, grew by only 2.2 per cent in the early 1980s (Evandrou *et al.* 1990). Nevertheless it is clear from figures calculated by Evandrou, Falkingham and Glennerster from the General Household Survey that the percentages of people over 65 using different social services in the previous month did not greatly change between 1975 and 1985. It is also interesting to note that, with the exception of the highest income quintile, there seemed to be the same sort of take-up of services by the elderly whatever their income (Evandrou *et al.* 1990). If around 20 per cent of over-65s generally use at least one service in any given month, this would suggest that a higher percentage would avail themselves of social services at some time during a year.

It has already been mentioned that a major government error has resulted in the DHSS paying for the residential care of many elderly people during the 1980s. The actual cost had been less than £11 million in 1977 but it rose to £500 million in the mid-1980s and £1000 million by 1989. Blunder or not, it meant that whereas local authorities had provided over 70 per cent of residential accommodation for the elderly in 1974 and the private sector only 13 per cent, by 1986 only 51 per cent was publicly provided and 37 per cent was in the private sector.

Community care

The policy of encouraging community care as opposed to care in large institutions illustrates the ambivalent response of government to social services in general. In the early 1970s the phasing out of hospital beds in mental institutions and institutions for the elderly was matched by a commitment to alternatives so that care could take place in the community. As resources became more scarce in the late 1970s and as government began to seek ways of reducing its statutory commitments, so care by the community became the focus of policy. Although it was clear, from Audit Commission and parliamentary reports, that effective community care required extra resources, the government's chief concern was to see that the role of the non-statutory sector was increased. It wanted the informal sector (in effect, female relatives), voluntary associations and private businesses to play a greater role in caring. The Griffiths Report endorsed this welfare pluralist approach but also recommended that local authorities be given the strategic function of regulating the contribution of all those involved.

This was important, given the government's hostility to local authorities. It had sought throughout the decade to earmark resources for specific projects through joint planning and joint finance with the NHS. Community mental handicap teams, community mental illness teams and the central funding initiative for drug misuse, were all examples of this approach – to ensure cooperation with the health authorities and to determine how the money was spent. But in the end, it seemed that it was only the local authority SSDs which could take on the task of coordinating the various community care packages which could be provided by a plethora of agencies, groups and individuals. While there is still some argument about whether the statutory or non-statutory services should be the main providers, there is wide support for the notion of pluralism if it means greater choice, flexibility and efficiency. The real worry is that care by the community will be inadequately funded; that mentally ill people will continue to be prematurely discharged from hospital with no alternative care arrangements having been made; or, as has happened with the elderly, private institutional care becomes a substitute for public institutional care.

As has already been noted in the previous section on health care, the financing of long-term residential homes for the elderly by the DSS has been an unforeseen consequence of the government putting the squeeze on local authorities. With the passage of the Community Care Act 1991, local authorities will again be put in charge of the financing of the caring aspects of residential care, leaving the DSS to pay for accommodation and living expenses. They will, though, be expected to 'encourage diversification' without any guarantee that the financial help they receive from government will be adequate for the task. The government will presumably hope that the social services expenditure on charities will continue to rise. By 1987 they were financing services whose expenditure had grown to the equivalent of 10 per cent of the local authorities' social services budget. The government will also hope that families and friends will continue to care with little financial support.

CONCLUSION

After thirteen years of a government committed to rolling back the frontiers of the state and reducing social expenditure, the persistence of major state responsibilities for health care, social security and social services, and the fact that they all continued to consume a similar share of GDP in 1992 as they had in 1979, would seem to suggest that the Conservatives had not succeeded in their aims. This would, in my view, be misleading.

The evidence would seem to suggest that had these public services continued to meet needs to the same extent as they had in the 1970s, then social expenditure would have been much higher. The governments of the 1980s had been very successful in restricting the growth of social expenditure. Many social security benefits had been reduced in value and charges for many services had been increased. The government had also advanced its aim of increasing the role of other sectors in welfare provision. Private employers were responsible for much of the administration of sickness benefit. Those in need were having to turn to charities, their friends and relations for help, where previously the state had assisted them. Private pension and health insurance schemes had increased in significance. Private-sector agencies were more likely to be used to carry out work previously the monopoly of public services. Business people took a greater part in the running of the

NHS while the views of employees and their organisations were ignored. The policy-making process itself now tended to exclude the professionals and relied on those voices more sympathetic to the ideological aims of the government. A new climate had been created in which the electorate no longer expected that welfare services would be greatly improved; the opposition parties had to be more circumspect about what they promised; and welfare professionals and bureaucrats could no longer expect an automatic right to be consulted. The dictates of the market now dominated where once social need had been an important criterion of welfare provision.

Conservative governments since 1979 have succeeded in moving towards a post-Fordist mixed economy of welfare. Within a few months of Major succeeding Thatcher as Prime Minister, it became clear that the initiatives taken under her leadership in the fields of social security, health care and social services would be continued and strengthened by the new administration. However, it was also apparent that the Conservatives had been less successful in emulating the Japanese in putting 'production first'. The state of the economy by 1992 and Britain's poor manufacturing record were the most likely guarantee of the future bleakness of state welfare provision.

CHAPTER EIGHT

Education and employment

INTRODUCTION

Britain is not renowned as a country which has attached a great deal of importance to mass education. Its élitist private schools represent a tradition which is class-ridden; its state schools have been preoccupied with the early selection of the most able and setting them apart; while its universities have guarded an exclusive academic tradition which has been wary of the dangers of rapid expansion. In spite of the fact that these and other factors have served as a brake on the nation's educational potential, the decades following the Second World War did see significant changes and considerable expansion in most areas of state education. Primary education became more child-centred, selection tests at the age of 11 were abolished and comprehensivisation introduced. The school leaving age was raised to 16 and tertiary education expanded. In part expansion was driven by a concern for the needs of a modern economy for a highly educated work-force; in part by the social democratic goal of equal opportunities; and in part by the demand from parents for more and better education for their children. The result by the mid-1970s was a state education system which consumed almost 7 per cent of GDP but which was the subject of considerable criticism.

Those on the left were critical of the degree of equality achieved. More generally there was a concern about the lack of vocational relevance of the school curriculum and the lack of accountability of the educational establishment. But on the right there was a dissatisfaction with the whole liberal, progressive, egalitarian ethos that, in their view, pervaded both state education and the vocational training of the young unemployed. The task, as Conservative critics saw it, was to reassert national and economic objectives in education and training policy; promote competition, choice and a greater degree of discipline amongst young people; and reduce the power and influence of left-wing teachers, local education authorities and the trade unions.

STRUCTURE AND CHANGE IN BRITISH EDUCATION

In Japan and Sweden, the role of the state in education had been regarded as a necessary part of the industrialisation process from the outset, whereas the industrial revolution in Britain was already over a century old before the state, amidst widespread controversy, began to establish a system of elementary education for all. Secondary education for some was introduced at the turn of the century and a tentative start given to technical education. A new period seemed to be heralded in 1944 when the Butler Education Act established free secondary education for all and a system in which all children would be encouraged to achieve their potential. Primary education was to last from 5 until the age of 11, when children would take an examination which decided which of three types of secondary school they would go to. The academically brightest would receive an education in grammar schools, the technically gifted would go to technical schools, while those with manual skills would go to secondary modern schools.

The original intention was that these different kinds of school would receive parity of treatment. In fact it soon became obvious that they were a crude duplication of the British class structure. Grammar schools provided places for only 20 per cent of the population, had a predominantly middle-class intake, and had superior resources because of the additional funding of children who stayed on after the school leaving age of 15. Technical schools did not develop a distinct identity of their own and catered for a small percentage of secondary-aged children. Secondary modern schools catered for the vast majority of working-class children but also received a number of middle-class 'failures'.

Criticism of this system began to mount in the affluent 1960s from parents, educationists and various government committees of inquiry. Parents whose children had the option of going into the private system did not have to worry too much if their children did not get grammar-school places. Less well-off middle-class parents and middle-class aspirants found it increasingly difficult to accept the early relegation of some of their children to schools with inferior resources and opportunities. Educationists with egalitarian sympathies became concerned at the arbitrary nature of an examination system which decided children's futures at such an early age and clearly cut off many working-class children from access to further and higher education. Government committees of inquiry, representing a wide range of professional, political and business interests, revealed not only the class inequalities of the system, but the waste of talent that occurred. The pool of ability which grammar schools presupposed was considered far too narrow. Not only did a much wider pool of ability exist, it was argued, but the economy demanded that it be exploited. This growing consensus, coinciding as it did with a period of economic growth, led to a considerable expansion of public resources for education. Only 2.5 per cent of GDP had been spent on education before the war. This rose to 3.2 per cent in the 1950s and to 5 per cent in the mid-1960s (Vaizey and Sheehan 1968).

The abolition of the selection at the age of 11 and the replacement of the tri-partite system by comprehensive schools began in the 1960s, and over a ten-year period led to a transformation of secondary schooling aided by the raising of the school leaving age to 16 in 1972. However, comprehensivation was never made legally compulsory with the result that grammar schools continued to survive in some parts of the country. The new comprehensives were preferred largely because they seemed to satisfy the need for a system which provided a wide range of subject choice and an economic way of providing the modern facilities and equipment required by secondary schools. It is important to note as well that the pre-comprehensive arrangment had also been characterised by single-sex schools, whereas comprehensives were co-educational. Whether the new schools created more opportunities for working-class children is still not clear, but they certainly eradicated many of the problems created by the tri-partite system and made it possible to introduce a more varied, more relevant and better resourced curriculum.

The expansion of further and higher education which took place in the same period was based upon a typically British class division. More universities were built, providing more places, but they were still characterised by an élitism which insisted on a high degree of autonomy. They were run by academics in an exclusive way which preferred the pure to the applied and the academic to the vocational. Polytechnics, on the other hand, which were created out of local government institutions of education, were both open to a wider range of the population and more responsive to the practical needs of society and the economy (Burgess 1977). As polytechnics themselves expanded, however, they seemed to imitate some of the features of universities through the process of 'academic drift'.

The upper reaches of secondary schools were also very influenced by universities since it was the universities which set the examinations which British children took at 16 and 18. While these set severe limits on what schools could do with their older and academically brighter pupils, children at primary school and in the lower part of the secondary school were experiencing major changes in the way they were taught. Even before the Plowden Report of 1967, which set the official seal of approval on a child-centred approach to learning, teachers and their training institutions had begun to move away from strict, traditional methods of teaching. The new curriculum meant that subject boundaries were broken down; new ways of teaching maths, science and language were used; classrooms, schools and relationships with teachers became more open and more flexible. While this approach was rooted in progressive educational philosophy, it took a politically more radical form in the hands of the post-1968 generation of teachers. Amongst some, there were hopes that education could indeed contribute to wider changes of a socialistic kind.

Similar hopes were vested in ideas of lifelong or recurrent education. By the early 1970s all the major areas of education had benefited from reform and expansion. Only the poor cousin, adult education, remained. Ideas of a participatory democracy which had not materialised through other changes, were thought to stand a better chance with the expansion of opportunities for adults (Houghton 1974). Hopes were raised by the recommendations of the last of the major government inquiries, published in the Russell Report of 1974. Unfortunately the report came too late. The egalitarian and democratic ideals of the recurrent educationists had to give way to the more prosaic goals of vocational re-training as unemployment grew and technological change accelerated.

In spite of the expansion of the educational system, there were many who still felt that it fell short of their expectations. Criticisms of the ways in which education had developed came from many quarters, but received most media attention when they came from the right. Socialists were disappointed by the persistence of inequalities (Rubinstein 1979), and left libertarians with the power of educational professionals and bureaucrats to further their own interests (Lister 1974); while those on the right were particularly critical of what they saw as a decline in academic standards and a left-wing bias in school teaching (Cox and Dyson 1971). Many of these issues were symbolised in the collapse of the William Tyndale primary school in London where the socialist headmaster and sympathetic colleagues came into conflict with a traditional teacher who resented what she considered to be a politically biased curriculum. The failure of the Inner London Education Authority to act decisively to defuse the situation, coupled with the intense interest of the press and Conservative MPs, led to a breakdown in the running of the school and a public inquiry (Gretton and Jackson 1976; Auld 1976). The report of the inquiry blamed almost everybody involved but the affair was used to highlight the complaints of those who felt that teachers and local authorities were insufficiently accountable for what went on in state schools.

In 1976 the Prime Minister and his Secretary of State for Education themselves tried to articulate some of these concerns by initiating a 'Great Debate'. Not surprisingly, given the growing level of youth unemployment at the time, one of the concerns expressed was about the need for a more vocational emphasis in the education of all young people. Another was the lack of accountability of educators and educational institutions. The Labour government took these concerns seriously as did the educational establishment. Schools themselves began to establish contacts with local businesses for both teachers and pupils; careers teaching was developed more thoroughly and the curriculum itself began to accommodate the demands of new technology. But it was left to the Conservative governments of the 1980s to interpret public concern in a more extreme way.

Education in the 1980s

The Conservatives came to office determined to expand the private sector in education, to teach the state educational establishment a lesson and to give 'power back to the parents'. One of their earlier actions was to introduce the Assisted Places Scheme which they claimed would provide state funds to help parents of limited means to obtain a place in a private school. The previous Labour government had discouraged measures which channelled public funds into private education but the Conservatives reversed that downward trend. The idea of educational vouchers came under considerable scrutiny but was eventually abandoned as impractical.

Apart from further concessions to private schools, which helped to reduce the cost of such education to upper- and middle-class parents, the early changes to education in the 1980s were not dramatic. Legislation was introduced in 1900 and 1986 to change the composition of school management bodies and to give them a greater say in the running of schools. Although the Tyndale affair had not prompted the setting up of the Taylor inquiry into the management of schools, the committee's recommendations were assumed to provide the answer to that and similar problems (Taylor 1977). Taylor had suggested that management bodies be made up of equal proportions of representatives of the teachers, the parents, the LEA and the local community. The formula finally accepted by the Conservatives was one which ensured that the teachers and the LEA representatives could never constitute a majority (Maclure 1989: p. 132).

The power of LEAs and teachers was threatened in another way. The Manpower Services Commission (MSC) – a government agency attached to the Department of Employment – had been established in the 1970s to administer employment and training services. Growing unemployment had led to its being responsible for the government training and job creation programmes for young people. At a time when local authorities were facing cuts in their central government grants, the MSC was able to put resources into the further education colleges to purchase training packages for the young unemployed. In the early 1980s the MSC began to use its financial power to influence what the young unemployed were taught and how they were taught. The MSC was also used by the government to challenge the power of the educational establishment by allowing it to use funds to encourage the adoption of a more vocational approach to education in secondary schools through the Technical and Vocational Education Initiative.

A different kind of impact was made by the steady erosion of local authority finance. The county and metropolitan borough councils which ran local schools and colleges were dependent for over 70 per cent of their funds on grants from central government. As the government sought to reduce public expenditure it was often local councils which felt the brunt. School buildings and equipment began to suffer and the impact on the ability of schools to buy books was seriously impaired. The value of teachers' salaries were also eroded and the consequent loss of morale was made worse by the government not only taking away their negotiating rights, but ignoring their professional advice. The voice of the teaching profession had always been represented on the committees of inquiry in the 1960s, and the years of consensus had assumed that major changes in education policy had to have the support of teachers and local authorities. The governments of the 1980s thought differently. So firmly did they believe that there was a conspiracy by the education 'industry' to feather its own nest, that they ceased to listen to professionals altogether, preferring right-wing think-tanks such as the Institute for Economic Affairs, the Adam Smith Institute and the Hillgate Group (Ball 1990).

An idea which found little support amongst the educationists was the creation of City Technology Colleges (CTCs). These were to be schools financed by the DES and industry to give high-quality scientific and technical education to young people living in inner city areas. Many LEAS were unwilling to cooperate with a venture which they saw as wasting resources on a privileged few that could be put to better use in local education budgets. Nor was industry keen to contribute much in the way of financing. By 1990 only 15 CTCs were in existence or planned. The government had contributed about 80 per cent of the capital cost, while industry had provided the rest (*Education* 1991a). Successful or not, the scheme was another indication of the lengths the government was willing to go to in order to challenge the dominance of LEAs in the field of education. The final and most significant consequence of this strategy was to be the 1988 'Great Educational Reform' Act.

The Education Act of 1988

According to Maclure this major change to the British education system was not prepared in consultation with DES officials or LEA chief education officers (Maclure 1989: p. 166). Others have claimed that a few typewritten sheets formed the basis of a short and narrow process of consultation in a few months in 1987 (Glennerster *et al.* 1991: p. 393). While it is too early to say how the implementation of the Act will work out, its intentions were clear from the beginning. The Act enhanced the powers of the Secretary of State, the business community and parents, at the expense of teachers and the LEAs. This fundamental redistribution of power and responsibilities might have seemed pluralistic at the time, even libertarian. But it could also be argued that the power of the centre had been strengthened while any forces that might oppose it had become weaker and more divided. Schools and their managers were to be given more responsibilities; a national curriculum was to be introduced; individual schools were to be allowed to opt out of LEA control; parents were to be allowed to choose schools for their children under a system of open enrolment; the Inner London Education Authority was to be abolished; polytechnics were to be allowed to be independent, but both they and the universities were to be subjected to tighter central control.

As far as school managers were concerned, the increase in their powers has to be considered in conjunction with the 1986 Education Act. The 1986 Education Act had sought to reduce further the control that local authorities had over schools by changing the composition of their management boards yet again. This time co-opted governors and parent representatives had a majority over representatives of the LEAs and the teachers. The managers were also given more extensive powers of supervision and were expected to produce a curriculum policy document for public perusal. With the introduction of the National Curriculum (see below), however, their powers in this respect were limited, but in one area at least their approval was essential – sex education. It was their job to have a school policy for such teaching and to ensure that it was firmly rooted in 'morality' and 'the value of family life'. In conjunction with other legislation it was clear that this was intended to prevent open discussions about homosexuality, a topic which progressive teachers had wanted to air in a society which has always had strong homophobic traditions.

The Local Management of Schools (LMS) was introduced, which gave the head teacher and the governors greater (and LEAs fewer) powers over school budgets. LEAs remained responsible for capital expenditure, debt repayments and government grants, while schools became responsible for staff salaries and other current expenditure. The LEAs still had a planning role but one which gave them little room for manoeuvre. By 1992, 41 of the 97 LEAs had delegated 85 per cent of their funds to schools, while the remaining authorities all came close to that target (*Education* 1992b).

LEAs were also to lose control over those schools which wanted to 'opt out'. A simple majority of those parents who chose to vote would be sufficient for a school to be able to gain independence. Such schools would be financed directly by the DES, thus complementing the earlier experiment to create City Technology Colleges. In contrast to LMS, this proposal, like that for CTCs, has been slow to excite interest. By the beginning of 1991, 104 schools had opted out while a year later the figure had increased to only 285 (*Education* 1992a). Set against a total of 30,000 state schools, these are not high figures, but they have set a precedent for schools which find their LEA plans for them unacceptable. It is assumed that the government's intention was to encourage schools to opt out of Labour LEAs.

In the event, schools in more Conservative LEAs have applied for grant-maintained status. To encourage opting out the government has forced LEAs to give grant-maintained schools an extra 16 per cent on top of their delegated grant. This has caused consternation amongst many LEAs, Conservative and Labour alike, since many of those schools which choose to opt out are already in an advantageous position, and are thus depriving schools with special needs of funds (*Education* 1991b).

Simon's view of these changes was that they would make the planning tasks of LEAs much more complicated, as would the right of parents to choose the schools their children would attend under the Act's regulations on open enrolment (Simon 1988). Schools which 'lost' pupils would lose funding, while schools which 'gained' pupils would be well funded. While the intention of this measure was to punish bad schools, the effect is more likely to be to punish schools in poor areas. Maclure has suggested that the effect of open enrolment will not be dissimilar to what the abandoned voucher scheme would have achieved (Maclure 1989).

While the Act does enable some parents to have more choice, it is important to consider which ones. Unpopular schools (and this won't necessarily mean those which are inefficiently run) will lose pupils and perhaps have to be closed down. If they are in poor areas they will lose funds. In contrast, 'better' schools will be full to capacity and gain more funds. Since another feature of the Act is to enable schools to charge parents for a wider range of services and equipment, it follows that schools with wealthier parents will become more wealthy themselves. Thus a range of measures at different levels – parental choice, charges, opting out, assistance for private education – are all likely to have the effect of increasing inequalities within the system, making educational attainment even more a matter of social class than of merit.

The Secretary of State also took on greater powers by introducing a national curriculum. The National Curriculum specifies what subjects are to be taught, the content of those subjects, targets which should be attained at particular ages, and the means by which the assessment should be carried out. Already, the practical implementations of testing have caused the Secretary of State to modify his demands, but the National Curriculum itself is firmly in place. The principle of a national curriculum has not been so contentious as the form it has taken and the methods of testing. The government clearly wanted to use a national curriculum to re-establish the priority of traditional subjects and traditional methods of teaching. History was to become much more a matter of great British dates and achievements as opposed to the more critical stance taken by history teachers. Even the arts were to become more a matter of recalling great moments of Western culture than the ability to paint, perform and compose. This stress on the academic and rote learning seemed to contradict the government's preoccupation with vocational education earlier in the decade, but what both had in common was an emphasis on discipline and authority in contrast to the permissiveness of the child-centred approach so popular amongst the teaching profession and educationists. While the Japanese authorities were questioning the ability of their education system to produce individual initiative and creativity, the British were emulating the Japanese obsession with rote learning and examinations.

A further attack on LEAs was symbolised by the abolition of the Labour-dominated Inner London Education Authority. This epitome of progressiveness for some (and bureaucracy for others) was wound up and the management of its schools handed over to individual London boroughs. LEAs were also to lose control of the polytechnics. Higher education institutions generally were to be much more accountable to their central funding bodies – the Polytechnic Funding Council (PFC) and the University Funding Council (UFC). The representation of the business sector was to be paramount in both. Business people were also to dominate on the governing bodies of individual polytechnics. New university lecturers were no longer to enjoy security of tenure. Thus, in a variety of ways, the autonomy of universities and polytechnics was reduced and the power of central government and the influence of business interests enhanced. Staff–student ratios began to deteriorate, first in the polytechnics and subsequently in the universities, as *per capita* funding levels were allowed to fall (*Education* 1992c). An amalgamation of the PFC and the UGC in 1992 was followed by a competition for research funds. This is likely to result in a hierarchy of higher education establishments characterised by a few with a strong research component and a larger number of teaching-only institutions. The intention of the government is that the former will be able to afford higher pay scales than the latter and national pay structures will become a thing of the past.

The government had, then, by the end of the 1980s achieved a fundamental change in the structure and character of the state education system. What did this mean in terms of opportunities for the mass of the population?

Achievement and opportunity

Boucher, in comparing the British system with that of the Swedes, said that at its most superior, British education produced excellent results but that at its worst it was very poor indeed. He considered Swedish education to be of better quality for the mass of the population (Boucher 1982). The same has been said of the Japanese system in comparison with that of the USA. International tests have shown that both Japanese and Swedish children have high average scores in certain subjects. No such claim is made for British children.

The 'excellence' of the British academic education is epitomised in the public-school system and the élite universities of Oxford and Cambridge. While it can hardly be contested that the children who go to these schools are likely to achieve better grades in examinations on average than their state counterparts, this can hardly account for their dominance of the country's economic, political and social institutions. The 3 per cent of the population that attend public schools are the major source of élite recruitment. Figures drawn on sources published in the 1960s, 1970s and 1980s all show that between 60 per cent and 90 per cent of leading figures in the world of industry and commerce, the law, the military, the church, Conservative MPs and governments were educated at public schools. High percentages exist in most other fields of public life (Urry and Wakeford 1973: p. 214; Boyd 1973; Reid 1989: p. 312).

Surveys indicating the persistence of other social class inequalities in education which were collected assiduously by committees of inquiry and academics in the 1960s and 1970s seem to have dried up in the 1980s. This is partly because recent Conservative governments have not attributed much importance to the issue of educational inequality. Reid also suggests that neither the advocates or critics of comprehensive education have been particularly willing to put their theories about such schools to the test (Reid 1989). He argues that another reason may have to do with a drift in the concern of social scientists with other issues. This in itself may be a reflection of the decreasing salience of class as a basis of social organisation. Certainly the issues of ethnicity and gender have received more attention in recent years than class.

Using data from the General Household Survey, Reid has shown differences in educational qualifications by occupational background while Brown has produced similar figures demonstrating differences according to ethnicity and gender (Reid 1989 and Brown 1984). For the sake of simplicity the extremes of *degree qualifications* and *no qualifications* will be presented here (see Tables 8.1 and 8.2). The figures illustrate the extent of educational inequality for different social groups in the population as a whole. Lower occupational groups, blacks and women are clearly disadvantaged compared with higher occupational groups, whites and men. It is clear also that occupational differences are greater than ethnic and gender differences. However, the figures cover such a wide age range that they tell us nothing about the present generation of young people. Similar figures for the population as a whole can be presented by ethnic group and gender category.

Using more recent data from the General Household Survey, Glennerster and Low have argued that while young people from white-collar backgrounds remain much more likely to gain educational qualifications than those from blue-collar backgrounds, the relative position of the former declined between 1974 and 1985,

Table 8.1 Educational qualifications by persons, aged 25–69, in particular occupational groups, Great Britain 1984–85 (percentages)

	1 [1]	2	3	4	5	6
Degrees or equivalent	65	14	11	1	1	–
No qualification	2	25	27	50	70	63

[1]Registrar General's occupational classification (1980): 1 Professional, 2 Intermediate, 3 Skilled non-manual, 4 Skilled manual, 5 Semi-skilled manual, 6 Unskilled manual
Source: Adapted from Reid 1989: p. 278

Table 8.2 Educational qualifications by persons, aged 25–44, by ethnic group and gender

	MEN			WOMEN		
	White	West Indian	Asian	White	West Indian	Asian
Degrees or equivalent	10	3	6	4	1	4
No qualification	38	64	56	50	54	71

Source: Adapted from Brown 1984

while the relative position of the latter improved. This applied to degrees, post-school and school qualifications (Glennerster and Low 1990: p. 72). Surveys carried out by the Rampton and Swann committees into the educational achievments of ethnic minorities suggest that Asian pupils gained as many school qualifications as whites and were as likely to study for degrees in higher education. Although the performance of West Indian children lagged behind both the other groups, there was some evidence that between the two surveys carried out in 1979 and 1982 West Indian children were improving their performance in terms of school qualifications (Rampton 1981; Swann 1985). What few surveys of ethnic differences do, however, is to control for occupational differences. The occupational background of Indian children, for example, is quite close to that of whites but parents of West Indian and Pakistani children are disproportionately in blue-collar jobs.

Figures on sex differences show that generally young men and women gain a similar number of school qualifications and are equally likely to go on to post-school education. One important difference between them is that young men are more likely to attend degree courses at universities than young women in a ratio of 4:3 (*Social Trends 1991*). Another difference is in what they choose to study, with more men opting for scientific and technical subjects, while women choose the humanities and social sciences. There can be little doubt, however, that the expansion of educational opportunities has benefited women *vis-à-vis* men even if their opportunities still remain unequal.

Inequalities may have increased in the last decade because of some of the present government's education policies but as yet it is impossible to be specific. The overall cost of the state education system has declined relative to GDP. From a high of 6.3 per cent of GDP in the mid-1970s, total UK expenditure on education fell to 4.6 per cent at the end of the 1980s (Government Statistical Service 1991). This may have been partly due to demographic changes which had resulted in declining school rolls, but it was also due to cost-cutting. Capital expenditure has been allowed to fall. Teachers' salaries have not risen in line with inflation. LEA support from central government has also fallen. Private enterprise has played a larger role in the financing of higher education, while charities and parents themselves have had to provide more resources for schools. It is likely that schools in poorer areas have suffered disproportionately from such cuts while schools catering for children with wealthier parents have been able to come up with additional resources. Student grants have also declined in value and the contribution assumed to come from parents has risen. This will also affect young people with poorer parents adversely.

Certainly the percentage of 16–18-year-olds staying on at school and in further education colleges has risen very slowly in the 1980s, from 52 per cent in 1981 to only 58 per cent in 1990 (Government Statistical Service 1991), leaving Britain well behind countries like Japan and Sweden. However, the percentage of young people under the age of 21 on first-year courses in higher education has risen from 14.6 per cent in 1979 to 20.2 per cent in 1989 (*Education* 1991c). Government figures also show that the absolute numbers of students in higher education have increased from 734,000 in 1976 to 1,094,000 in 1990. This is reflected in the number of grants awarded which amounted to 509,000 in 1976 and 707,000 in 1990 (Government Statistical Service 1991: p. xii). It could well be that the main beneficiaries of this expansion are the children of those middle-class and affluent working-class parents who have benefited from the more favourable developments of the 1980s. In the face of government cutbacks they would still be able to afford higher education for their youngsters. But those young people with parents who have experienced unemployment, the increased polarisation of the labour market, the decline in public services and benefits, and growing wage differentials, are hardly likely to be in a position to benefit from an expansion of educational opportunities that require substantial private resources to take advantage of them. If in the 1990s there is going to be a widening gap between schools themselves because of policies of opting out and open enrolment, then it is hard to see how the situation can improve.

So far, we have concerned ourselves with the experiences of young people prior to their entry into the labour market. We must now turn our attention to a set of services which in the 1970s and early 1980s were created to help a wide range of people to adjust to the changing requirements of the labour market.

EMPLOYMENT AND TRAINING SERVICES

The sort of employment and training services which had existed in Britain prior to 1973 were residual in nature. They were there to help the hard to employ and were not seen as central to governments' economic and social strategy. Labour exchanges had been established in 1909; public works schemes had been used in the 1930s; Government Training Centres were introduced after the Second World War. In the post-war years, then, there were opportunities for those who required help to find a job, or to acquire a skill. But however adequate they may have been when they were introduced, by the 1960s they came to be seen as shabby and inadequate. Training in particular was seen as something which British employers had neglected for too long. In 1964 the Industrial Training Boards were set up to combat this neglect. Each industry was represented by a board consisting of representatives of government, employers and trade unions, which had the task of raising the level of training in their industry and the awareness of employers of the importance of the issue. The device used to goad them into action was the levy-grant system. Each firm paid a levy, a small percentage of its labour costs, to the board, which then redistributed the levy in the form of grants towards training costs. Firms would either invest in different levels of training for different categories of employees and recoup the expense of the levy, or not train and lose what they had contributed.

This programme was followed by the setting up of committees within the Department of Employment to investigate the need for improving not only training services but employment services as well. Their reports were severely critical of the existing set-up, and proposed expansion and modernisation of these services to bring them into line with what were perceived as being the needs of a modern economy. Santosh Mukherjee at this time wrote a study of the Swedish Labour Market services for the research group – Political and Economic Planning – suggesting that Britain would do well to emulate the single administrative board which the Swedes had used since 1940 to coordinate all its employment and training programmes.

The rise of the Manpower Services Commission

A Conservative government introduced the employment and training legislation which was passed in 1973 and created the Manpower Services Commission (Showler 1976). The MSC was a quasi-government agency which was run by a commission consisting of representatives of the TUC, the CBI, and government civil servants with one or two members drawn from local authorities. The succeeding Labour government was only too happy to use this new device for updating Britain's archaic employment and training services. Whereas the old labour exchanges had been attached to unemployment benefit offices in shabby backstreet offices, the new job centres had offices of their own on prime high-street sites. It was intended that they should look inviting, and that they should attract a wide range of job-seekers. Jobs were advertised on display boards so that people could drop in and look around. The relatively plush surroundings were staffed by personnel who could help you establish contact with an employer or direct you to a range of advice, guidance and training services which might help you to find work appropriate to your skills and talents.

The Training Opportunities Scheme (TOPs) was created to provide training places for adults who were unemployed or seeking new forms of employment. An approved list of training courses, manual and non-manual, skilled and professional, carried out by a variety of private and public colleges, was backed by training allowances for the trainees. The aim was to provide up to 100,000 places a year.

Unfortunately the work of building up employment and training services was interrupted by the recession following 1973. Unemployment grew, particularly amongst young people, and the MSC was the obvious agency for government to turn to to manage the problem. This new demand meant that the MSC grew in terms of resources and responsibilities but it also meant that the updating of the other services could no longer be the priority. The Job Creation Programme (JCP) was the first response to the youth unemployment problem followed by the Youth Opportunities Scheme (YOPs). The aims of YOPs as set out by the Holland Report were generous and humane, recognising that young people were unemployed through no fault of their own, that they needed a combination of work experience and training to help them find a place in the labour market. The allowance paid to them while on the scheme compared well with what they would have received in supplementary benefit.

In practice neither JCP nor YOPs were seen as that successful at the time. JCP was criticised for creating makework jobs of little value to the community and as simply a device for keeping young people off the streets. YOPs work experience placements were accused of providing exploitative employers with cheap labour, while the training provided was often regarded as minimal. The replacment of JCP by the Community Programme (CP) and YOPs by the Youth Training Scheme (YTS) in the 1980s did little to stem the criticism.

A change of direction

When the Conservative Party came to office in 1979, it was widely thought that the MSC might be wound up. There had been growing criticism of corporatist bodies like the MSC as being examples of 'creeping socialism'. Nor was the government keen to cooperate with trade unions on major policy issues. However, the rapid growth of unemployment over the next three years from 1.3 million to over 3 million made it difficult for the government to abandon the only agency which had the powers to alleviate the plight of the unemployed. Paradoxically, the MSC continued to grow. It had established a Special Programmes Division alongside its divisions for employment and training services, which had the responsibility of dealing with both the young and adult unemployed. But while staff and resources for the Special Programmes Division continued to grow, other services remained stable for a while and were subsequently reduced.

The anti-state intervention policy style of the government saw the private sector as the appropriate locus for the provision of employment services. In particular there was seen to be little justification for the MSC to use expensive town-centre sites to provide information on job vacancies. Nor were they considered to need the high staffing levels they had acquired. The Industrial Training Boards were greatly reduced in number. Again, it was felt that employers were the best judge of whether they needed to train their own work-forces; it was not the job of civil servants to make decisions for them. Moreover, it was felt that the grant-levy system had become redundant. Employers were either merely claiming back what they had already paid in or, worse, manipulating the system with dubious claims. The TOPs scheme was also abandoned. It had never reached a total of more than 60,000 places annually, and was now abandoned as an unnecessary and wasteful exercise. TOPs, after all, had met the needs of the individual, not those of employers.

Although the existence of the MSC had not been threatened, its philosophy was. As an agency based on the enlightenment of the corporatist consensus, it had been run by people used to trying to meet the needs of both sides of industry. Even if such an approach was often rhetorical it had a certain reality. The MSC as constituted in the early 1980s was not accustomed to the notion of compulsion, nor to an over-emphasis on employers' needs. As the government sought to use the MSC for its own political ends, the commitment of trade-union representatives, and even some of those on the employers' side, came under strain. The allowances and benefits enjoyed by those on government schemes were reduced in value. The Young Workers' Scheme had the explicit aim of encouraging employers to reduce the the wages offered by employers to their young employees. YTS, CP and other schemes came to be used as a form of workfare whereby the unemployed were told that they had either to accept a place on them or be deprived of benefit. While the government claimed that it was devising training schemes to prepare the unemployed for the opportunities of a post-industrial economy, critics deplored the low standard of the schemes and the controlling mentality which guided them (Davies 1986). Instead of providing young people with a broad-based vocational education, schemes provided a narrow job training which emphasised the needs of the employer for docile, obedient workers. Courses in colleges could not discuss the causes of unemployment. Indeed courses were structured in such a way as to imply that unemployment arose because of the inadequacies of the unemployed themselves rather than as resulting from economic change and government policy. The monitoring of work experience placements became so poor that accidents and fatalities began to increase.

As successive ministers began to restructure the MSC so that the government and employer representatives were prepared to adopt the new harder line, trade-union representatives found themselves in an increasingly invidious position. If they threatened to withdraw from the MSC it would look as though they had no interest in helping the unemployed. If they remained, their principles were compromised as they cooperated in the manipulation and exploitation of the unemployed. They finally withdrew in 1988. The MSC was immediately replaced by the Training Commission (TC), a body on which employers but not trade unions were represented. This in turn was abandoned and all the former activities of the MSC and the TC reverted to the Department of Employment, under the direct control of the Secretary of State. Local Training and Enterprise Councils now exist throughout the country, dominated by employers whose task it is to continue to encourage the spirit of enterprise without the necessity to carry trade unions along with them.

The achievements and shortcomings of the MSC

The history of the MSC illustrates the dilemmas and the deficiencies of social policy in Britain. The corporatist elements in British society strove to overcome the class-divided politics of the past. They could not satisfy the participatory and egalitarian politics of the left, nor could they appease those elements of the right which saw any kind of collectivism as socialist. For a while, though, there was a confident vision of an approach to the labour market which could be both efficient and humane; which could provide opportunites to individuals while providing employers with a labour force which was well trained.

It was sabotaged by the circumstance of growing unemployment and the meanness that faces a society in recession. Instead of reactionary attitudes being challenged, they were reinforced. Instead of a vocational education, young people got narrow job training on the cheap. Young black workers found it difficult to get on the more ambitious programmes. Young women were still channelled into routine clerical, service and caring jobs. MSC became the secondary modern of post-school education while bright youngsters from affluent backgrounds went to polytechnics and universities.

CONCLUSION

The advanced welfare state vision of educational opportunities for all and comprehensive labour market services provided by the state which heralded the 1970s barely survived the decade. By 1980 the social-democratic state had come to be regarded as insatiable and Keynesian policies of demand-management as unworkable. A new vision was promoted by the British Conservatives which emphasised the values of free enterprise and self-reliance. The irony was that this new order also required a strong conception of the state in order to dismantle old institutions and replace them with new ones (Gamble 1988). Nowhere was this more important than in the area of education and training. Future generations of young people had to re-learn the values of labour discipline and enterprise. That was not to be achieved by relying on a progressive educational establishment nor on a philosophy that insisted that social and economic problems were created by an unjust economic system. Individuals had to be taught to adapt to the system and learn that any failure to do so was theirs.

At times government policy seemed beset by contradiction. In education there were those who were calling for individualism and free choice on the one hand, while on the other, adherents to the notion that the state should take more responsibility for the curriculum. There were the old humanists who wanted to

> return to some kind of pre-Fordist idyll, based upon the public school, the grammar school and some kind of sponsored mobility. The industrial trainers are pushing towards a post-Fordist, decentralised,

open, contest mobility and thus an education system compatible with the desocialisation of production and the individualisation of living labour, and flexible work practices, wages and labour markets.

(Ball 1990: p. 130)

Certainly new education and training policies have more than one source. In place of the old accommodation with labour, a new one had to be found; and in place of the old alliances, new ones had to be forged. What is important is whether the different strands can be made to work. The Japanese had managed to combine a pre-Fordist, traditional education system with an emphasis on discipline and rote learning in schools with flexible post-Fordist training at work; the Japanese had combined state control of the curriculum with the expansion of a private market in education; the Japanese had encouraged open contest mobility and a respect for traditional values. If it worked in Japan, why not in Britain?

CHAPTER NINE

Perspectives and evaluations

INTRODUCTION

Critiques of the British welfare state as it existed prior to 1979 have already received considerable attention and many of the main points in such critiques have been alluded to in previous sections. This chapter will refer to attempts to evaluate the achievements and shortcomings of post-1979 Conservative governments in the field of welfare. How have different commentators responded to the welfare activities of governments which have often espoused a free-market, libertarian ideology while at the same time centralising state power and using it in an unashamedly authoritarian manner? The existence of conservative authoritarianism should not be surprising when set in the context of the emergence of Japan. The Japanese state saw its main task as the creation of a strong market economy and was prepared to use its considerable powers to achieve this. At the same time it also used state power to defend traditional institutions and practices and weaken those countervailing forces in society which opposed it. A parallel to Japanese authoritarianism can be found in the writings of the British political journalist Worsthorne.

Prior to the election in 1979, Worsthorne expressed considerable doubts about the then Conservative opposition's rhetoric of laissez-faire liberalism. He claimed that the Conservatives were mistaken if they thought that the problem with British society was that there was too little freedom. In his view there was too much. The state had allowed organised labour too much influence and had been unable to resist pressures for increased public expenditure. British Labour governments had shown a lack of concern about crime, sexual immorality, the spread of pornography, and about discipline in schools, universities and the home. Parts of the Labour Party are against the police, the armed forces, and corporal and capital punishment as well as spurning the disciplines of the market, the boss and the landlord.   (Worsthorne 1978: p. 148)

There was a 'lack of supervision, lack of interference, excessive tolerance' (Worsthorne 1978: p. 151). In a Nietzschean attack on compassion for 'the weak, the sick, the poor and the miserable, the plight of whom we are never allowed to forget' (Worsthorne 1978: p. 153), he called for a new emphasis upon the needs and values of the strong:

The urgent need today is for the State to regain control over 'the people', to reassert its authority, and it is useless to imagine that this will be helped by some libertarian mish-mash drawn from the writings of Adam Smith, John Stuart Mill, and the warmed-up milk of nineteenth century liberalism.   (Worsthorne 1978: p. 149)

This powerful rhetoric may not have figured prominently in the public statements of Thatcher and her colleagues, but the evidence would suggest that Worsthorne's sentiments came more closely to reflect the values upon which subsequent Conservative social policies were based, than the anti-state ethos of neo-liberalism.

WITHER THE WELFARE STATE

The emergence of the New Right in Britain was initially associated with neo-liberalism. Post-war Conservatism was seen to have become bogged down in a consensus which endorsed a strong role for the state in economic and social policy. The result of this consensus had been a spiralling of public expenditure and a welfare state that was constantly striving to achieve a greater degree of equality. The task of Conservative governments after 1979 was to get government off the backs of the people, to roll back the frontiers of the welfare state. The welfare state was seen as wasteful in its use of resources, ineffective in achieving its goals. It sapped the incentive of those who were employed and created dependency amongst those who were not. People needed to be encouraged to provide for themselves and their families and not to rely on the state. Seldon, a key spokesman for the Institute for Economic Affairs (IEA), an organisation committed to free market economics, argued that the welfare state had destroyed the welfare institutions that ordinary people had created in the nineteenth century – friendly societies, cooperatives, educational associations – which had provided them with health coverage, social security and education. The state, instead of building on these voluntary activities, had chosen instead to take them over and gradually replace them with monopolistic state services over which they had no influence or control. The expansion of the public sector generally had resulted in a situation in which poor families were paying more in tax and contributions to the state than they were receiving in state services and benefits. Seldon's answer was for the role of the state to be diminished. This was to be achieved by encouraging private insurance schemes for pensions and health care, a system of vouchers for services like education, and increased charges for local authority services. The state needed to wither away (Seldon 1981).

A parallel organisation, the Social Affairs Unit (SAU), saw, as an important part of this task, the need to 'break the spell of the welfare state' (Anderson 1981). The welfare state had assumed a charmed status in political debate. It was assumed to be a force for the good, by its very nature. Its defenders did not have to justify its merits and its critics were uncaring by definition. Those who researched its performance were employed by institutions who were part of the welfare state conspiracy. The spell which had been woven around the welfare state needed to be broken, so that people could see its inefficiencies, its lack of accountability, its self-seeking salariats for what they were.

Such were the views of critics from the right at the start of the decade. Their hopes were clearly that a series of radical Conservative governments would create a slimmer, more efficient, more accountable set of social policies.

REACTIONS FROM THE RIGHT

By the end of the decade, with a new Prime Minister, an economy in recession and a general election in prospect, spokesmen for the IEA and the SAU looked back over the Thatcher years with only qualified satisfaction. Thatcherism, according to a paper written by two IEA members, had retained a strong streak of collectivism. While they were pleased that the private sector in health care had grown, they were critical of the reforms to the NHS. They felt that the reorganisation following 1988 might result in better value for money but that there was little evidence that consumers were to have more choice. The NHS continued to be financed out of general taxation within cash limits set by the Treasury. Community care reforms were similarly judged. They might result in less bureaucracy but this was 'no substitute for choice' (Green and Lucas 1992). Education reforms were regarded as having achieved a greater degree of choice for better off parents, but otherwise as having done too little to reduce the power of the LEAs and not enough to empower the vast majority of parents. Trends in pension policy and housing policy were applauded but the authors could not disguise their overall disappointment. Social policy in the Thatcher years had become 'an incoherent compromise' and from a classical-liberal point of view had to be judged 'a failure' (Green and Lucas 1992: p. 46).

This view was confirmed by the Director of the Social Affairs Unit in his comments on a conference paper delivered to the Social Policy Association in the summer of 1991. Instead of a radical transformation of welfare provision, the Thatcher governments, he claimed, had chosen to try and regulate the system. The consequence, he implied, had been a costly bureaucratic nightmare. Peacock, another champion of free market economics, has expressed dismay that the State Earnings Related Pension has been retained and that education vouchers were never introduced. He agreed that there had been a reduction in collectivism, but expressed the view that classical-liberal policies had little chance of being implemented (Peacock 1991: p. 52).

In an account of modern conservatism which sought to demonstrate that the collectivist and liberal wings of the party complemented each other, Willetts, the Director of the Centre for Policy Studies, has suggested that conservative attitudes towards welfare had been misunderstood. Although it might seem that Conservatives often claimed only that they were more able to produce the wealth which financed the welfare state and to manage it better, their real position was more positive than this. Conservatives recognised, he claimed, that advanced capitalist societies needed a welfare state in order to function. Unemployment benefit and pensions made it easier for employers to shed labour. Homelessness prevented adults from working and children from studying. It impaired their economic efficiency and it was therefore rational for Conservatives to want to do something about it. State-run social insurance schemes were a sensible way of reallocating resources through different stages of the life cycle. Too great a reliance on means-testing was administratively complex and inefficient. The poverty trap was a 'terrible disincentive to personal advancement' (Willetts 1992: p. 146).

Conservatives, he went on, only objected to welfare policies when they had egalitarian aims; when they sought to erode mediating institutions like the family and charities; and when they destroyed values such as prudence and self-reliance. If volunteers could provide a service as well as paid workers, then why not use volunteers? After all 'volunteers don't strike, but paid employees can' (Willetts 1992: p. 148). Recent Conservative policy had sought to strengthen mediating institutions. It had sought to reorganise state education and health care so that there was a higher degree of choice and competition. It had also been concerned to help people in need to participate in the life of society but in a way which did not encourage pauperism.

This strange little section of Willetts' book is interesting in the light of the role that Willetts played in providing the Thatcher governments with ideas and intellectual inspiration. There is no evidence of either the authoritarian rhetoric of Worsthorne or of the free-market rhetoric of the classical-liberal school. But for all its sweet reason, there is a clear sub-text to Willetts' defence of the welfare state. What Willetts calls the welfare state is primarily justified only in so far as it makes a contribution towards the economy. It should therefore not be involved in redistributive policies but only in the reallocation of resources between different parts of the life cycle. State welfare must be disaggregated and the voluntary sector encouraged because 'volunteers don't strike'. Those without incomes had to have recourse to state benefits but these must not be so high as to encourage people to become paupers, i.e. be able to survive on them for long periods. This more strident tone, which had been prominent during the 1980s, may have been softened because of the approach of the general election of 1992, in which Willetts himself was standing as a candidate.

SOCIAL DEMOCRATIC RESPONSES

The gap between the classical-liberal aims of early Thatcherism and the experience of the 1980s also left some social democrats bemused. In a study of all the major areas of social policy from 1974 to 1988, carried out by academics involved in the Welfare State Programme of the London School of Economics, the editor concluded that reports of the death of the welfare state had been greatly exaggerated. Particular services might have been reduced; standards of service and benefit might not have been maintained, but the welfare state had not been 'rolled back' as might have been expected from the Conservatives' ideological opposition to the public sector. Another contributor, Glennerster, expressed the view that a consensus on the welfare state had rarely existed in the post-war years anyway. Substantial differences between the major parties had always existed and all that the economic crisis of the mid-1970s had done was to 'sharpen and deepen that debate' (Glennerster 1990: p. 27).

A more speculative consideration of the significance of the last decade occurred in another paper to which Glennerster contributed. Had the New Right brought about fundamental changes in the character of the welfare state, the authors wondered; had a new Leviathan been created to dominate and control people's behaviour; had a more pluralistic approach to welfare provision made new forms of participatory democracy possible; had there been any real change at all? The answer, following an analysis of the major pieces of social legislation in 1988 and 1990, was unambiguous. The increased powers for central government in the field of education were 'disturbing'; the future of local government finance and expenditure was firmly under central government control; and local government services were subject to greater central government interference. While Glennerster and his colleagues agreed that there had been devolution to bodies like school managers, managers of housing estates and community care agencies, they concluded that this had been at the expense of local government. There was therefore, in their view, 'nothing to set between small-scale semi-representative bodies and a very powerful central state' (Glennerster *et al.* 1991: p. 413).

Others like Field who, before he became a Labour MP, had for many years been an influential member of the poverty lobby, and who was not so even-handed. He was of the opinion that increased inequalities of incomes and wealth, combined with unemployment, homelessness and poorer social benefits, had conspired to create in Britain a distinct underclass. Neither the unemployed, single-parent families nor poor pensioners could be said to be able to play their full role as citizens in British society. Many of them had become victims of a 'political, social and economic apartheid' (Field 1989: p. 4). Not only were the poor separated from the wealthier members of society but because of changes in public attitudes, they had become separated from the working class itself.

WELFARE PLURALISM

Pinker, whose favourable comments upon the Japanese welfare system have already been mentioned (see chapter 5), has referred in more critical terms to the growing welfare pluralism of the Thatcher years. Too powerful a welfare state, in his view, had indeed been a threat to people's personal liberty. The pressure towards collectivism from the producers and consumers of welfare had needed to be curbed. An expansion of private, voluntary and informal provision had taken place in Britain which in one sense brought the British welfare system into alignment with those of its European neighbours. But whereas their systems had been accompanied by a growing decentralisation of state power, Britain had been moving in the direction of 'increasing central government control' (Pinker 1991: p. 296). The Thatcher governments exercised 'even stricter control' over what remained of statutory services. This was clearly worrying for someone who had advocated welfare pluralism in preference to the state monopoly of welfare provision.

Like Pinker, many of the advocates of welfare pluralism had had liberal and humane hopes of a form of welfare which gave the state a less dominant role. As Beresford and Croft had pointed out some years earlier, the welfare pluralists did share certain concerns with socialist critics of the welfare state, 'notably democratisation, decentralisation, non-hierarchical working and different kinds of services'. However, they also claimed that 'Welfare pluralist proposals . . . tend to be piecemeal and . . . unrelated to political, economic, cultural and other structural issues' (Beresford and Croft 1984). While Johnson too considered that the future lay with welfare pluralism, he was concerned that without additional resources, voluntary and informal providers would be unable to cope with the problems that they faced. Welfare pluralism had become a justification for cuts in state expenditure and the expansion of the private sector (Johnson 1987). In a later study he concluded that Britain had become a more divided society during the 1980s. There were greater 'divisions in the labour market, divisions of race and gender, and divisions between the rich and the poor' (Johnson 1990).

DIVISION AND CONTROL BY EMPLOYERS

The division referred to by Johnson is referred to in a different way by Mann. Recognising that individualist ideology itself was a weak explanation for the growth of occupational welfare that had occurred in the last two decades, Mann examined other factors such as the paternalism of employers or their desire to create a positive image for their companies. But other factors also played an important part.

157

One was that employers who wanted their work-forces to give up certain work practices and accept more flexible ones would offer welfare benefits in negotiations with trade unions. Moreover, some British unions were keen to demand such benefits for their members. Such developments were reinforced by government fiscal policies that made such schemes attractive. Coupled with the decline in state welfare provision, occupational welfare was increasingly becoming an issue in industrial relations. Mann's work was based on a small survey and he was reluctant to address broader issues. None the less, he suggested that Titmuss was probably right when in his discussion of 'the social division of welfare' he claimed that when welfare benefits became a matter of industrial relations, the result would be 'a socially divided society' (Mann 1989: p. 102). If what Mann has observed is as widespread as he clearly suspects, then it would suggest that many employers are keen to use occupational welfare to gain more control over their workers.

The increased role of employers in the administration of Statutory Sick Pay (SSP) has also been the subject of investigation by Dean and Taylor-Gooby. This scheme – whereby employers were responsible for the payment of sickness benefit for the first 8 weeks of sickness originally, but subsequently for 28 weeks – began with legislation in 1982 followed by further legislation in 1986. The scheme could not be judged a success, they argued, in terms of financial savings for central government, and was only a modest success in administrative terms. Its major achievement was in terms of labour discipline, the control it gave employers over the absenteeism of their workers. SSP legitimised the introduction of new methods of surveillance by management through interviews with those returning from sick leave or special forms which had to be completed. No 'privatisation' as such had occurred since employers simply deducted what they had paid out in sickness benefit from the total of National Insurance Contributions which they had to pay to the government. In the view of Dean and Taylor-Gooby, what had occurred 'did not diminish the state's role in welfare as redirect it' (Dean and Taylor-Gooby 1990: p. 65).

'THE FREE ECONOMY AND THE STRONG STATE'

Gamble, in a study not of the British welfare system as such but of 'Thatcherism' in general, has effectively linked the paradox of the Conservatives' libertarian rhetoric and authoritarian practice by insisting that a free market economy needs a strong state to create the conditions for its survival. Although the New Right had been liberal in origin, it had become a predominantly conservative movement, much to the 'embarrassment of the intellectuals who contributed to its early development' (Gamble 1988: p. 30).

A strong state was necessary to dismantle the institutions created by the years of consensus and social democracy, to police the market order and to modernise the economy. It is clear from Gamble's analysis that the Thatcher governments were successful in meeting the first two of these requirements but less so in the third. In the course of reconstructing Britain's Fordist society to meet the technological and organisational challenge of the new post-Fordist order, Gamble says that:

> the Left is threatened not only with exclusion from the possibility of power, but also with the reversal of the gains which had been won during the rise of the Labour movement and which at one time had seemed inviolable. (Gamble 1988: p. 185)

How much more true does this statement appear now, after the Conservatives' fourth consecutive success in the 1992 election.

Gamble also credits the Conservatives with having furthered the interests of the City and British transnational companies, not intentionally but through the maintenance of the openness of the British economy. But in doing so the domestic economy has been weakened. British manufacturing industry has continued to decline. The shake-out in the early 1980s which resulted in high unemployment and the consequent weakening of the trade unions had also severely damaged British industry. Gamble goes on to argue that the modernisation and strengthening of British manufacturing industry has yet to be carried out. Thatcherism, he argues, has merely prepared the ground for that particular task. It remains to be seen whether the new administration will be able to implement a national industrial strategy to reverse Britain's economic decline.

CONCLUSION

There would seem to be substantial agreement that the Conservative governments of the 1980s have reduced state collectivism in the provision of welfare, but not to the degree promised by their rhetoric nor to anything like the satisfaction that their supporters on the libertarian right had been led to expect. The scale of social expenditure has been stabilised if not significantly reduced. The major institutions of welfare provision still exist, albeit with their powers curtailed and their functions altered. Moreover, it is unlikely that any foreseeable future government would have the resources to make major improvements in state welfare provision – partly because the economy is unlikely to improve sufficiently but also because a climate has been created which makes the necessary tax increases politically impossible. But the major change which has resulted from the last decade is that a more authoritarian state has used its power to weaken those forces which, in the post-war settlement, had redistributed economic and political power in favour of a strong labour movement and a progressive state welfare establishment. The result is a more divided and a more easily controlled society.

British welfare institutions do not resemble Japanese welfare institutions, but the same principles now underlie them. A strong state has been created to limit the extent of state welfare and to ensure that it functions in the interests of British capitalism, just as a strong state in Japan created a Japanese-type welfare system to meet the needs of its economy. Reconstructing state welfare will not be enough, however. What is now required is a new industrial strategy to regenerate British industry. The Conservatives have yet to learn the most important lesson from Japan.

PART THREE
Sweden

CHAPTER TEN

Economic, political and social context

Swedish society was regarded by many as something of a model for capitalist countries from the time that Marquis Childs wrote his book *The Middle Way* in 1936, to the publication in the mid-1970s of Furniss and Tilton's *The Case for the Welfare State*. It seemed to some that Sweden had achieved an impressive balance between the needs of the business community to respond to the changing conditions of private markets, thereby generating profits, and the demands for employees for security and a good standard of living. Even in the middle of the 1980s it was possible for journalists to applaud Sweden's ability to maintain both a prosperous economy and a generous welfare state. To others Sweden had held out the possibility for decades of a country that was creating an evolutionary path to a democratic socialist state. Only as the decade came to an end did it become clear that the country's economy was facing the sort of crisis that was bound to lead to a profound questioning of the size and function of the public sector.

It has been pointed out that attempts to analyse the forces that gave rise to the Swedish welfare state have alluded to the persistence of pre-industrial features of Sweden, the influence of social reforms in other countries, the Social Democratic concept of 'the People's Home' in the 1930s, and the post-1945 years of reconstruction (Olsson 1990). None of these can in fact be ignored. A complex web of social, political and economic factors has conspired to create the conditions that made the Swedish experiment possible. But it is principally the force of international competition which has in the last few years brought about the most profound questioning of the 'Middle Way'.

163

INDUSTRIALISATION AND NEUTRALITY

Few would have predicted the Swedish model from the conditions that prevailed for most of the nineteenth century. Poverty had often been the lot of those eking out a living on the land, but the consequences of the agricultural and industrial revolutions towards the end of the century were so severe that 1 million Swedes were said to have emigrated to the United States between 1880 and 1910 (Wilson 1979). It may even be that this mass exodus alerted even the most conservative to see the need for improving social conditions sufficiently to encourage the remaining population to stay (Heckscher 1984: p. 37).

But within Swedish society a number of conditions had already been created which were to make social and political reform less difficult than in many other countries. A strong centralised state with sophisticated administrative machinery had existed for some centuries. Those working on the land had not experienced the same subjection that those in more feudal societies had. There existed institutionalised procedures for government to consult the major classes of pre-industrial Sweden, and farmers played a more independent part in politics than in other countries (Tomasson 1970). Castles has suggested that the non-conservative nature of Sweden's rural population is the principal explanation for the country's not developing a powerful political party of the right (Castles 1978).

Popular education was widespread in the nineteenth century and literacy high. In the manufacturing workshops, or *bruks*, that had slowly become established in the dispersed towns and villages, employers had already started their own paternalistic brand of welfare, often providing housing, health care, education and pensions to their workers (Huntford 1971). The population, in terms of religion and ethnicity, was fairly homogeneous, and remained so until well into the latter half of the twentieth century. It was perhaps therefore not surprising, with the problems brought on by industrialisation, that class emerged as the clear basis for both conflict and, ultimately, compromise in the century that lay ahead (Tomasson 1970: p. 5).

Sweden's economic development was made possible by the existence of rich sources of raw materials, principally timber, iron ore, and copper. Both these and its manufactured goods provided the basis for export-led development towards the end of the nineteenth century. The process of industrialisation created the most appalling conditions for many of those who worked on the land and in the factories and mines. In response to the problems of dislocation, poverty and alcoholism, three popular movements arose to represent the views of the growing urban mass – the labour movement, the free church movement, and the temperance movement. Membership of all three was not uncommon and they provided the basis for alliances pressurising for reform (Lundqvist 1975).

By the end of the century both the Social Democratic Party (SAP) and a federation of manual workers' trade unions, Landsorganisationen (LO), had been established. A few years later the employers created a federation of their own – SAF. For the first thirty years of the century the conflicts between employers and workers were often severe, resulting in major strikes and lock-outs. During the same period, however, political and social changes were introduced: universal suffrage was completed when women were given the vote in 1921; capital punishment was abolished; changes were made to the old poor law; unemployment insurance through trade-union associations was established; and temperance legislation was introduced.

The first, albeit minority, socialist government was elected in 1920 but the major breakthrough for the SAP came in 1932. The depression years led to increased unemployment in Sweden as they did in most other capitalist countries. The victory in 1932 was to begin an uninterrupted series of social democratic governments until 1976. In the early years it was the support of the Agrarian Party which provided the SAP with parliamentary majorities. In return for subsidies to protect the farmers the Agrarians accepted the need for major relief projects for unemployed workers – the first 'historic compromise'.[5] Unemployment was not the only major social question faced by the new regime, however. The decline in the population led to widespread concern that resulted in support to a whole range of measures to encourage larger families and ameliorate family hardship.

Within a few years Childs was heralding the Swedish middle way between capitalism and socialism, a way of prosperity and security which was given a further boost in 1938 by the second historic compromise – that between the two sides of industry. Under the threat of state interference in the wage negotiations LO and SAF reached an agreement at Saltsjöbaden in 1938 which was to be the first of many basic agreements concerning wage rises, providing a basis for cooperation between capital and labour which became an important factor in subsequent productivity.

Sweden was to remain neutral during the Second World War. Its economy was thereby spared the devastation suffered by so many other industrial nations. But the war provided Swedish industry and the steel industry in particular with the same sort of opportunities that the Korean War was later to give to the Japanese economy. It would seem that it was the war which helped to provide the basis for the impressive economic development after 1945.

POST-1945 ECONOMIC DEVELOPMENT

Despite its neutrality during the Second World War, the mobilisation made necessary by the threat of war had the effect on the Swedish economy of raising public expenditure and taxation (Olsson 1990: p. 115). The governments were subsequently able to redirect this expenditure to meet social and economic goals. For the next two decades the economy grew at an impressive rate. Swedish industry became highly concentrated, a situation encouraged by the governments' labour market policy and LO's negotiating stance.

The strength of the labour movement was demonstrated by the continuing support given to the SAP by the working class and by the high degree of unionisation that has remained a characteristic of the Swedish system. According to Scase, around 80 per cent of manual workers voted for the SAP throughout the 1950s and 1960s. A similar proportion of male manual workers were members of trade unions affiliated to LO (Scase 1977) (a figure which subsequently rose to 90 per cent).

The implementation of an active labour market policy from 1948 onwards, with the cooperation of the trade unions and the employers' federations, meant that economic and social goals could be pursued in relative harmony. The solidaristic wage policy pursued by the trade unions was aimed at ensuring that the lowest paid manual workers received disproportionately higher wage rises than the higher paid workers. This had the effect, through centralised industrial agreements, of forcing inefficient and less profitable firms out of business. For many years redundant employees were encouraged to re-train and move about the country to take up employment, which again obviated the need to maintain less prosperous firms in the declining regions. The combination of trade unions pursuing security and solidarity, governments taking an active interest in the welfare of the people, and of industry and employers willing to cooperate with government and trade unions, seemed to provide the Swedish economy with a cohesion and harmony that led to prosperity and productivity. Industry had an adaptable and flexible work-force, the labour movement had members satisfied with their wage packets and their security.

Cracks in the consensus

From the late 1960s onwards, however, this happy combination began to falter. Increased competition from abroad and the recession following the oil crisis of 1973 led to a serious decline in certain sectors of industry, notably steel and shipbuilding. Government policies were leading to increases in taxation and social security contributions. Trade unions, goaded by discontent amongst rank-and-file manual workers, began to make more radical demands upon government for the protection of and participation by employees in industry. In response to these changes, a significant proportion of the electorate began to shift its preference to the political parties of the right.

The essence of the Swedish model had been the coexistence and co-operation of both sides of industry, with the state, albeit in the hands of the Social Democrats, playing a neutral role. This neutrality was jeopardised by demands from LO for greater industrial and economic democracy. LO and SAF had been unable to reach an agreement on an extension of industrial democracy. Pressure was put on the government by the unions to pass legislation, the Codetermination Act 1976, which would give trade unions rights to information and negotiation and reduce management prerogatives. At about the same time the SAP adopted another LO scheme, the wage-earner fund, whereby 20 per cent of a firm's profits would be paid into a fund, with the result that after twenty years significant parts of the Swedish economy would be collectively owned. In the event neither the Codetermination Act nor the form the wage-earner funds eventually took when they were established in 1983 had anything like the radical outcomes their devisers had hoped for (Fulcher 1991). But even in the form of a proposal the wage-earner funds in particular galvanised SAF into outright hostility.

The unions and to an extent the SAP, in the years approaching the 1976 election, seemed to be moving away from an accommodation with capitalism towards democratic socialism, while the employers became more intransigent in their relationship with labour. The Swedish model of centralised, corporatist collective bargaining was beginning to show signs of strain. White-collar workers and their union federation TCO did not always see eye to eye with LO, particularly on wage issues. Moreover, there were clear signs of conflict between the growing army of public-sector employees and employees in the private sector. Not only was it becoming more difficult for LO and SAF to agree, but fractions within labour organisations were beginning to emerge (Fulcher 1991).

In contrast to the model industrial relations of the early post-war decades, the 1970s were ridden with conflict. By the 1980s SAF had begun to reject centralised bargaining on the grounds that it was leading to wage rivalry rather than wage restraint, with a consequent spiralling of labour costs. In recent years, agreements between employers and employees have been made at the level of individual industries with increased local flexibility. Some of these have resulted in a strengthening of the link between

> company profits and workers' pay, [which have] started to weaken the traditional consensus amongst workers. Productivity-based deals, profit-sharing and convertible loan stock (which give employees the option of buying shares in their company on favourable terms) are spreading like wildfire. (*Economist* 1990: p. 6)

Others have taken the form of cooperation between blue- and white-collar workers to establish 'single status' agreements, a phenomenon which SAF has described as a British development worthy of emulation (*SAF-Tidningen* 1992). It is ironic that this practice has arisen in Britain largely due to the influence of Japanese companies there.

Continuing economic problems

The problems facing the Swedish economy had begun in the mid-1970s when

> wages rose by rose by some 45 per cent in two years, world demand for Swedish capital goods simultaneously slumped dramatically after the OPEC crisis of 1973-4 and *Japanese* [my italics] competition . . . hit them. (*Economist* 1981: p. 87)

The disadvantages of increased wage costs and tougher international competition were not helped by the Bourgeois governments of 1976 and 1979. These not only wasted public resources in a vain attempt to rescue ailing companies, but proved incapable of encouraging the growth of high-technology industry amongst small firms. Meanwhile Sweden's large, successful multi-national companies such as Asea, Volvo, Electrolux and Ericsson were beginning to invest more resources and employ more people outside Sweden than within.

These developments were not reversed when the SAP was returned to government in 1982. Initially, a 16 per cent devaluation seemed to stimulate the economy. Between 1982 and 1986 industrial production grew at a much greater rate than the OECD/European Community average (*Economist* 1987). Profits were at record levels, manufacturing exports grew by 7 per cent, productivity by 8 per cent and industrial investment by 15 per cent. The economy was booming (Linton 1984). But it was not to last. Stagnation set in after 1988. Inflation rose to 11 per cent; economic growth and living standards declined and unemployment began to grow. Although inflation came down to 2.4 per cent in 1992, unemployment looked set to grow from 4.5 per cent in January (double the rate of the previous year), to 6 per cent by the end of the year according to the Labour Market Board (*DN* 1992d). GDP and net investment contracted by 1.3 per cent and 8.5 per cent respectively in 1991 and were expected to contract still further by 0.2 per cent and 7.5 per cent in 1992.

Increasingly, the size of the public sector in Sweden has also come to be seen as a principal factor in the country's economic stagnation. Public expenditure had risen from 30 per cent of GDP in 1960 to over 60 per cent in 1980 where it remained until the end of the decade (Olsson 1990: p. 120; *Economist* 1990: p. 15). Social expenditure, which had amounted to less than 20 per cent of GDP in 1970, had climbed to over 30 per cent in 1976 (SCB 1990). Since 1988 it has been above 35 per cent (SCB 1992). Public-sector employment, which had been about one fifth of total employment in the 1960s, rose to one quarter in the mid-1970s and continued to climb. By 1980 it constituted one third of all employment (Olsson 1990: p. 124). By the end of the 1980s the figure still stood at over 35 per cent (SCB 1992).

If the attempt to stabilise these figures has been a feature of government policy during the 1980s, it would seem that their reduction is to be the task of governments in the 1990s.

THE POLITICAL SCENE

The dominance of the SAP in government from 1932 has perpetuated the fragmented right in Swedish politics. While the Centre Party (as the Agrarian Party came to be called) had cooperated with the SAP in the early stages of their rule, the small Communist Party, VPK, had latterly come to support the SAP whenever they lacked a clear majority in Parliament. As a result the only way in which the right could form a government was through an alliance of the three 'bourgeois' parties – Center (Centre), Folk (Liberal) and Moderata (Conservative). Perhaps because of the prevailing paternalist culture, but certainly because of the SAP's success, all three had supported strong state welfare in the post-war years. They might have criticised trade-union power, public bureaucracy and the high tax burden, but they did not attack the welfare state as such.

As can be seen from Table 10.1, the socialist and the bourgeois blocs in the Riksdag, the Swedish Parliament, were evenly balanced throughout the 1970s and the 1980s. From 1973, elections have been held every three years, to a single chamber based upon proportional representation. Any party that receives over 4 per cent of the vote gets seats in Parliament. In 1976 and in 1979 the parties of the right were able to form governments with a small overall majority. But it was clear that none of them was in a position to challenge the SAP as the single, largest party in the Riksdag.

The two elections in 1976 and 1979 resulted in bourgeois governments which by most accounts were not a success. On many issues the three parties remained divided. Not only were they unable to make significant reductions in social expenditure, but their rule coincided with a particularly difficult time for the economy. The ironic result was that two right-wing administrations succeeded in nationalising and subsidising weak industries, something that

Table 10.1 Results in Riksdag elections 1976–88: number of seats

	1976	1979	1982	1985	1988
The bourgeois parties					
Conservative	55	73	86	76	66
Liberal	39	38	21	51	44
Centre	86	64	56	44	42
Total	180	175	163	171	152
The socialist parties					
Social Democrat	152	154	166	159	156
Communist	17	20	20	19	21
Total	169	174	186	178	177
Green					20

Source: Brunnberg 1991

the Social Democrats had resisted (*Economist* 1981). Their failure to cooperate or to improve the economy's performance would seem to have led to a rapid disenchantment amongst the electorate. The SAP was returned to government in the next three elections, 1982, 1985 and 1988. The only other significant change was the emergence of a Green Party (Miljö) in 1988.

The organisational strength of the SAP

The strength and significance of the SAP was vividly described by Linton in the mid-1980s. In 1982 the party had a membership of almost 1.25 million people. Nearly 1 million were collectively affiliated through their trade unions but 300,000 were individual members. The latter figure was almost identical to that of the Labour Party in Britain, a country with a population six times greater than Sweden's. Even the youth section had a membership of 45,000, six times greater than its British equivalent. Nor was this membership passive. Linton suggested that through consultation and political study circles the party 'succeeded in harnessing the intelligence of its membership to the task of policy-making' (Linton 1985: p. 17). Linton described how a system of press subsidies helped to sustain newspapers which reflected a wide range of political views. Social Democratic daily newspapers amounted to 21, a figure that had remained stable for many years. He went on to describe a whole network of organisations which seemed to encompass all aspects of an individual member's life:

> In Sweden people can lead their lives in the warm bosom of the labour movement, reading a labour paper, shopping at the co-op, taking evening classes at the [Workers' Educational Association], going to a dance at the People's Hall, joining in the social activities of their trade union or the SAP branch, leaving their children at the Young Eagles while they go out to their study circle. They can completely envelop themselves in the environment of the movement. (Linton 1985: p. 22)

The strength, cohesion and organisation of the labour movement in Sweden were indeed impressive, but times were changing.

From decentralisation to crisis

The SAP government in the 1980s found it increasingly difficult to avoid policies more associated with parties of the right. As a consequence the relations between the party and LO were often fraught. The growth in public expenditure was halted, local authority expenditure was limited, financial markets deregulated and exchange controls lifted. An ambiguous development in the 1980s was the policy of decentralisation. Ideologically it was justified as a means of restoring democracy to the people by making services less remote and more effective. Elander and Montin have cited a number of examples. Framework legislation for social services, health care and planning replaced detailed prescriptive regulations; the national administrative boards abandoned their directive role for a more advisory and evaluative one; free *kommunes* (municipalities) were set up on an experimental basis to allow some local authorities to have greater autonomy over their finance and organisation; other municipalities experimented with neighbourhood councils; and lastly business methods were increasingly used. The latter also took the form of local authorities setting up 'companies, foundations and trusts'. Elander and Montin imply that these were not full-blown examples of profit-making free enterprise (Elander and Montin 1990). They fell short of the outright privatisation advocated by the bourgeois parties but they were clearly a step in that direction.

But these decentralisation measures were occurring at the same time as central government was placing more controls on local authority expenditure. The two processes actually complemented each other. If you were going to reduce the resources going to local authorities, the least you could do would be to place less financial and administrative restrictions on them, in the hope that they would find ingenious ways of managing with less. Unfortunately, local experiments in reorganisation were not enough on their own to reduce the scale of the public sector or to promote economic growth.

From 1988, a series of economic crises were met by austerity packages which so offended the SAP's Riksdag ally, the Communist Party, that Bourgeois support was required. In 1989 an increase in VAT was passed through the Riksdag with the support of the Centre Party. Further tax reforms were carried with the support of the Liberal Party. The old, high marginal rates of income tax were abolished; a standard rate of 30 per cent on all incomes was levied as a local income tax; while central government was to receive an additional 20 per cent from those who had annual incomes in excess of SKr170,000. This simplification was welcomed by many, but the parties of the right complained that the overall burden had not changed. LO meanwhile was more concerned with the regressive direction of the SAP's taxation policy. LO successfully opposed the introduction of waiting days for sickness insurance and resisted a government attempt to introduce a wages and prices freeze in 1990. As will be seen in the next two chapters, important changes were being undertaken in all areas of social policy throughout this period.

In the months approaching the general election of 1991, opinion polls saw support for the SAP decline to less than 30 per cent, only a few points ahead of the Conservatives. Moreover, a new party of the right emerged, New Democracy, more committed to cuts in public expenditure and immigration controls than the established parties of the bourgeois bloc. The Conservative and Liberal Parties published a joint programme called 'A New Start for Sweden' which had a clear neo-liberal message. The aim was to promote 'the market economy, competition and individual ownership'. As far as social policy was concerned, the intention was to carry out a revolution in freedom of choice:

> In concrete terms, this means that citizens will get the opportunity to decide for themselves even in the field of social services. Starting from a system of common finance, money ought to a large extent follow the choices made by individuals themselves.   (*Ny Start för Sverige* 1991)

The time for a 'system shift' seemed to have arrived.

The 1991 election and its aftermath

By the time the day of the election came, the SAP had regained some of its lost support but polled the lowest percentage of votes cast in a national election since 1932. But the three main Bourgeois parties also had a disappointing result, receiving less than 40 per cent of total votes cast and little more than the SAP. The final distribution of seats appears in Table 10.2. Subsequently, Carl Bildt, the Conservative leader, was able to form a four-party coalition government (Conservatives, Liberals, the Centre Party and the Christian Democrats), but this had no overall majority in the Riksdag. His government was dependent upon the maverick behaviour of New Democracy, a party with which none of Bildt's partners in the coalition wanted to cooperate.

During the months following the September election the new government began its task of producing a 'system shift' within Swedish society. Its intention was to reduce public expenditure by SKr10 billion each year for the next three years and to reduce the overall tax burden. The difficulty which the government faced was that only the Conservatives had a clear ideological determination to roll back the frontiers of the state. Bildt coined the phrase 'Den enda vägen' – the only way – to describe the policies he would

Table 10.2   The election of 1991

	Per cent of votes	Number of seats
Bourgeois parties		
Conservative	21.9	80
Liberal	9.1	33
Centre	8.5	31
Christian Democrat	7.1	26
Total	46.6	170
New Democracy	6.7	25
Socialist parties		
Social Democrat	37.6	138
Left (former Communist)	4.5	16
Total	42.1	154

Source: Brunnberg 1991

like to see. Unfortunately this single path seemed to branch out in different directions. The Liberal leader, who had become the Minister for Social Affairs in the government, spoke against the scale of public expenditure reductions proposed; the Liberal, Centre and Christian Democratic Parties all rejected certain cuts in adult education; while New Democracy voted with the SAP and the Left against the abolition of the partial pension.

None the less, as will be seen in the next two chapters, there are clear moves in the Swedish system towards deregulation, decentralisation, a market economy approach to social matters, and a mixed economy of welfare. Moreover, privatisation plans for postal, telephone, airline and rail services were due to be announced later in 1992.

More significantly, the complex network of Social Democratic institutions was slowly being undermined by events and reinforced by government action. Unionisation amongst manual workers had fallen from 90 to 80 per cent, the same percentage as for non-manual workers. Individual unions could not afford to contribute as much money to LO as they had in the past, with the result that LO was having to lay off employees. The new government abolished tax allowances on union membership fees, cut the state contribution to study associations, and reduced press subsidies by 5 per cent. Local authorities, faced with cuts in their own budgets, were unable to fund social and political associations (many of which had strong links with the labour movement) to the extent that they had done previously. The labour movement's own insurance company, Folksam, faced considerable losses, while the socialist newspaper group, *A-Pressen*, had recently become bankrupt, leaving the SAP with a large debt to pick up.

While some of these changes may seem of minor significance in isolation, together they form a pattern which suggests that the Swedish model is undergoing substantial change. However, the new set of forces behind this change has yet to make a clear mark on some of the more enduring features of the society.

CORPORATISM AND CONSULTATION

Economic growth after 1945 benefited enormously from the institutional cooperation implicit in the Swedish system. This cooperation was demonstrated in many ways by the composition of administrative boards and the consultative processes by which many government policies were formed. While government ministries have employed relatively few civil servants to prepare legislation, to manage the state budget and to play a key role in the policy-making process, it has been left to the administrative boards to take on the responsibility of policy implementation. These boards have been corporatist in essence, consisting of representatives from business, the unions, and any other groupings in society which have had a major interest in the area being administered. The staff employed by these boards have, in the past, been considerably greater in number than those employed by the ministries. The important point is that at a significant point in the policy-making process, organisations outside government have played an important role. Moreover the organisations represented are the same ones with which outside government often found themselves in conflict. Membership of the boards undoubtedly enabled them to come together with government in a formal way to agree on both the implementation of, and recommendations of changes to, government policy. Significantly, trade-union and professional associations representatives have often constituted the majority on such boards.

It is also important to note that it has been customary for the party in government to ensure that senior posts in state administration are shared between senior representatives of the main political parties. Although the Social Democrats have been in office for most of the years since 1932, it would be unthinkable for them to have a monopoly on all offices of state. Thus the opposition parties are also involved in the policy-making process.

Perhaps the most systematic form of making sure that a wide range of views are heard by government has been the 'commission' and 'remiss' systems. New policy initiatives have usually been initiated by the appointment of a commission to investigate an aspect of policy that seems to require change. The members of such commissions are usually people outside government whose expertise would seem to make them qualified to investigate a particular area. Such commissions seek to evaluate available evidence, carry out new research, establish experimental schemes before coming up with a report with a set of proposals. The latter are sent out 'on remiss' to as broad a range of interested groups as possible, asking them to respond. The final set of proposals and the responses from affected organisations are then dealt with by a cabinet committee which comes up with an amended set of legislative proposals to put before Parliament. This process can take between anything from two to ten years. It is a process which is intended to take into account, as far as is possible, the different interests that characterise a complex capitalist society.

While such a system seems to have performed very well in times of economic growth, with the different parties prepared to be reasonable and compromise as long as their interests merited some consideration, it has been put under considerable strain in years of low and sometimes negative growth. Reconciliation of the demands and needs of manual workers, salaried workers and employers in the private sector, all the employees in central and local government and the whole range of voluntary organisations dependent on state assistance, has become increasingly problematic. It has proved very difficult to make significant public expenditure cuts in a society where the cultural expectation of improved state benefits and services has become deeply entrenched.

CULTURAL CHARACTERISTICS

The success of the Social Democrats for many decades after 1932 must in part have been due to the fact that their aims and aspirations were in tune with a large section of Swedish society. When we look at the way in which others have described the cultural characteristics of that society, it is not difficult to see why there should have been such a close fit. 'The Social Democratic project has become the nation's project' (Heclo and Marsden 1986). This quotation was followed by a description of those qualities which the authors felt characterised Swedes – pragmatic, ideological, adaptable and moralistic. They are said to take a pragmatic approach to their laws and institutions and are prepared to adapt these to changing circumstances as long as the changes are justified by logical, painstaking and rational argument. The ideological and moralistic commitment to state welfare would seem to run deeply amongst many groups in the society; as indeed does a commitment to internationalism and an antipathy to alcohol and drugs. Perhaps sobriety would best describe the approach of many to life in Sweden, though exceptions to this rule are quite visible.

Work and social lives are dominated by large organisations. In their free time many Swedes would expect to participate in and through study organisations, leisure organisations and pressure and interest group organisations. They are described as being rather conformist in such participation, subordinating their individuality to the needs and interests of the organised group. So much so that others have implied that, as a result of excessive paternalism and authoritarianism, Swedes have become self-policing.

In contrast and, according to Heclo and Marsden, as a consequence, their private lives are very private indeed. 'Just as American individualism creates a land of the gregarious, so Swedish communitarianism creates a land of the truly solitary' (Heclo and Marsden 1986: p. 22). Jenkins, complaining about the reluctance of Swedes to invite foreign visitors into their own homes, dismissed the explanation that they were shy, and claimed that they were simply indifferent. Jenkins also insisted that the Swedes were better at organising 'things' than they were at relating to people.

These particular insights would seem to explain a number of features of Swedish society that puzzle observers. On the one hand foreign visitors on business are given a great deal of cooperation and information in a friendly and polite manner, but little interest is shown in them subsequently. Swedes have a very internationalistic outlook on life as a matter of principle, but immigrants, while receiving many benefits and services to help them cope with their new country, feel totally isolated from what seems an unfriendly, cold culture. Similarly in the field of welfare. Considerable resources go into the provision of staff, space and equipment, whether it be in the care of the elderly, the handicapped or children; but one is often left with the feeling that the relationship between the client, patient or disadvantaged individual and the welfare bureaucrat is formal and rule-governed.

SOCIAL DIVISIONS

Sweden would seem, then, to be a society in which compromise and cooperation have been a hallmark of both its institutions and its culture. Major compromises between significant social actors have enabled the society to function and progress in a rational, pragmatic way without too many traumatic cleavages. It has for long been described as socially homogeneous, particularly in terms of religion and ethnicity. Protestant Swedes were able to build a 'People's Home' for a people who were not riven by ethnic and religious conflicts. With a Social Democratic government which proclaimed a non-aligned internationalism abroad and a spirit of egalitarianism at home, the Swedes have been in a good position to tackle major social inequalities.

The fact remains that Sweden is a capitalist society which inevitably generates inequalities of income and wealth. The continuing control of many of Sweden's most powerful companies by the Wallenburg family is a good example of the latter (Burton 1989). It is a hierarchical society in which incomes are distributed according to market-place and bureaucratic values. Recent research has shown that income inequalities by social class were reduced considerably between 1965 and 1975, largely as a result of redistributive public policies; that this process continued at a more moderate pace over the next ten years; but that since the mid-1980s inequalities have begun to widen (Persson 1990).

Recent medical research has illustrated a similar though somewhat earlier pattern with regard to occupational differences in mortality rates and health. Death rates for manual and non-manual workers and differences in their children's mental health and physical heights narrowed up until the 1960s and thereafter began to diverge (see chapter 11). The evidence would seem to suggest that by the 1980s a range of class inequalities was beginning to widen.

Sweden also remains a country in which gender inequalities persist. It is more likely that women will gravitate towards humanities courses in education and to caring, clerical and part-time jobs in the labour market; take time out of work to have and rear children; and perhaps ultimately care for the elderly. None the less a high proportion of women, 80 per cent, were employed in the 1980s, and although almost half were in part-time employment compared with a small proportion of men, the ratio of women's hourly earnings to those of men was a high 86 per cent (Wernersson 1989). There is a high degree of segregation in the job market, however, with a larger proportion of women than men being employed in the public sector and vice versa for the private sector. It is therefore not surprising that women have achieved high occupational status in the public sector while few have reached élite positions in the private sector. In political terms, however, it cannot be denied that women have considerably more power in Sweden than in many other countries. While the election in 1991 resulted in a drop in the number of women MPs (from 132 in 1988 to 100), even in a right-wing coalition cabinet women were well represented – 8 out of a total of 21. Nor were their ministerial posts 'soft' ones, since both the Finance Minister and the Minister for Foreign Affairs were women. There would seem to be overwhelming evidence of a reduction in gender inequalities in Sweden.

Sweden is also a society to which immigrants and refugees have been attracted from other parts of Scandinavia and, for the last three decades, from Southern Europe and troubled parts of the globe such as the Middle East and South America. Inevitably many of these people have found it difficult to get decent jobs and promotion and, as in Britain, the unemployment rate for ethnic minorities is twice as high as for the indigenous labour force. If they do not feel particularly discriminated against, they do not feel particularly welcome either. Moreover, it is true that in recent elections immigration has played a negative role, especially with the advent of New Democracy in the Riksdag. The emergence of small nationalist political parties and an increase in racially motivated attacks on (and even murders of) members of ethnic minorities have been the cause of recent concern. It is to the credit of the Swedish authorities, however, that not only have all party leaders in the Riksdag been prepared to join an anti-racist march, but even leading military officers have written a joint letter to the press rejecting the misuse of military uniforms and insignia by nationalist groups. Similar reactions by élite figures in Britain and Japan are hard to imagine.

Swedish egalitarianism has not always lived up to high expectations, but it cannot be said that it has failed. On the contrary, the following chapters will show the extensive lengths to which the authorities have gone to try and alleviate the more obvious and grinding inequalities. Few would deny that the status and material standards of the low-paid, women and ethnic minorities have been higher in Sweden than in most other countries.

The solidarity of the labour movement, the commitment to full employment and public-sector expansion by successive Social Democratic governments have been the principal egalitarian forces in Swedish society. Full employment has prevented the development of a substantial underclass and has ensured that both women and minority groups have had plenty of employment opportunities. The LO policy of wage solidarity has protected the low-paid and has ensured that immigrant workers have not been used to undercut the wages of indigenous workers nor been used as a divisive force as has so often happened in other countries. Lastly, public-sector expansion has provided a whole range of jobs, especially for women, while child care provision has made it easier for young women with families to take up paid work.

But this egalitarianism is now threatened by the economic and political changes which have already been described. A weakened labour movement, decentralised bargaining and increasing unemployment are likely to create a divisiveness in which solidarity with the low-paid, women and ethnic group employees will not have the same importance as before. Moreover cuts in the public sector, increased charges and privatisation are likely to hit the vulnerable groups in receipt of benefits and services, while reduced employment opportunities in central and local government may well affect women disproportionately.

DEMOGRAPHIC CHANGE

Sweden does not have to cope with the density of population experienced in Japan and Britain. A population of only 8.5 million people inhabit a country twice the geographical size of Britain. Nor are its principal cities large. Greater Stockholm has 1.5 million inhabitants; Gothenburg, 700,000; and Malmö fewer than 500,000. One would hardly therefore expect the sort of social problems that are associated with really large conurbations – with or without an extensive system of state welfare.

Another important demographic fact is that the proportion of elderly people in Sweden has been high for some time – 18 per cent at the time of writing. Given the high standards of pensions, health and welfare services for the elderly which have been developed, and the difficult economic circumstances of recent years, this proportion is presenting the politicians with some difficult policy choices. Moreover, the proportion is set to rise, as in Japan and Britain, to over 20 per cent around the year 2020.

In the last few years there has also been a 20 per cent rise in the numbers of children born, an unanticipated rise which forced the last Social Democratic government to revise its policy of guaranteeing state nursery provision for all those who needed it. Demographic changes, then, are beginning to put even more pressure upon an economy already in severe difficulties and at a time when public welfare is coming under close scrutiny. It is not surprising that the new government should be looking for alternatives to state provision.

CONCLUSION

Those factors which led to Sweden's post-war success were particularly well suited to the requirements of a Fordist society. The centralised relationship between the employers and employees enabled large-scale organisations to reach agreements concerning pay, working practices and working conditions with relative ease and little conflict. The state's active labour-market policy guaranteed low levels of unemployment and a flexible, well-trained labour force. Consistent Social Democratic government created a welfare state which has provided considerable protection and security to the whole population. The methodical, rational planning mentality of Swedes, their institutions and their culture enabled the system to function with an impressive degree of consensus and cooperation.

But these same factors have become something of a hindrance in a post-Fordist world. In spite of persistent economic difficulties in the last twenty years, successive governments, both Social Democratic and Bourgeois, have been reluctant to embrace the structural and ideological changes which have occurred elsewhere in Europe.

Opinion polls leading up to the 1991 election strongly indicated that the electorate felt that taxes were too high, the public sector too large and inefficient, and that the Bourgeois parties would be more likely to bring about the right conditions for economic recovery than the socialist parties – yet the result gave four parties a minority mandate, and a fifth party an unpredictable influence on events. The Swedish electorate is clearly reluctant to embrace unbounded conservative rule as the Japanese and British have done.

However, it is clear that major changes are taking place. Industry and commerce, operating internationally, have adapted to many of the changes taking place around them and have pressed for entry into the European Community. The Social Democratic governments of the 1980s, particularly after 1988, have reluctantly recognised that the public sector must cease to grow and become more flexible and efficient – a view endorsed by LO (Fulcher 1987). Moreover, it is clear that a lot of thought has been given to the harmonisation of tax and finance policies with those of Sweden's competitors. Privatisation, market orientation, competition and effectiveness have become key concepts in political debate. Decentralisation is occurring in collective bargaining and political structures. Deregulation is taking place in the public and the private sectors.

The Swedish welfare state is a formidable set of institutions and practices which is not easy to dismantle, not least because so many have come to depend upon it for benefits, services and jobs. It has had considerable support from a strong labour movement and public-sector unions and professional associations. But economic developments and social change are slowly breaking up the alliances which have sustained 'the People's Home'.

CHAPTER ELEVEN

Health, social security and social services

INTRODUCTION

Only towards the end of the 1980s was Sweden forced to re-examine its social policies seriously. It is currently involved in a major revision of public and social expenditure and the role of the state in the provision of welfare. Commitment to the institutions of the welfare state have been seriously tested throughout the rest of Western Europe. Some governments, like the British, have embraced the opportunity to erode the principles of full employment, universalism and high-quality public services only too willingly. Others have done so with great reluctance. But none has found it as difficult to jettison the principles of the welfare state as has Sweden. This is partly due to the fact that the 'People's Home' is more a source of national pride than elsewhere; because so many people have something to lose in terms of jobs or benefits; but also because in Sweden the welfare state was an integral part of the whole modernist project. No institution was left untouched by the idea that a strong Social Democratic state in collaboration with centralised organisations representing major interest groups could create a 'Good Society'.

THE SWEDISH WELFARE STATE: AN OVERVIEW

We have seen that Sweden had already begun to earn a reputation for its social policies even before the Second World War. Extensive provision for employment relief and measures to stem the decline in the birth rate were established in the 1930s. But much of the rest of welfare provision was in the form of poor relief or subsidies to non-statutory organisations. In the early years of the century, the poor relief associated with a rural society had to give way to a system more appropriate to an industrialised, urban society. Not surprisingly the early measures were strict, moralistic and repressive (Holgersson 1981) although, according to Heclo, they did not suffer the same swings between outdoor relief and the workhouse that had characterised the British system (Heclo 1974). Legislation covered the care of children, the poor, and, almost unique to Sweden in terms of emphasis, those with drink problems. The inter-war years saw improvements in the management of those institutions which took children, the poor and alcoholics into care. In particular the state took greater responsibility for both the provision of welfare services and the regulation of those provided by others.

A universal, but means-tested, old-age pension was established in 1913 but the benefits were very low. State subsidies were increasingly given to voluntary sickness benefit societies, but no state scheme was established. Similarly with unemployment. The state preferred to provide subsidies to unemployment benefit societies run by trade unions than introduce a system of national insurance. Only for work injury did a compulsory national insurance programme exist.

It is clear, however, that during industrialisation there had not been the same degree of hostility towards either the labour movement or the idea of state intervention as had existed in many other capitalist societies. Moreover employers' and employees' organisations had already begun to cooperate over national wage agreements in the 1930s. With the ending of the Second World War, a strong economy and a government which had, because of the wartime environment, been able to raise public expenditure and tax levels, Sweden was in a better position than either Japan or the UK to begin to expand social programmes.

With the introduction of flat-rate old-age pensions, child allowances, and a national earnings-related health insurance scheme in the early 1950s and the controversial state earnings-related old-age pension (ATP) in 1960 and major reforms in employment services, education and housing, Sweden began to achieve a formidable reputation in the social sphere. ATP in particular was the clearest indication of the third 'historic compromise', that between manual and non-manual workers. The Swedish welfare state was to be predicated upon the idea of high-quality services and benefits for all. If everybody benefited from state welfare provision, it would gain universal support. It became difficult in the 1960s and 1970s to find areas of welfare where the Swedes did not excel. In spite of economic difficulties, shared with the rest of the Western world, after 1973, the Swedish authorities continued to improve on the scale, scope and quality of welfare provision until the early 1980s.

SOCIAL SECURITY

It must be said that, compared with most other countries, social insurance benefits generally have not only been higher in Sweden in both relative and absolute terms, but that they have covered a wider range of contingencies and have aimed to give those who are insured benefits to cover almost any eventuality where income capacity has been impaired. Moreover most benefits have been linked to a base amount which in turn has been index-linked to price changes. While in the 1960s and 1970s these arrangements were regarded with envy by foreign observers, in the 1980s they came to be seen as highly problematic.

Social insurance in Sweden has been provided through a unified system administered nationally by *Riksförsäkringsverket* (RFV, the Social Insurance Board) and locally by social insurance offices. Contributions to the insurance scheme since 1974 have been paid for by a payroll tax on employers. Since employers regard their contributions as non-wage labour costs, it can be argued that employees are paying indirectly for their benefits. It may be significant psychologically that employees do not actually see such contributions, or increases in contributions, as deductions from their wage and salary packets. However, as payroll costs have risen, employers have no doubt insisted that these be taken into account in awarding pay increases.

Pensions

All Swedish citizens are entitled to a basic old-age pension regardless of contributions. Those dependent upon the basic pension alone have also been entitled to a means-tested but generous housing allowance and a substantial supplementary pension to compensate them partially for not having an earnings-related pension. The state earnings-related pension (ATP), together with the basic pension, was intended to give old people about 65 per cent of what they had been earning in the best fifteen years prior to retirement. To qualify for a full ATP pension,

185

contributions needed only to be made for a maximum of thirty years. Many manual and non-manual workers have also been contributing to occupational pension funds which give them a further 10 per cent of their income in retirement. As these various schemes have come to maturity so many workers have been able to expect an income in old age ranging from 65 per cent to 85 per cent of their pre-retirement incomes.

Wilson, writing in the late 1970s, was clearly of the opinion that the fifteen-year rule – whereby one's pension was related to the *best* rather than the *most recent* fifteen years of income – would benefit manual workers whose earnings capacity might not, as is the case with non-manual workers, occur towards the end of their working lives. She was also concerned that in being over-generous to the existing generation of pensioners, the Swedish economy might be building up problems for the future (Wilson 1979).

In some ways Wilson has been proved right, in other ways not so. Ståhlberg's analysis of ATP, thirty years after its introduction, has shown that the rule whereby to qualify for ATP only thirty years of contributions were necessary has advantaged higher-income groups more than the fifteen-year rule has advantaged manual workers. Their combined effect has been regressive. Manual workers are likely to make more years' contributions than those white-collar workers who spend a greater amount of time in full-time education. Women have also been advantaged by the need to pay contributions for only thirty years since many of them have been forced to take time out of the labour market to bring up children (see Table 11.1).

Table 11.1 The ATP benefit/contribution ratio for the cohort born in 1944–50 by social class and gender

Social class*		Benefit: contribution ratio	Social class		Benefit: contribution ratio
Men	II	0.88	Women	I	0.94
	II	0.80		II	0.82
	III	0.78		III	0.65

Source: Adapted from Ståhlberg 1991: p. 228
*Social class in official Swedish statistics uses the following categories: social class I, higher-grade salaried employees and large-scale businessmen; social class II, lower-grade salaried employees and smaller-scale businessmen; social class III, manual workers.

Ståhlberg points out more significant ironies, however. The originators of ATP imagined that Swedish prosperity would be longer-lasting than it has proved to be. They thought, wisely it seemed at the time, that to link ATP benefits to wage rises would prove costly. Benefits were therefore linked to price rises. But with sluggish growth in both the economy and in real wage rises, financing state pensions is becoming more and more expensive. In 1960 ATP contributions came to 1.9 per cent of the payroll. In the 1980s they rose to 11 per cent. This rise will continue as the ratio of those in employment under retirement age falls relative to those aged 65 and above. But Ståhlberg shows that the payroll contributions will have to increase to massive proportions unless the economy can grow at an annual rate of 3 per cent (see Table 11.2). Moreover, with price-indexed pensions rising faster than real wage growth, the value of pensions relative to wages will increase, with the result that pensioners could be much better off than those in work (Ståhlberg 1991: p. 10).

Ståhlberg has suggested one policy option which may offer future governments a way out of the problems raised by ATP. The earnings-related element in ATP applies only on incomes up to a certain level. If this ceiling were to remain fixed while wages rose, more and more employees would find themselves with incomes above the ceiling.

> Today 13.1 per cent of men and 1.7 per cent of women have incomes above this ceiling. According to the National Social Insurance Board's [RFV] calculations, 75 per cent of men and 50 per cent of women will have incomes above this ceiling by the year 2025, given an annual real wage growth rate of on average 2 per cent. If growth is less, say 1 per cent, the figures will be 40 per cent of men and 10 per cent of women. (Ståhlberg 1991: p. 229).

Since the cost of raising the ceiling would be high (and if the economy continues to prove sluggish, very expensive in terms of payroll

Table 11.2 The national pension schemes'
(basic pension, special pension supplement and
ATP) contributions as a percentage of payroll

Year	Real wage growth			
	0%	1%	2%	3%
1995	27.5	23.9	22.8	20.2
2015	44.1	32.0	24.0	16.5
2035	52.5	37.9	21.8	12.5

Source: Ståhlberg 1991: p. 220

contributions), Ståhlberg argues that it would be better to let the real value of the ceiling fall. The effect of this would be a decline in the real value of the ATP pension. A policy for the future income-related pensions could then be based upon the *funded* occupational schemes rather than ATPs *pay-as-you-go* system (Ståhlberg 1991: p. 234). Ironically this is precisely the sort of system advocated by the Liberals and the Conservatives at the time that ATP was debated in the 1950s and one which is likely to appeal to them increasingly in the future.

While all insurance systems based on a pooling of risks lead to some groups benefiting more than others, any major systematic inequities have to be sorted out. In the Swedish case the growing proportion of elderly people allied with poor economic performance is going to produce anomalies. The Swedish government is faced with the difficult choice of, in effect, reducing real wages in order to pay for pensions, or of appeasing the work-force at the expense of the pensioners. Either way a significant body of voters will be alienated. The original aim of ATP was to help cement a sense of solidarity between blue-collar and white-collar workers. In the event that aim has been difficult to achieve.

Flexible retirement and partial pensions

Not only have old-age pensions been more than adequate for many to live on, but there have been other built-in advantages. Swedes have been able to choose whether to retire early (minimum age 60) and have a lower pension, or retire later (maximum age 70) and have a higher pension. This flexibility was further increased by the possibility of having a partial pension. Having reached the age of 60, old-age pensioners have been able to choose to work part-time and supplement their incomes with a proportion of their pension. Both these measures have provided old people with a degree of choice that has been impressive by most other countries' standards. Laczko has shown that where partial pensions have been introduced in other countries it has been because governments have been looking for ways of encouraging older workers out of the job market – as a short-term measure to cope with serious unemployment problems. In Sweden they have been implemented to give older workers a degree of choice and flexibility in their lives (Laczko 1988).

The future of the Swedish pension system

The recently elected Bourgeois government has set up a commission to investigate the state pension system with a view to substantial reform. The opposition parties have suggested that ATP should be subsidised by the proceeds of the wage-earner funds which the government has abolished. Although this proposal has been resisted by the government, it is well aware of the fact that on present economic performance it is going to be impossible to finance its pension commitments. For that reason it has already proposed the abolition of the partial pensions scheme and is raising the minimum number of years that individuals have to contribute to ATP.

Health insurance

Another major area of social insurance, that of sickness benefit, has also been the centre of debate and controversy. All employees are part of the national sickness insurance scheme which employers contribute to in the form of a payroll fee. Until recently employees were entitled to 90 per cent of their pay when absent from work because of sickness. This amount, in 1991, was payable up to a ceiling of an annual salary of SKr241,500 (approx. £24,000) (Swedish Institute 1991).

Similarly, parents could claim 90 per cent of their income when they took time out from work to give birth or to look after a child during its first four years. The father could, in addition, take ten days' leave after the child was born. Either parent could also claim parental leave of up to 60 days a year to look after a sick child; take care of the other children while the mother was having another child; or take a child to a medical examination. All of these benefits amounted to 90 per cent of income lost or SKr60 minimum. A survey of employees by Arbetslivscentrum has shown that 73 per cent experienced no difficulty in obtaining parental leave. The research also showed that although women took nearly 95 per cent of the total days of leave, 20 per cent of fathers had taken taken parental leave at some time (*SvD* 1989c).

Concern about the rising costs of sickness benefit has led to a major investigation and calls for reforms which will help reduce the costs. In 1979 Wilson suggested that the average number of days lost in Sweden because of sickness was the highest in Europe. By the end of the 1980s the RFV was claiming that 25 days per worker were being lost per year on average. It was claimed that there had been a 35 per cent increase in the total cost of sickness benefit since 1987 (*SvD* 1989d). Wilson had suggested that the ageing of the work-force and the increase in the numbers of women employed might have been having a disproportionate effect (Wilson 1979: p. 55). The same

189

concerns existed at the end of the 1980s, but also focused on the growing numbers of those receiving early retirement or disability pensions because of long-term health problems and those claiming because of injuries received at work.

A commission investigating sickness insurance recommended a number of reforms in 1989. Some of these were administrative – paying benefits at the end of the month rather than every fortnight, and making employers responsible for the first fourteen days of sickness benefit. Other changes were more concerned with rehabilitation measures, claiming that benefits were being paid out for long-term injuries and sickness when effective rehabilitation could enable claimants to return to work. In this connection, experiments have been carried out in some parts of Sweden to pay sickness benefit on a part-time basis to encourage sick workers to go back to work as soon as they can manage to cope with some employment (*Folksam* 1988).

In 1991, the former Social Democratic government cut the value of sickness benefit from 90 per cent to 65 per cent of income for the first 3 days of illness and 80 per cent thereafter for 90 days. Parent benefit was also reduced to 80 per cent of income. This has been followed by a proposal from the new government to introduce 2 'waiting days' for which the sick would receive no benefit. Moreover employers have been given responsibility for the administration of the first 14 days of benefit and for investigating the rehabilitation needs of those who experience long periods of absence from employment due to sickness. No longer is it felt that a doctor's certificate is sufficient proof of an absentee's medical condition.

Health insurance also covers patients for the major part of the costs of medical care. Until recently, visits to the doctor on an outpatient basis cost SKr60 (approx. £6). This covered the visit, the writing of any prescription, and any X-rays and consultancy visits that resulted. Any medicines prescribed cost the patient up to SKr65, although live-saving drugs were free. For hospital care, the local social insurance office would deduct SKr55 a day from the sickness benefit the patient received. Pensioners received free hospital care for a year but also had to pay SKr55 subsequently. There were also charges of SKr35 for visits to different kinds of therapist – e.g. occupational therapists, physiotherapists and psychotherapists. The new government has increased the fee for a visit to the doctor from SKr60 to SKr100 and the charge for a prescription from SKr65 to SKr90 (with an additional SKr30 for extra items). Presumably many of the other charges mentioned above have been raised correspondingly.

Dental care is also covered by health insurance but not so well. Patients have had to pay 60 per cent of the costs up to a total of SKr2,500 and 25 per cent for costs in excess of SKr2,500 (*Folksam* 1988). Dental charges have also been increased drastically recently.

Child allowances

Child allowances have long existed for each child in the family in Sweden. During the 1970s it was suggested that the value of these allowances had been eroded by the failure to raise them in line with the cost of living as happens with other benefits such as the basic pension (Wilson 1979; Elmér 1983). Although increases have continued to be erratic in the 1980s, child allowances had, until 1992, maintained their value at roughly one fifth of the base amount, against which many benefits are calculated. The recent large increase, for 1991, from SKr6,720 per child per year to SKr9,000 was quite extraordinary. It was even more impressive when set against the additional allowances that larger families received. A three-child family received an extra SKr4,500 per year, the fourth child entitled the family to an extra SKr9,000, while the fifth and subsequent children attracted a further SKr13,500 (*Folksam* 1990). However, one of the first measures taken by the new government has been to postpone the annual rise of the child allowance due at the beginning of 1992 in an attempt to save SKr1.7 billion.

Unemployment benefit

Unemployment benefit, in spite of the emphasis upon state provision in Sweden, has remained the administrative responsibility of the trade unions. Contributions are made by the employers and subsidised by central government, but 43 unemployment benefit societies, closely associated to trade unions, administer the benefit. The value has borne a constant relationship to the base amount and in 1990 varied from a minimum of SKr174 a day to a maximum of SKr495 a day. For many unemployed workers who are members of trade unions their benefit comes to 75 per cent of the income lost. Benefit can be drawn for up to 300 continuous days, or 450 days for older workers. For newcomers to the labour market or those who are not members of trade unions, an inferior system is administered by the Labour Market Board. The daily amount of benefit paid is roughly equivalent to the lowest amount paid out by the trade unions, i.e. SKr174.

This system is also about to undergo significant change. There is a proposal for a general, obligatory scheme to replace the present arrangement. It is not intended that the trade unions should continue to administer unemployment benefit. On the contrary, that task might even be given to a private agency. In the meantime, unemployment benefit contributions have been doubled for 1992 and will be tripled for 1993.

MEDICAL CARE

The Swedish medical care system is largely state-dominated. Over 90 per cent of the Swedish medical system is in the public sector and only 5 per cent of doctors are in private practice. It is an expensive system. Sweden devoted 3 per cent of its GDP to its medical care system in the early 1960s and employed the same proportion of the total work-force within it. In the early 1980s the proportion for both exceeded 10 per cent. While a considerable part of these resources was necessitated by the growing numbers of elderly people, they also reflected a commitment to a high standard of public services. Those standards came under increasing scrutiny in the 1980s, as it became clear that the economy would be unable to maintain them and as the needs for and demands on services grew. Measures have been taken to reduce the overall cost of medical care, to increase efficiency and competition and to decentralise services and decision-making.

While the Ministry for Health and Social Affairs and Socialstyrelsen – the administrative board – have the responsibility for overall legislation, supervision, policy and planning, the 23 county councils, whose local autonomy was strengthened by the Health Act of 1983, have the major responsibility for medical care provision. The county councils are empowered to levy a local income tax which finances 60 per cent of the health care budget.

It has been argued that while different county councils might have different parties controlling them, there has been a cross-party consensus on the need for a good public-sector medical care system. The conflict at local level has been between the politicians and the medical profession rather than between different political parties (Ham 1988). The end result has been the creation of an impressive array of services. County hospitals provide the whole range of medical specialisms for their populations, but they also have access to the facilities of a regional teaching and research hospital of which there are six throughout the country. Primary care, which for many years was neglected in Sweden in favour of hospital provision, is now extensive. Medical centres can be found in most localities. These provide the services of doctors, nurses and a range of therapy specialists. While health indicators are only partly attributable to health care provision, these services must take some credit for the fact that Sweden has the second lowest infant mortality rate and the second highest life expectancy in the world.

However, in spite of the fact that the medical care system is both comprehensive and universal, inequalities in health and health care persist. While Sweden has a low rate of mortality amongst men between the ages of 45 and 64 compared with other industrialised countries and the rate has improved for many non-manual groups since 1970, it has worsened for many of those in manual occupations (Diderichsen and Lindberg 1989). Diderichsen and Lindberg go on to show that manual workers, both men and women, are more likely to be hospitalised for lung cancer, cardiac infarct, strokes, alcohol-related injuries, psychoses, attempted suicide and motor vehicle accidents. The Swedish Medical Institute has shown that whereas death rates for manual and non-manual workers had been almost identical in the early 1960s, since that time death rates for the former had increased while for the latter they had decreased (*DN* 1990c). An official report into children's mental health has similarly demonstrated that whereas there had been a narrowing of differences between socio-economic groups in the 1950s, the children of manual workers now were four to five times more likely to have serious social and mental problems than those from other socio-economic groups (*DN* 1991a). A similar pattern held for children's heights. In 1960 there had been hardly any difference between the heights of 7-year-old children with parents in manual and non-manual occupations; such differences had increased significantly since that time (*DN* 1991c).

It is important, however, to remember that Swedish standards, even in spite of internal inequalities, might still be superior to those of other countries. Vågerö and Lundberg, for example, claim that class differences in mortality and sickness exist in both Britain and Sweden, but that not only are the class differences not so acute in Sweden but Swedish workers have a lower mortality rate than socio-economic groups I and II in England and Wales (Vågerö and Lundberg 1989).

The pressure for reform

The cost of maintaining Sweden's high standards are an increasing cause for concern. An international team of health economists has claimed that Swedish medical care is characterised by overstaffing and low productivity. Pointing out that the number of doctors in the system had doubled since 1975, it went on to say that increasing costs could not be attributed to the need to treat more elderly people but had arisen because age had become over-medicalised (*DN* 1991j). This sort of argument had already led to experiments to improve the efficiency and competitiveness of hospitals. A report in the *BMJ* (*British Medical Journal* 1990) has described how some hospitals have organised themselves into relatively autonomous base units which manage their own budgets and make their own decisions. This does not sound very different from the recent attempts by the British government in both the National Health Service and education to create more localised management systems.

However, an article in *The Economist* refers to two-year waiting lists for minor operations and a disinclination amongst hospital staff to reduce inefficiency (*Economist* 1988a). The article went on to say that some county councils were paying fixed price fees for cases sent to Sophiahemmet, Stockholm's largest private hospital. Olsson describes how Sophiahemmet was revived by a private insurance company in the 1980s, insures 3000 persons and has a potential for insuring some 30–50,000 more. The premiums for such insurance can be set against an individual's tax liability and is proving popular with corporate management and the self-employed (Olsson 1990: p. 270). He describes another experiment in the private sector as the 'City Clinic Ltd' – a scheme for busy business people who preferred to pay for quick treatment near their places of work in the city centre than queue 'half the day for a consultation in the suburbs' (Olsson 1990: p. 271).

Under the last Social Democratic government, hospitals were having to rationalise and prioritise in order to cope with their lengthy waiting lists, which varied from a few months to in excess of two years for certain operations (*SvD* 1989b). The Diagnosis Related Groups (DRG) system borrowed from the USA was beginning to have an impact. DRG enabled hospitals to cost operations and types of treatment with the aim of improving management, planning and evaluation. Units within hospitals were setting themselves up as private entities selling their services to other departments, hospitals and areas. While the government claimed that more efficiency was needed rather than more resources, the Conservative and Liberal Parties insisted that competition from an expanded private sector was required.

It is too early to say whether the results of increased competition within the public sector has resulted in greater efficiency, but other consequences are more evident. Many hospital departments were having to close and staff, particularly temporary ones, were laid off even before the Bourgeois government came to office. There was evidence too of increased pay differentials, with some counties able to pay their nurses more than others. Belatedly, the use of generic drugs was being considered in an effort to make savings (*DN* 1990b). These trends have been reinforced by the new government. Market principles have now been widely adopted within the health care system. Primary care doctors in Stockholm have been given control over their own budgets. The government has not been able as yet to promote the private sector in a big way but it has provided extra money to reduce waiting lists, on the understanding that services from the private sector should be bought in to help with this process.

As in Britain it may be that the aim of expanding the private sector in health care may not prove that successful, but there does seem to be a necessity and a willingness to experiment with a variety of measures to curb and reduce health expenditure and to make better use of existing resources. What divides the SAP from the Bourgeois parties is not so much the need for markets and competition, but the role and size of the private sector.

SOCIAL SERVICES

Social services are also having to consider ways of improving their effectiveness within the constraints of increasing responsibilities and dwindling resources. But this is occurring after a prolonged period of change and expansion.

With the abolition of its old poor-law legislation in the 1950s, Sweden began to develop a more humane and modern approach to social services. Legislation remained based upon three divisions: (a) the administration of means-tested social assistance, (b) the care of children, and (c) the care of those with alcohol problems. In the view of many liberal commentators, however, the new laws continued to reflect the patriarchal and repressive traditions of the laws they had replaced (Holgersson 1981). Whereas the rest of the Swedish social policy was based upon the labour movement's philosophy of solidarity, social services were still rooted in the capitalist work ethic. An investigating commission in the 1970s, backed by widespread support from within local authorities and amongst social workers,

195

Capitalist Welfare Systems

recommended a liberalisation of social services legislation. New legislation finally came into effect in 1982. It was one of the first examples of the law providing a general framework for public agencies to work with, rather than detailed regulation of their activities. The foundation of the new approach was to be found in the preamble to the Social Services Law (SoL), which made it clear that assistance was to be given to those in need in a way which respected their integrity and independence. This law, which covered help sought voluntarily by the client, dealt not only with cash benefits but also with the care of the elderly, of pre-school children, the handicapped, those with substance misuse problems, and other forms of advice and assistance. Two additional laws governed the circumstances in which children and adult substance misusers could be taken into care compulsorily. In each it was clearly the intention that such care should only be used as a last resort. Legislation towards the end of the 1980s, however, reversed the liberal trend and compulsory care was made easier (Gould 1989). If the legislative changes of 1982 were a belated response to the permissive climate of the 1960s, then the more recent changes can be seen as a response to the harsher social and economic climate of the 1980s.

The principles of SoL remained relatively unaltered although there have been calls for its revision. It is possible that to an extent the permissive nature of SoL encouraged a greater expansion of social services and social assistance than was affordable in the 1980s. It is certainly the case that the Social Democrats remained opposed to private ventures in child care throughout the period. For them the principle, state provision for all, also meant higher standards for all. If a public service became identified solely with the needs of the deprived, it was felt, then the service itself would deteriorate. To no group has this been felt to be more applicable than the elderly and the care and services they were entitled to receive.

The care of the elderly

It has already been made clear that the income replacement levels of Swedish pensions are very high. In addition to their pensions, elderly people in Sweden are likely to receive housing allowances which have made it unnecessary for all but a few to claim social assistance. It was the opinion of Wilson and Greve in the 1970s that poverty amongst pensioners was much more rare than in the UK (Wilson 1979; Greve 1978). Part of the credit for the circumstances in which the elderly live is due to the work of the local municipality, or *kommun*, social

196

services departments. These have had the responsibility for providing not only accommodation for those elderly people who cannot live by themselves unaided, but also for providing services to help those who live in their own homes.

It is said that over 90 per cent of those over 65 live in their own homes and a small percentage with their adult sons or daughters (Swedish Institute 1989). Three per cent live in old people's homes; 3 per cent receive long-term care in hospitals; while a further 3 per cent live in *servicehus*. Service houses consist of up to a hundred flats and are a form of sheltered accommodation. They have been designed to enable old people who are fairly independent but who find living alone difficult, with those support services which enable them not to have to go into old people's homes. The services will often consist of a cafeteria and those services associated with day centres. Indeed in large majority of local authorities the services located in the service houses are available to other elderly people in the community. With the conversion of old people's homes during the 1980s, or their closure, service houses have come to play a greater role in the care of the elderly.

Home helps have continued to be provided to about a quarter of elderly people, but during the last decade the number of recipients of this service has decreased while at the same time the number of hours provided has increased. It is those above the age of 80 and others in greater need who benefit from this greater targeting of resources (Sundström 1988). Sundström found, over the three-month period she investigated, that quite small percentages seemed to take advantage of the subsidised community services provided, such as chiropody, hair-dressing, meals and taxis. She also claimed, however, that over half of all elderly people used these services at some point during their retirement.

For some time there has been confusion about the divided responsibility in the care of the elderly that has existed between the county council health authorities and the social services departments run by the municipalities. After much deliberation the last Social Democratic government transferred the principal responsibility to the municipalities, a measure which took effect from the beginning of 1991. One of the first difficulties faced by some municipalities was a lack of accommodation. The premature closing down of old people's homes had left them without sufficient means to take on old people being discharged from hospital. Another was financial. Although central government had transferred resources to the municipalities for their extra duties, they none the less faced growing responsibilities at a time that their overall financial situation was deteriorating. With the cost of home helps and social assistance doubling in the 1980s, municipalities were being driven to find new ways of organising their services.

The new government's approach is to emphasise the plurality of provision with a much greater reliance on the informal and private sectors. The Social Affairs Minister has said that the elderly themselves should decide where they get their care from, implying that resources should follow the customer. Many municipalities are beginning to privatise their home help services and even the *servicehus* complexes. The hope here is that there are cheaper and more effective forms of provision than those traditionally provided by the municipalities. Whether or not this proves to be the case, there has been a clear abandonment of the principle that it is the state's responsibility to provide a high quality-service for all.

In the last few years it would appear that the one of the consequences of the austerity measures taken by both the Social Democratic and Bourgeois governments has been a deterioration in the financial situation of elderly people, with the result that many are now having to resort to social assistance.

Social assistance

In Sweden it is the municipalities which also administer means-tested social assistance. This is done by social workers employed in social services departments. SoL makes it clear that such assistance should be given where people's needs fall below a reasonable level and they are unable to provide for themselves in any other way. Typical situations where social assistance might be given are:

- as a top-up to families on low incomes;
- to the unemployed (where other unemployment support is not granted or is insufficient);
- to the sick (where sickness benefit is insufficient or not granted);
- to those drawn into an industrial dispute;
- to those house-bound with young children, unable to get child care and therefore unable to seek employment. (*Folksam* 1990)

An ambiguous feature of SoL is its reference to the fact that assistance ought not to be entirely without conditions. While this may have been intended simply to ensure that the system was not abused, it has led some authorities to take a very proactive stance in 'encouraging' claimants to try to provide for themselves (Gould 1988: ch. 6).

In the early 1980s Elmér was able to claim that the proportion of the population living on social assistance had declined from 10 per cent of the population in the 1930s to 4 per cent in the more prosperous of the post-war years. This he attributed to the way in which the social insurance system had helped to maintain the living standards of the old, the sick and the unemployed in a more effective manner. The old in particular, he insisted, hardly had to resort to social assistance at all because of the high level of pension provision (Elmér 1986). It can also be argued that the extensive provision of child day care made it possible for many single parents to seek employment. Official statistics show that the proportion of the population claiming social assistance was between 4 and 5 per cent from 1977 and 1981. Of the 250,000 households in receipt of benefit in 1983, about 40 per cent were single men, 40 per cent single women (half of whom had children), and 20 per cent couples (three quarters of whom had children) (SCB 1986).

For many the experience of being on social assistance was short-lived or occasional. During the early 1980s, only 1 per cent of social expenditure was devoted to social assistance. The benefit itself, for an adult, was similar to the basic income of pensioners and was uprated annually in line with prices. It is interesting to note that social assistance rates corresponded fairly closely to the systematic calculations made by the state agency Konsumentverket as to what constituted a reasonable standard of living (Socialstyrelsen 1985).

Many of the more positive features of Sweden's social assistance are now changing, however, particularly as a result of the increased demand caused by unemployment but also by the municipalities'

Table 11.3 Revised social assistance rates, SKr per month, October 1991

	Old rate	New short-term rate	New long-term rate
Single person	3,570	2,825	3,285
Single parent with two children	6,860	5,631	6,171
Family with three children	11,670	10,070	10,800

Source: DN 1991h

financial difficulties. The cost of social assistance doubled during the 1980s and in the first quarter of 1992 it grew by 25 per cent compared with the same period the previous year. Not surprisingly, many municipalities have reduced their benefit scales accordingly and Socialstyrelsen has claimed that there are those who are paying benefits below the existence minimum which it recommends (*SvD* 1992). Even in Stockholm, where the rates are higher than in other parts of the country, severe reductions have occurred. In October 1991 a decision was taken to reduce social assistance rates and to introduce a new short-term benefit for the first three months. For a single person this was a reduction in benefit of over 20 per cent. According to Vinterhed, the proportion of unemployed claimants of all those who received social assistance in Stockholm rose from 8 per cent in 1990 to 20 per cent in 1991. Moreover, not only were benefits being reduced in value, but stricter demands were being made on claimants (Vinterhed 1991).

CONCLUSION

There can be no doubt that it will take considerable effort to change the structures and policies of the Swedish welfare system. The range of services and personnel, the scope and generosity of the benefits, the all-embracing pervasiveness of the programmes testify to a formidable structure. It is hardly surprising, given the institutional, electoral and ideological support the system has received in the past, that some should be 'pessimistic about the chances of a real withering away of the welfare state' (Olsson 1990: p. 285).

However, within the space of a few years a bewildering array of changes has taken place. It is clear that the future might result in a greater commitment to private and occupational pensions, and a lesser reliance on a state earnings-related scheme. Sickness benefit has been reduced and greater control over its administration given to employers. Conversely, trade unions are about to be deprived of their role in the administraion of unemployment benefit. Health charges and insurance contributions for employees have been massively increased. The private sector is being encouraged in child care, the care of the elderly and in medical care. The informal sector will be relied on more in the future to take care of old people. Dependence upon social assistance is increasing, while the benefit is being reduced and the eligibility rules toughened up. And last but not least is the fact that public-sector workers are facing a much more insecure future than ever before. There are too many similarities in these measures to pretend that Sweden is not going down the same path as the British system. The question is, how far will Sweden travel?

CHAPTER TWELVE
Education and employment

INTRODUCTION

The social democratic aims of the Swedish welfare state have been stamped on every aspect of social policy, not least the education and employment services. Equality of educational opportunity for different social groups has shaped many educational reforms and programmes. In the 1960s it was important to give working-class children the same opportunities as those from middle-class backgrounds; women opportunities the equal of men's; and ethnic minority pupils similar chances to those which indigenous pupils have enjoyed. In the 1970s there were attempts to redress the imbalance of educational opportunity that had grown up between the generations, and programmes were introduced to provide adults with a second chance. The aim of equality was also linked with the idea of promoting democracy, of providing all citizens with the knowledge and expertise which would enable them to play a full part in democratic processes.

Employment policy has been characterised by the commitment to full employment. Citizens were seen as having the right not only to work but also to decent wages and working conditions. Subsequently these aims were extended to include the right to *meaningful* jobs and to have some democratic influence over employers' decision-making.

Moreover, both sets of policies, in the past, have been seen as establishing the necessary conditions for economic growth. The Swedish active labour-market policy was seen at one time as a model for other capitalist societies to follow and certainly influenced the creation of the British Manpower Services Commission (see chapter 8). Similarly with education. An OECD report, in 1969, described Sweden as a lead country in educational policy-making:

> Educational concepts in Sweden, such as extended postponement and flexibility in school career choices, equalization of social participation in higher education, insistence upon a rapid expansion of numbers and a simultaneous increase in quality in an already highly developed school system and the introduction of scientific investigations into educational policy issues, are only representative of this position.
>
> (Quoted in Boucher 1982: p. 193)

While the major programmes of both education and employment services have expanded in the last two decades, their achievement of the social and economic goals expected of them has in recent years come under more critical scrutiny.

Social Democratic governments in the 1980s began to return to more prosaic, more instrumental aims in education, while the newly elected Bourgeois government is losing little time in its attempt to dismantle the Social Democratic inheritance. As full employment is being relinquished as a policy goal, so there are moves to erode the employment rights built up through previous legislation.

EDUCATION

The Swedish post-war educational reforms were able to build on a system that reflected a deep commitment to popular education at all levels. Adult education in study circles and folk high schools established by the labour, free-church and temperance movements and their educational associations had firm roots in Swedish society. Indeed it has often been argued that it was the experience of leading Social Democrats in the study-circle tradition that made a democratic, non-élitist approach to mass education possible. Moreover, the state education system has been a highly centralised one, with national administrative boards accountable to the Ministry of Education having the responsibility of running it. In a structural sense this made major educational change all the more easy to achieve, especially as even the curriculum of schools was directed from the centre.

The Swedes had begun to think in terms of comprehensivisation as far back as 1940, but it was only in 1969, after various reports, research projects and experiments, that the country had a basic all-through comprehensive school serving children from 7 to 16. The principles and aims behind that lengthy process have in the last twenty years years been applied to the rest of the education system with varying degrees of success. Initially, comprehensivisation was intended only to bring equality of opportunity to all of the country's children, but by the end of the 1960s other more ambitious aims were on the cards.

Education, it was increasingly argued, should be used to bring about positive social change in society and to extend the principles of democracy in all areas of organised life. Adults who had not had access to educational opportunities earlier in their lives should be given the chance of returning to the system. Access at all levels should be increased. Another set of demands, made by those dissatisfied with the way in which the educational system was operating, concerned the isolated nature of educational institutions. Educationists were seen as people divorced from the real world and therefore unable to prepare young people for it. The outside world, it was argued, should impinge more on the school and the school venture into the outside world. In particular this was associated with demands for a more vocational approach to education. The term *recurrent education* came to be used to represent these new contributions to educational policy-making and the Swedes set about implementing it with enthusiasm and commitment.

New structures of opportunity

Considerable resources have been devoted to education. The percentage of GDP spent on education had risen to 7.8 per cent in 1970; remained between 7 and 8 per cent until the late 1970s; reached 9 per cent around 1980; and in the 1980s fell back to below 8 per cent (SCB 1990). Large numbers of staff have been employed in schools, particularly teachers but also medical and counselling staff. The staff–pupil ratio in the early 1980s was reported by Boucher to be 10:1 (Boucher 1982) but class sizes may often be nearer to 30 pupils, because of teachers being on leave, engaged on non-teaching duties, or involved with very small groups, e.g. home language teaching for immigrant children (*Economist* 1988). Conditions in educational establishments were described by Boucher as extremely good, with spacious, well-furnished rooms, plenty of books, resources and equipment (Boucher 1982).

As has already been mentioned, Sweden had spent the 1960s establishing a fully comprehensive system for the compulsory years of schooling – *grundskola*. Children's education is organised in three stages, for 7–10-year-olds, 10–13 and 13–16. Classes are organised on a mixed-ability basis. All pupils pursue the same subjects or have the same choices. The subject range remains broad throughout *grundskola*, with all children studying Swedish, English, maths, sciences and arts as well as working life orientation courses in the later years. There are no formal national or entrance examinations taken by pupils during or at the end of *grundskola*. However, marks are awarded based upon continuous assessment in the last two years.

When young people leave *grundskola*, few of them seek work or find employment. A varying proportion will find themselves on government schemes for the young unemployed. The vast majority (around 90 per cent) stay on to attend the upper secondary school – *gymnasieskola*. The reform of the *gymnasieskola* in 1971 brought together three different types of school – the old, academically orientated *gymnasieskola*; *fackskola*, which provided courses that were both academic and vocational; and *yrkesskola*, in which courses were more specific and vocationally orientated. These three divisions continued to form the basis of three *lines* which young people could choose from on entry to *gymnasieskola*. Initially there were five 3–4-year academic lines which led to university entry; four 2-year general theoretical and vocational lines which might lead to other forms of post-secondary education; and thirteen more specific 2-year vocational lines, which tended to lead straight to the labour market.

Students were faced with a free choice of lines regardless of their school performance to date. Their teachers might have encouraged them to choose particular lines, but if they and their parents disagreed then they were at liberty to choose what lines and courses they wanted. The only restriction was availability. According to Boucher, this meant that about 25 per cent of young people failed to get into their first choice of lines, with a consequent sense of frustration (Boucher 1982). In spite of the obvious conflict between the idea of a centrally planned set of courses and free choice by the consumer, Boucher claimed that planning did not determine people's choices. Students were not required to meet simple manpower requirements. The choice they had was a genuine one even if a substantial minority might not get exactly what they wanted. Under this system, all students would choose some vocational lines and from 1981 were expected to complete a substantial amount of work experience (Boucher 1982: p. 102).

The last of the major reforms of the education system came in 1977 with changes in higher education. Higher education was reorganised on a regional basis around the six universities of Stockholm, Lund,

Umeå, Uppsala, Göteborg and Linköping. Together with 'university colleges' (similar to the British polytechnics), they make up the 31 *högskolor* providing various forms of higher education throughout the country. Not only do 35 per cent of those leaving the upper secondary school attend *högskolor*, but also a large number of mature students who may follow their courses on a part-time basis or through distance learning, or a mixture of these plus a full-time component. The total number of students registered in higher education has risen from below 50,000 in the early 1960s to over 150,000 in the 1980s. New enrolments in 1950 were only 3500 while in 1987 they amounted to 52,200 (Askling 1989: p. 291).

All higher-education students need to have reached a certain standard of Swedish and English to qualify for entry. In addition, good grades in academic lines at upper secondary level are the most certain route to a university education. However, there are other routes which may qualify a candidate for entry: completion of two year lines, certain kinds of adult education, or simply reaching the age of 25 with at least four years' work experience.

The old faculties have gone, to be replaced by a structure based upon occupational sectors: (i) technical, (ii) administrative, economic and social welfare, (iii) medical and nursing, (iv) teaching, and (v) cultural and information (Askling 1989). This vocational emphasis is also mirrored in the way in which many courses are orientated towards the needs of the local economy. Moreover, *högskolor* are managed by boards which include a majority of members who represent 'the public interest', many of them from the local area served. In this way, a system which is run centrally by the National Board of Universities and Colleges (UHÄ), can also respond to local needs.

Adult education, always a strong part of the Swedish tradition, also expanded in the 1970s. Local authorities, both municipalities and counties, provide a range of general and vocational education courses. According to the Swedish Institute, each year about 160,000 participants (100,000 of whom are women) take courses which lead to improved job or educational opportunities (Swedish Institute 1990a). Official statistics certainly suggested that sort of figure for 1982 when 154,000 students were quoted as attending municipal courses. However, that figure steadily declined to 129,000 by 1988 (SCB 1990: p. 344). Residential adult education colleges – 130 *folkhögskolor* – provide a wide range of short courses to 250,000 people, according to the Swedish Institute, but only 15,000 attend courses lasting 15 weeks or more (Swedish Institute 1990a; SCB 1990: p. 354). Last but not least, over 300,000 study circles organised by 11 study associations cater for the more recreational education needs of more than 650,000 adults.[6]

The recognition of adult educational needs has also been extended to immigrant workers, who have been given a right to paid educational leave from their employment for up to 240 hours, to learn Swedish. While it could be argued that such a measure has benefited employers and society as a whole, there can be little doubt that it was intended to redress the educational and linguistic disadvantage many immigrants have.

Part of the general increase in adult participation in all forms of education must also be due to the law on educational leave passed in 1975. This gave adult workers the right to request leave from their employers to attend educational courses. Employers had to comply with the request within six months or could be taken to an industrial court. The Act did not include any provision for financial maintenance, however. This was *educational leave*, not *paid educational leave*. But when students were in a position to get state support to attend a course or were prepared to finance themselves, leave was relatively easy to get. Few adults would have used educational leave to read for a degree full-time, but more were able to use it to obtain a university education on a part-time basis. Trade unions, which had pressed for educational leave, used it to organise short courses for their members. These might be for no more than two hours a week and last six to eight weeks. Topics covered might be to do with industrial relations, health and safety, negotiating skills, or cover topics of social and political interest. With trade-union backing it was relatively easy for employees to obtain educational leave (Gould 1984). Within the trade- union movement this sort of education was seen as an opportunity for people to rise 'with their class' not 'above it' (Viklund 1977). It was also one of the few clear illustrations of education being used to redistribute cultural power.

Achievements and shortcomings

What has all this expansion meant in terms of the aims set out by various government commissions in the 1960s and 1970s? It is clear that Sweden has been committed to mass education at every level. All social groups are represented not only throughout *grundskola*, but *gymnasieskola*, *högskola* and in adult education in a way that few countries could match. Tuition fees have been non-existent for the individual, with the exception of study circles where small charges have been made. The staffing and facilities are usually of a high standard. Buildings and classrooms are spacious and well designed. Teaching and non-teaching staff have been plentiful and equipment in good supply. Education has also clearly taken a more vocational direction. Work orientation in *grundskola*, work experience in *gymnasieskola*, occupational 'faculties' in universities and colleges have all sought to ensure that education has occupational relevance. However, this should not be taken to mean that education is narrowly geared to the labour market. Recreational, sporting and cultural activities have had an important part to play at all levels.

The expansion in the 1970s, which slowed right down in the 1980s, has not achieved all that it aimed for, however. Equality and democracy have not been as successfully accomplished as have greater access and the emphasis on the vocational.

One of the more significant egalitarian goals has been the provision of tuition in 'home' (mother tongue) language for the children of immigrants and refugees. Between 60 and 80 per cent of most of Sweden's ethnic minorities have availed themselves of the right to home language tuition under the new national curriculum for *grundskola* in 1980. Similar percentages have been given extra help with Swedish. These efforts have been made to help the children of ethnic minority parents become bi-lingual – maintaining their ethnic identity as well as becoming Swedish speakers. Critics have suggested that the end results are semi- rather than bi-lingual children; inadequate, rather than competent, in both languages (McNab 1989: pp. 80–3). Complaints have also been levelled at the scale of resources going to a doubtful project which also has disruptive effects on other aspects of school education. On the whole, however, research seems to show that these measures have contributed to greater educational achievement amongst the children of Sweden's ethnic minorities.

Women too have certainly benefited considerably from the expansion of Swedish education. The national curriculum of 1969 aimed to create not only more educational opportunities for girls, but also to discourage subject and ultimately occupational stereotyping by gender and to enhance the awareness of gender issues in the classroom. In terms of participation, equality has been more than achieved with more women than men to be found in *gymnasieskolor* as well as *högskolor* and more impressively in adult education, but there remain marked differences in gender choices in upper secondary-school lines and in courses chosen in post-school education. Askling shows that whereas 78 per cent of those in the technical sector of higher education are men, similar proportions of women can be found in the medical and education sectors (Askling 1989: p. 296). Similar segregation is also found in programmes for the unemployed and in jobs themselves, where men are more likely to be found in the private sector and women in the public. While some may attribute these differences to the influence of the labour market or to choices of young people or to the influence of teachers (Wernersson 1989), what is undeniable is that educational institutions themselves have not been able significantly to erode such segregation.

Much the same might be said concerning class differences. Obviously the opportunity for large numbers of children to stay on after the compulsory school-leaving age and to go on to some form of higher education means that more working-class children than ever before achieve higher levels of education. Even in adult education it has been reported that when asked if they had taken part recently in some form of adult education 43 per cent of unskilled workers said they had. Moreover, this did not compare unfavourably with 58 per cent of professional workers and 54 per cent of other white-collar workers (*Economist* 1988b). However, some writers have commented disappointingly upon the persistence of class inequalities in educational achievment. Härnqvist noted that in 1968 the 'free choice' of lines in the last year of *grundskola* showed that the great majority of children from all social groups with high grades chose the academic line, and children from manual and routine white-collar backgrounds with low grades did not. But even when their grades were low, high percentages of children from the higher occupational groups chose the academic line (Härnqvist 1989: p. 22). Svensson showed that while the chances of children from SEG (socio-economic group) III had improved relatively to those from SEG I in terms of the choice of the *gymnasieskola* academic line, large differences between those from different occupational groups remained (see Table 12.1). The big improvement would seem to have taken place for the children

Table 12.1 The percentage choosing 3- and 4-year university preparatory upper secondary education in different birth cohorts as related to sex and socio-economic group

SEG	Male students				Female students			
	1948	1953	1958	1963	1948	1953	1958	1963
I	52	57	62	65	47	50	50	58
II	26	32	33	31	23	28	32	32
III	11	17	19	18	10	16	13	17
All	21	28	33	31	19	25	24	29

Source: Quoted in Härnqvist 1989

of manual workers starting the upper secondary school between 1965 and 1969. The ensuing ten years hardly made any difference at all in the life chances of different occupational groups except to see an increase in the proportion of those from SEG I.

Jonsson and Arman focused not on the choice of 3- and 4-year lines but on their completion at the end of *gymnasieskola* in 1984 and found that 59 per cent of young men and 48 per cent of young women from SEG I completed compared with 18 per cent and 17 per cent respectively from SEG III. Jonsson and Arman were particularly concerned about the way in which the rules governing entry to neighbourhood comprehensives seemed to reinforce social segregation through spatial segregation (Jonsson and Arman 1989).

Figures on social class differences in higher education are much more difficult to interpret since there is an enormous difference between those following degrees in medicine and engineering at one of the six main univerisities and those doing much shorter vocational courses at provincial colleges. None the less, it would seem that males from SEG I are seven times more likely to start higher education than those from SEG III (Härnqvist 1989: p. 296). Moreover,

> students from theoretically-oriented upper secondary school lines and with academic home backgrounds still dominate in long and prestigious programmes, such as the training of physicians. . . . Students with non-academic backgrounds and from vocationally-oriented upper secondary school lines dominate in shorter programmes.
> (Askling 1989: p. 297).

In adult education, Arvidson has suggested that the study associations which grew out of the old popular movements have become simply a part of the establishment. Whereas the old study circles provided their members with knowledge to strengthen their cause, today they have become the focus of leisure pursuits for the already-educated (Arvidson 1989). Rubenson claimed that while there had been a large expansion in adult education in the 1970s, it had begun to decline relative to the other sectors of education in the latter years of the bourgeois government and continued to do so under the Social Democrats from 1982. He suggested that municipal adult education, which catered for the already-educated to an even greater extent in the 1980s, was beginning to gain resources at the expense of the study associations (Rubenson 1989).

But a more significant decline took place from 1976. From the time that the Bourgeois government was elected the whole notion of a 'general redistribution of cultural and economic resources was allowed to lapse' (Rubenson 1989: p. 127). This trend was allowed to continue after the Social Democrats were returned to office in 1982. Education was seen much more in terms of the facilitation of technological change than the democratisation of working life (Rubenson 1989: p. 127). Ball and Larsson have argued that this trend was also evident in the retrenchment of education generally in Sweden, in the way in which the employers' views concerning educational change began to take precedence over those of the trade unions. They argued that this was also a part of an international trend which emphasised the need to get back to basics and for excellence (Ball and Larsson 1989). As Englund argued, the scientific-rational model of education had won over the democratic one (Englund 1989).

If some social democratic and socialist writers have expressed disappoinment with the pace of egalitarian and democratic reforms, Boucher has perhaps expressed a wider view. He described how the optimism of the 1960s had become the doubts of the 1970s which in turn had become the uncertainties of the 1980s. Writing as he did in the early 1980s, he knew that education was about to face economies. While he felt that it was unlikely that there would be a return to the principles and traditions of the years prior to 1960, there was, he felt, no longer a general recognition that education could solve major social problems and inequalities. But what the Swedes had achieved, he admired – the broad, balanced curriculum, with all young people studying science, culture and the environment right up to the age of 19; the commitment to very successful language tuition throughout the comprehensive system; the help given to ethnic minorities to retain their children's linguistic identity.

> It may be that the very best schooling in England is very good indeed. The very worst can be very bad. In Sweden, the range is narrower. But faced with the choice of average school matched with average school, there is little to regret and much to be grateful for in the Swedish experience. (Boucher 1982: p. 204).

This view has been reinforced by tests carried out by the IEA (International Association for the Evaluation of Educational Achievement) between 1964 and 1985, which have shown that differences between schools are not so marked in Sweden as elsewhere. Swedish children also score particularly well in tests of scientific knowledge, comprehension and English language compared with children from other countries. However, they do poorly in tests of mathematical ability (*SvD* 1989a).

How such evaluations will be affected by more recent developments in Swedish education remains to be seen.

Recent developments

Policy changes in education have reflected changes going on elsewhere in Swedish society since 1989. The worsening economic situation has been a major factor in these changes, but they have not all resulted in cuts to services and expenditure. The last Social Democratic government began, for example, to encourage local authorities to lower the school starting age from 7 to 6 but there has been a reluctance on the part of both parents and the municipalities to take up this opportunity. One of the attractions of this measure to central government may have been that the cost of a school place was lower than that of a place in municipal child care. Similarly, in the midst of its economic problems, the government also decided to lengthen the two-year vocational lines in *gymnasieskolor* to three years (*DN* 1991e). The Bourgeois government accepted this reluctantly but has postponed financing the measure, leaving some municipalities to finance the expansion themselves (*DN* 1992a). This was attacked as short-sighted by the Director-General of the Labour Market Board, as the cost of the extra year at school was a quarter of the cost of attending a labour-market course, which in a time of growing unemployment was the likely destination of the premature school-leaver (*DN* 1992c).

What expansion there is now in numbers, at any stage of the education process, is likely to be at the lowest possible cost. Decentralisation of the responsibility for the running of schools to the municipalities by the Social Democrats, reinforced by the Bourgeois coalition's policy of deregulation, has certainly given local education authorities more autonomy, but that autonomy has to be used to try and find more cost-effective ways of providing the same (if not greater) level of services for less money. Stockholm was forced to reduce its educational psychologists and counsellors in 1990 (*DN* 1990a). Linköping undertook a similar exercise over a year later when it created a pool of care staff (nurses, counsellors, psychologists, etc.) from which schools were expected to purchase specific services (*DN* 1991g). Adult education and the home language tuition for ethnic minorities were also pruned by these and other municipalities, under the Social Democratic and the Bourgeois governments. It is also clear that reduced resources and the growing birth rate is going to mean larger classes in the future and less scope for meeting the special needs of small groups of children with learning difficulties (*DN* 1992e).

Administration is another area where it is felt that cuts can be made. With more autonomy at the local level there is less need for administrative staff at the national level. Skolöverstyrelsen, the national board for schools, has been replaced by a smaller unit. Seven hundred and fifty staff were made redundant and only 230 re-appointed (*DN* 1991d) to the new body.

Parents are to be given greater choice as to where they send their children to school. As with child care and care for the elderly, so the new government has decided that resources should follow pupils whatever school they go to, whether it be run by local authorities or privately owned. Private education in Sweden has traditionally catered for less than 1 per cent of the school-age population, considerably less than in Japan or Britain, but that could change. When plans for the privatisation of a school in Nacka, Stockholm, were announced, the pupils went on strike, worried about the consequences. Since the school was to have become a company with two owners, the pupils wanted to know where the profits were to come from; whether class sizes would grow; and whether they would have to pay for school dinners (*DN* 1991k). Even the educational reforms of the British Conservatives fell short of outright privatisation. It will be interesting to see the results of this, seemingly drastic, policy change.

Educational aims and the curriculum may also be about to change. The Assistant Minister for Schools of the new government has already said that she expects a future national curriculum to have a 'clearer knowledge profile', to be more subject-based, and to be purged of its social tasks (*DN* 1991f). A directive from the minister to the committee considering the national curriculum has already criticised theme- and project-based work (*DN* 1992d). The Education Minister has also indicated that he wants to remove the aims of democracy, equality, vocational relevance and regard for the environment from legislation governing universities. The key words in his policy document are instead 'freedom and competition with quality' (*DN* 1992b).

This will fit in nicely with plans to allow universities like Umeå to become private institutions. There will be more competition for the best students and the best teachers so that universities will have to enhance their reputations. To get to university, if the minister's proposals are accepted, it will be necessary to cover the three years of the high-school curriculum. It will no longer be acceptable to qualify for entry by demonstrating that one is 25 years old and has had four years of work experience (*DN* 1992b).

We can thus see that the new government would like to introduce structural, curriculum and ideological changes which would reverse the progressive and socialist tendencies of the past. As in Britain, pluralistic policies at the local level have been complemented by tighter central government control over finance and the curriculum. There is a new emphasis on markets, competition and traditional subjects on the one hand and a playing down of egalitarian and democratic aims on the other. The Schools Minister may claim that parents' choice of school for their children will not be determined by the size of their wallets (*DN* 1991f), but there are others who believe that that is the inevitable logic of the government's new policies (*DN* 1992f).

EMPLOYMENT POLICY

If the Swedish system has, in the past, tried to provide educational opportunities for all, it has also tried to provide decent employment opportunities for all its work-force. This has been achieved by a strongly corporatist, interventionist approach to industrial policy and the labour market. An impressive range of measures has been aimed at providing jobs; decent working conditions and job security; opportunities for training and retraining; advice, guidance and information on the state of the job market; help for people to move to areas where there are more jobs available; and opportunities for those who for one reason or another have found themselves at a disadvantage in the labour market. In the years of unparalleled economic growth, these measures were often seen as generous ways of ensuring that nobody suffered the adverse consequences of a free market without some support and opportunity. In Keynesian terms they were seen as counter-cyclical and economically stabilising. The combined strength of the trade unions and the Social Democratic government behind such measures was hard for employers to resist. Nor did they wish to do so as long as their own profitability was not unduly threatened.

However, as economic growth has slowed down and as the competitiveness of the Swedish economy has been weakened, the inexorable inequalities of the occupational structure have asserted themselves, in spite of labour-market policy measures. In consequence, the very solidarity that was the keystone of the labour movement has been eroded. Private-sector workers have different interests from those in the public sector; white-collar workers do not always share the same interests as blue-collar workers. These differences have become increasingly obvious in pay negotiations in the last decade and a half (Fulcher 1991). Fears of an underclass have already begun to emerge (*DN* 1991b; *DN* 1992g); others talk of Sweden becoming, like so many others, a two thirds/one third society. In a country which has prided itself on a commitment to full employment many must now be feeling threatened by the spectre of growing unemployment.

In what follows, some of the principal measures that have become important parts of the active labour-market policy will be outlined, together with some details concerning its development in recent years.

The Labour Market Board

The Labour Market Board (AMS) is an administrative board established to carry out the policies established by the government and under the jurisdiction of the Department for Labour Affairs. It came into existence to regulate the labour market in 1940 as a wartime measure, but was subsequently used to ensure that labour-market problems were adequately dealt with by a partnership of the government, employers and trade unions. The membership of the board has reflected the dominance of trade unions in Swedish political and economic life. Trade unions have had six representatives on the board, over one third of the total, while the employers have had only three. This pattern was replicated at county level to take responsibility for county-wide services, and at a local level for employment services. In 1991, SAF decided to disengage itself from much of the state apparatus and relinquished its membership of AMS at government, county and local levels.

The principal aim of AMS has been to make an important contribution to post-war Keynesian macro-economic policies through the use of selective employment measures. These have been designed to provide training places when unemployment rises, to encourage the mobility of labour, and to avoid bottlenecks in labour supply. In doing so AMS was supposed to ensure that full employment did not lead to inflation, and to alleviate the experience of unemployment (Hedborg and Meidner 1984).

The main tasks of AMS are to provide employment services, training opportunities, job creation places and employment subsidies. Cash support for those unemployed people not covered by the unemployment benefit schemes administered by the trade unions is also the responsibity of AMS.

Employment services

Employment services are provided in most localities as a state monopoly and employers are required to register vacancies with local offices. In fact employment agencies deal with 90 per cent of vacancies and are credited with filling over 66 per cent of the job placements that take place in a year ('Taylor 1989). Staff give help and advice not only on the jobs that are available but also on opportunities for training, relief work, sheltered workshops, aptitude testing and rehabilitation. In the 1970s, Wilson claimed that the service was being criticised for concentrating too much on the hard to employ (Wilson 1979). In the 1980s there has been a greater concern for efficiency. The service is now completely computerised and it is hoped that waiting times will be reduced. In the mid-1970s, Butt Philip was impressed by the 1:15 ratio of employment agency staff to unemployed people (Philip 1978), but more recently it has been felt that staff have concentrated too much on administration and not enough on face-to-face contact with clients (Swedish Institute 1988). There has also been a great concern about matching job-seekers to the jobs available, since the combination of low unemployment and an increasing demand for more qualified and highly specialised labour has resulted in bottlenecks in the labour market, illustrated by an excessive demand for technicians (DsA 1988:3).

The service faces two other problems: first, a decline in the ratio of vacancies to the numbers of unemployed people. In 1975 there were 63 vacancies for every 100 unemployed; in 1980, 57; and in 1985, 26 (DsA 1988:3). Even in Stockholm the ratio of unemployed to vacancies had, by the end of 1991, become 5:1 (*DN* 1991i). The second problem is a trend in increased long-term unemployment:

> In Sweden the long-term unemployed are defined as people having been unemployed for at least six months. . . . In 1964 the share of long-term unemployed was 8 per cent. In 1975 this share had grown to 15 per cent and in 1986 to 22 per cent.   (DsA 1988: 3)

With the prospect of growing unemployment, these percentages are likely to grow still further.

Training and retraining

Training measures for the unemployed and those seeking to re-enter the work-force or change their employment have always been provided on a considerable scale, but this has varied according to the economic climate and the size of unemployment itself. Wilson reported that

10–12,000 were on training schemes at any one time in the 1960s (Wilson 1979), but that rose to an all-time high of 56,000 in 1979 (DsA 1988:3). Women in particular have benefited from the expansion of training programmes. Whereas they made up only 14 per cent of trainees in 1960, they constituted 46 per cent in 1970 and 53 per cent in 1989 (Wilson 1979; Swedish Institute 1990b).

From 1979, young workers began to be provided with separate schemes under the aegis of the education authorities, which led to a reduction in the monthly total of training places to between 30,000 and 40,000. The reduction was also partly due to a greater unwillingness to give training allowances to those under the age of 25 since 'since people of this age ought to be educated through the regular school system' (DsA 1988:3: p. 57). The daily training allowance which workers received in 1990 was between SKr297 and SKr495, which compared well with unemployment benefit (SKr174–495). In spite of these high income replacement levels, it has been reported that funds for training have been underutilised because of the reluctance of the unemployed to take advantage of them. Moreover between 1980 and 1986 the statistical probability of unemployed people getting training was halved (DsA 1988:3: p. 57).

Opportunities for the young unemployed

The rise in youth unemployment in the 1970s brought a similar concerted response from the Swedish authorities as it did from those in Britain. In 1980, a youth opportunities programme was started for 16- and 17-year-olds, while in 1984, a Youth Team Law came into force for unemployed young people between 18 and 19. Teenage unemployment was over 11 per cent in 1983 when the figure for the work-force overall was at a height of 3.5 per cent. By 1988, total unemployment had come down to 1.6 per cent and that of youngsters to 3.3 per cent. In 1984 when the Youth Team Programme began, 14,000 were on the youth opportunities programme at any one time, while 30,000 took part in the Youth Team Programme.

The administration of these schemes is the responsibility of the education services, although some assistance is given by AMS. The youth opportunities programme consists of an induction course, training and work experience with an employer, usually but not always in the public sector. Wages are not set at market rates and the employer receives a grant of 60 per cent of wage costs. Those who take part in the Youth Team Programme receive market-rate wages while employers are compensated in full (from 1989 a new but similar programme guaranteed employment but compensated employers for only half of their wage costs). It is local municipalities who guarantee young unemployed people a place on the scheme and in the majority of cases provide the employment. An attempt to promote induction courses in the private sector would seem to have floundered on employers expecting to pay youngsters at lower than market rates (with 50 per cent coming from the state), while unions were insisting on such rates in full. AMS has insisted that that young people should devote a specified period of time to job-seeking while on such schemes (Jonzon and Wise 1989).

Jonzon and Wise also report that not only are there more women than men participating in such schemes – 60 per cent and rising – but also that women spend more than the average time of seven months on youth teams before finding employment. There is no right to unemployment benefit if young people refuse to participate in youth teams. In accordance with Sweden's Lutheran attitude towards work, Jonzon and Wise suggest this rule was intended to prevent dependency. A similar argument has been used by the British Conservatives. It is perhaps not surprising to find that research has shown that employers tend to stigmatise youth team participants as failures (Jonzon and Wise 1989).

Hartmann argues that Sweden has moved from being a country where education was encouraged not only for its own sake and for its contribution to the economy, to one in which full-time education for young people is a cheap way of keeping them off the labour market. In a similar way the exclusion of the young from relief programmes and restricting them to youth opportunity programmes and youth teams is also an attempt to reduce the cost of youth unemployment. This treatment of young people, following legislation in 1974 which gave regular adult workers security of employment while stipulating that young workers could only work at the same rates as adults, has combined to marginalise the role of many youngsters in Swedish society. He argues that young people would prefer apprenticeships or employment with proper vocational training. Instead they are offered inferior government palliatives – an 'unemployment career' (Hartmann 1985).

Opportunities for the hard-to-employ

Recruitment subsidies amounting to 50 per cent of wage costs for a six-month period were introduced in the 1980s to encourage employers to take on the long-term unemployed. A greater proportion of these placements are in the private sector and lead sometimes to private jobs. Most of those taken on in this way tend to be men. In contrast the youth teams which operate in municipalities consist predominantly of young women who finish up working for local authorities anyway (Jonzon and Wise 1989). On average the number of job subsidies operating in 1984 was 20,000, declining to 10,000 in 1986 (DsA 1988:3).

Public works, or job creation schemes, have been a feature of Swedish labour-market policy for over half a century, and remain an important part of the way in which the difficult-to-employ are handled. Before 1984 young people were able to take advantage of these schemes and the numbers on them rose to 59,000 in 1983. With the young pushed towards youth teams and with an improvement in the employment situation, the number declined to 19,000 in 1986 (DsA 1988:3). Again the wage offered was the going rate for the job.

With the increase in immigration in the 1960s and 1970s, there was concern that immigrant workers could easily become disadvantaged because of language difficulties. For some years AMS financed the right of immigrant workers to have 240 days of paid leave for tuition in the Swedish language. This responsibility was transferred to municipalities in 1986 (Elmér 1986).

Help for handicapped workers

The number of wage subsidies to employers who take on disabled workers, combined with those in sheltered workshops, rose from 48,000 in 1979 to 79,000 in 1988 (SCB 1990). Comparative research carried out in 1974 showed that whereas 29,000 were employed in 250 sheltered workshops in Sweden, in the UK the equivalent figures were 8700 in 94 workshops (Moores, *et al.* 1987: p. 132).

There is little doubt that under Social Democratic governments labour-market policy employed a wide range of measures to complement macro-economic policy but also to further social goals, to alleviate unemployment and to help disadvantaged groups. It is also clear, however, that when faced with growing unemployment, particularly amongst the young, there has been a tendency to take a tough line with trainees. If that tendency was apparent under Social Democratic governments in the 1980s, it is likely to be reinforced in the 1990s under the new Bourgeois government.

New policies

Swedish active labour-market policy has been predicated upon full employment. It has also assumed an *arbetslinje*, which means that it is better for a worker to be usefully occupied on a training scheme, a job creation programme or in a sheltered workshop than passively to receive cash benefit. According to the Director-General of AMS, this is now under threat He predicted an unemployment rate of 6 per cent for autumn 1992 (and more recently 7 per cent for the summer of 1993). AMS training and job creation places amount to 3 per cent of the work-force and are now full to capacity. 'One can justly ask whether we are on our way into Europe through a Europeanisation of Swedish unemployment. Is it time to say farewell to full employment?' (Bernhardsson: *DN* 1992d.)

There would seem to be little evidence of a Bourgeois government determination to keep unemployment low. However, like its pre-decessor in Britain in 1979, it cannot afford to allow unemployment to rip and at the same time reduce labour-market measures. In its January 1992 budget, it gave AMS the SKr20 billion it needed to continue to provide 3 per cent of the work-force with training and job creation places. Resources for handicapped workers and deprived regions have been made a priority. Money has also been given to reduce the social security contributions of employers in poorer regions.

But if other aspects of employment policy are anything to go by, it will not be long before AMS faces changes. Subsidies to company health schemes have been abolished, as have training and information grants for the Co-determination Law. Work injury insurance is to undergo drastic revision. More significantly, the wage-earner funds are to be abolished and employment rights to be reviewed. SAF has already made it clear that it wishes to see higher fines for wildcat strikes, compulsory membership ballots before a strike, compulsory arbitration, less job security, fewer rights to leave employment and more protection for employers (*DN* 1991m). Trade-union leaders are obviously fearful that these measures will become government policy (*DN* 1992g). Moreover, there has been a clear message coming from SAF and the Labour Market Minister that wages will need to be reduced to keep small firms in business and young people in employment.

CONCLUSION

Even if the present scale of AMS programmes has been protected, there can be little doubt that they operate in an increasingly hostile environment. There are clear signs that both government and employers want a more flexible, less demanding, more docile work-force. The attempt to achieve this is taking place on a number of fronts. Unemployment is being allowed to grow, wages are being depressed and employment rights eroded. Each of these reinforces the other. SAF is encouraging both single union deals and decentralised pay bargaining (see chapter 10). At the same time education is becoming more market-orientated and instrumental in its aims and organisation. Education is now about the competition for good jobs and the disciplined knowledge required to get them. It is now clear that the concepts of equality, recurrent education, industrial and economic democracy, have become diluted and that the likely driving force behind education and employment policies in the future will be, as neo-Marxists so neatly put it, 'the reproduction of labour power and the maintenance of the non-working population' (Gough 1979).

For years other countries felt they had much to learn from Swedish experiments in the fields of education and employment policy. But even in Sweden, social democracy is on the retreat and the imported policies and principles of the New Right are in the ascendancy.

CHAPTER THIRTEEN
Perspectives and evaluations

INTRODUCTION

Events have moved too rapidly in Sweden in the last two years for there to be a substantial literature which considers their significance. It is none the less instructive to look at how different writers have examined and explained developments in the last two decades. The whole nature of the debate about Sweden has shifted from one which concerned the success or otherwise of the 'middle way' to whether or not Sweden was on an evolutionary path to socialism – 'the socialist way'. Currently the debate is about whether a reduction in the public sector and stimulation of the private sector represent 'the only way' for Swedish governments of the future. What had appeared to be *the* unassailable welfare state is now on the path towards post-Fordist welfare pluralism.

THE MIDDLE WAY

During the post-war years in which the middle way enjoyed such a strong reputation, it was difficult for critics to carry much conviction. Those who claimed, like Parkin, that Sweden was not particularly egalitarian or socialist (Parkin 1971), or that it was, on the contrary, both too socialist and authoritarian (Huntford 1971), seemed to miss the point. The Social Democrats, it was argued by others, had long since abandoned any revolutionary pretensions. They were concerned simply to manage capitalism in as efficient and effective a way as possible while ensuring that the vast mass of the population enjoyed a high standard of living and a high degree of security. American reformists in particular were pleased to find a country where gross national product *per capita* was similar to that of the USA, but in which there was little evidence of the slums and primary poverty which disfigured their own society. Tomasson had described Sweden as a 'prototype of modern society'. Furniss and Tilton saw Sweden as 'the archetype of the modern welfare state' (Tomasson 1970; Furniss and Tilton 1977). When post-modernists today refer back to the 'modernist project', it ought to be remembered that Sweden was seen as the supreme example at the time.

Furniss and Tilton were also impressed by the political consensus which surrounded social programmes. The Swedish welfare state had its origins in the paternalism of employers; the moral obligation of Christian traditions; a pragmatic and preventive approach to social problems which regarded them as wasteful and inefficient; as well as a social democratic ideology which emphasised liberty, equality and solidarity. Social Democratic governments had not sought to nationalise large sections of the economy but had helped it function efficiently and equitably. The trade unions, in their view, had used their strength wisely to help maintain full employment while at the same time developing an anti-inflationary strategy without which full employment would be jeopardised. The active labour-market policy gave workers a sense of security and made them willing to accept rationalisation and re-structuring. Extensive counter-cyclical measures, such as state regulation of investment, ensured that the economy did not suffer the booms and slumps experienced elsewhere. All the indicators seemed to suggest that the effect of social programmes on the life chances of ordinary Swedes, quantitatively and qualitatively, were extremely beneficial. The expansionary attitude towards social policy that prevailed in Sweden contrasted with the more restrictive approach of the British. In the view of Furniss and Tilton, 'Sweden's accomplishments make it natural that other nations should strive to imitate it' (Furniss and Tilton 1977).

Furniss and Tilton were writing too early to be able to consider the implications of some of the more radical reforms introduced by the Social Democrats in the mid-1970s. But in their wake other commentators began to express doubts about the more idealistic representaions of 'the People's Home'. Wilson, writing in the latter half of the 1970s, admitted that on many aspects of social policy, Sweden compared well with other countries, but she expressed concern about the extent to which high social benefits, taxes and social security contributions were becoming a disincentive for employees to work and for employers to invest (Wilson 1979). She even went so far as to question whether too much was being done for the elderly. Shenfield had no such doubts. To him it seemed that a major change had taken place in Swedish social democracy. Whereas, initially, Social Democratic governments had cooperated with capital, now they seemed set on milking it. The degree of influence that trade unions were beginning to have in economic and political life struck him with horror. Workers were being brainwashed by trade-union education programmes and children in day nurseries by socialist teachers. The state was making too many decisions about people's welfare and company investment. The degree of state dependency was stifling individual initiative (Shenfield 1980).

Socialist writers had also criticised excessive state interference but from a different standpoint. There were those who felt that reformism had done too little to reduce the power and wealth of individual capitalists, and too much to manage and manipulate the work-force on behalf of the employing class (Sjöström 1979). Ronnby put it differently when he criticised the state technocracy which the Social Democrats and the trade unions had established. Democracy was a façade, he argued. People had too little control over their own lives. They were controlled by welfare bureaucrats and professionals. The state apparatus preferred to pursue a policy of adapting individuals to the system rather than change the system for the benefit of individuals. Capitalism created casualties, and the welfare state merely mopped them up (Ronnby 1981). Similar attacks were made on the nature of Swedish corporatism. Panitch argued that capitalism employed corporatist approaches to social and economic policy in order to incorporate trade unions and diffuse their demands. Corporatism in Sweden was used to reduce the wage pressure that resulted from full employment in an attempt to sustain profitability and competitiveness (Panitch 1981).

In the 1960s, criticisms such as the above might have been easy to dismiss, but by the late 1970s it was more difficult to do so. The SAP had lost two elections in a row; the Swedish economy had severe problems; labour relations were no longer stable; and the Bourgeois governments of 1976 and 1979 had not been able either to improve economic performance or to tackle public spending. None the less, with the re-election of the SAP in 1982, it was still possible for its more radical supporters to hope that the forward march to socialism would be resumed.

THE SOCIALIST WAY

For theorists of social democracy there was a battle to be fought over the importance of politics in the determination of levels of welfare spending and the characteristics of welfare systems. Many Marxist accounts of the welfare state had implied that it was an institution which to a large extent functioned to meet the needs of capitalist societies. Although social democratic reformism could improve the lot of the working class at the margins, it was argued, the political complexion of a government was of no great significance. The balance of class forces within the capitalist state ensured that whoever was in government, capital held the reigns of power. A similar argument, though not a Marxist one, had emerged in the more empirical work of Harold Wilensky. Using regression analysis, Wilensky had claimed that his data demonstrated that the main determinants of the level of health and social security expenditure were economic growth, the age of the population and the age of the social security system. Factors such as political ideology and political system seemed to account for a very small degree of the variation between countries (Wilensky 1975).

What is important about these different analyses from our point of view is that they seem to have stimulated a vigorous defence of Swedish social democracy. Castles, a political scientist, criticised Wilensky for the 'futility' of his sociological approach to politics and claimed that all that Wilensky's methodology showed was that rich countries had more to spend on welfare than poor countries. In an analysis of similar data, but making use of different criteria, Castles claimed to demonstrate that it was not so much the presence of a government of the left which was important as a predictor of welfare spending and equality, but the absence of a strong party of the right. Sweden's small Conservative Party, it could be concluded, was a significant factor in the development of the welfare state (Castles 1978; Castles and McKinlay 1979).

Others, however, took a more positive stance. Stephens argued that whereas other countries' welfare states were pursuing a corporatist path, the Swedish welfare state might be on the road to socialism. The creation of a welfare state, which, through measures like the ATP pension scheme, had commanded the support of working-class and middle-class electors alike, gave social democracy greater strength than elsewhere. The near permanence of Social Democratic governments, the high degree of unionisation, the degree of political consciousness in the population – all provided necessary preconditions

225

for socialist development. Moreover, the labour movement had moved away from the 'welfare state reformism that had dominated its policy for almost forty years back to the original programme of the party – democratic ownership and control of production' (Stephens 1979: p. 177). The Co-determination Law of 1976 had given unions a greater influence over management and the employee-investment funds, if enacted, would bring about greater control of private-enterprise decision-making. His examination of the Swedish case had cast an 'optimistic light on the possibility of a parliamentary transition to socialism' (Stephens 1979: p. 200).

Korpi, in spite of the loss of the 1976 election by the Social Democrats, which he put down largely to the exploitation of the issue of nuclear energy by the Centre Party, also remained basically optimistic about the future for socialism in Sweden. LO's wage-earner fund proposal showed that 'the collective power resources and social consciousness of the workers had developed to a point where the dominance of capital in the sphere of production was no longer accepted' (Korpi 1978: p. 332). In Korpi's view internal competition amongst wage-earners was 'on the verge of being abolished' (Korpi 1978: p. 4). The grave-diggers of capitalism were still at work, he claimed.

In another publication following the return of the Social Democrats to office in 1982, Korpi was even more optimistic about the future of socialism. High unionisation; the working/middle-class support for the Social Democrats; and the possibility of economic democracy through the Co-determination Law and the wage-earner funds – all gave support to the idea that the power resources of labour transcended those of capital. Sweden had not suffered the welfare backlash experienced by other countries. On the contrary, the welfare state seemed to be 'well-entrenched among the voters' (Korpi 1983: p. 207). Korpi continued to demonstrate the importance of his power resources argument throughout the 1980s. In a study of the rights to sickness benefit in OECD countries from 1930 onwards, he yet again attacked those pluralists and Marxists who took a pessimistic view of the democratic potential for radical change. Social rights, he concluded, could not be regarded a function of capitalism or state bureaucracy. His data showed that 'class-based left parties' played a significant role in their development (Korpi 1989: p. 325).

Meanwhile, a parallel argument was being developed by Esping-Andersen. In a number of publications from 1980 onwards, Esping-Andersen developed the concept of 'decommodification' (Esping-Andersen 1985, 1987, 1990). Under early forms of capitalism the wage-earner had had to earn a living to survive. Without alternative means of sustenance workers were totally dependent upon their ability to sell their labour. Labour became a commodity. With the evolution of social security, rights to unemployment, work injury and sickness benefits there was a lesser degree of commodification, but the level of these benefits, their duration and the rules which governed their eligibility varied considerably from one welfare system to another. In Esping-Andersen's work, Sweden stands out as an example of the society in which the greatest strides have been made towards reducing an employee's reliance on the market's demand for labour, i.e. in which there is a high degree of decommodification. This has been achieved by making the greatest efforts to maintain full employment; and by ensuring that income replacement levels are high, benefit duration is lengthy, and the take-up of benefits is widespread. Moreover, the generous provision of disability benefits, educational leave, maternity and parental leave, means that there are a variety of ways open to employees to lessen their market dependency.

It is not surprising, given the pervasiveness and thoroughness of the work of people like Korpi, Esping-Andersen and Kolberg, that social democratic literature on the welfare state in Sweden should have remained so optimistic throughout the 1980s, especially in the context of the three election victories experienced by the Social Democrats in 1982, 1985 and 1988. With this background in mind, we can now turn to the work of Sven Olsson. This work is important because a number of studies of welfare developments in capitalist countries during the 1980s seemed to carry a chapter by Olsson on Sweden (Olsson 1986, 1987, 1988, 1989). Although the concepts of power resources and de-commodification are hardly mentioned, Olsson's acknowledgement of the work of Korpi and Esping-Andersen and his own optimism suggest that he was not out of sympathy with their studies. Writing in the middle of the 1980s, Olsson claimed that inequalities of living conditions had been significantly reduced between 1960 and 1981. Although he was critical of the persistence of educational inequalities and was reluctant to pronounce on the variability of health services and their outcomes, he thought it significant that while unemployment had grown elsewhere in Europe, in Sweden it had not risen above 4 per cent in the early years of the decade: 'Despite the reported shortcomings in actual welfare the welfare state must be regarded as not only being fairly successful, but also . . . an irreversible feature of Sweden for the foreseeable future' (Olsson 1989: p. 303).

In another paper written at about the same time and certainly after the 1985 election victory of the Social Democrats, he noted that the outside world no longer seemed to hold the Swedish model in the same esteem as before. Of the 1982 election he said that it demonstrated the strength of the social forces behind the welfare state, and of 1985 that the election was fought on a consolidation platform. With some satisfaction he noted that while Sweden's Conservative Party had become more hostile towards state welfare, it had gained less electoral support in 1985 than in 1982. Nevertheless it was clear that the welfare state was becoming a more contentious issue politically, between the forces of consolidation and those which sought to dismantle it. There was, however, no major retrenchment and Olsson again reiterated his belief in the welfare state's irreversibility (Olsson 1987: p. 78).

A subsequent paper remains optimistic, but one senses a gathering of the clouds. Olsson noted the deterioration in welfare provision in other developed countries but claimed that there was no evidence of a national welfare backlash or of an anti-welfare coalition. One local authority had attempted major cutbacks in welfare expenditure and a few isolated cases of privatisation had broken out, but otherwise, he suggested, there was little to suggest that the welfare state was under threat. The Social Democrats had even expanded child care, and improvements to parental benefit were also being proposed. He concluded that the prospects for social welfare were 'rather favourable in Sweden especially as the economy is recovering in the mid 1980s . . . the national backlash still seems far away' (Olsson 1988: p. 90). Only in the introduction to his collected papers did he at last permit himself to wonder whether regression was a possibility (Olsson 1990: p. 35).

While it is possible to understand the optimism of Korpi and his colleagues, given the electoral success of the Social Democrats in the 1980s, one is also entitled to wonder whether their theoretical framework obscured the possibility of a more pessimistic inter-pretation of events. For two commentators on Swedish social democracy and its system of industrial relations, there were clear signs of strain throughout the 1980s. Pontusson, writing for the *New Left Review* in the early 1980s, claimed that Korpi, and others who saw Sweden as maturing towards socialism, had failed to appreciate the nature of the economic crisis Sweden was facing. Swollen welfare expenditures were simply adding to that crisis. The Swedish welfare state was becoming dysfunctional for capital. Korpi, he argued, neglected global economic developments, and the need for Swedish firms to compete in world markets. Korpi may have been right to say that Social Democratic rule had resulted in a redistribution of resources from capital to labour, and Esping-Andersen was certainly right to claim that citizens had been decommodified to a significant degree. But these developments, combined with full employment, had led to a decline in the kind of labour discipline that Swedish capital required to adapt to world markets (Pontusson 1984).

In a subsequent paper, Pontusson admittted that the adoption of the idea of wage-earner funds in the 1970s was a direct challenge to capital. But precisely for all these reasons, he argued, Swedish capital had begun to fight back. SAF had become much more politicised and was beginning to speak out on what it saw as the waste and inefficiency of the public sector. It was using the mass media more effectively to advocate 'the restoration of market forces and corporate profitability' (Pontusson 1987: p. 22). Perhaps the most telling part of Pontusson's analysis was his statement that the internationalisation of major Swedish firms had made them less dependent upon a 'welfarist recovery strategy based upon domestic demand stimulation' (Pontusson 1987: p. 24). Inevitably, the wage-earner funds, when legislation was finally introduced, were a pale reflection of the original radical proposal. They may have saved the face of LO and the SAP government, but it could not be pretended that they were a major threat to capital.

While Fulcher – a specialist in the field of Swedish industrial relations - recognised that there was a radical side to the labour movement which corporatist thinkers like Panitch perhaps neglected, he too saw little radicalism in the co-determination legislation and the wage-earner funds. By the time they were on the statute books, he argued, they had become mildly reformist – neither a great threat to capital nor a great bonus for labour (Fulcher 1987). In a review article, Fulcher continued to express his doubts about 'labour movement theory'. The success of the Swedish system, he insisted, depended not simply on the policies advanced by the labour movement, but on the success of Swedish capitalism and the cooperation with labour that for many years had been the chief characteristic of the Swedish model. The corporatist consensus may have broken down, but that was not because power now rested with the labour movement. Employers and SAF had resented the radical direction the labour movement had taken in the 1970s and early 1980s and had begun to fight back. Private-sector employers were no longer interested in centralised negotiations and were introducing company-level schemes for bonuses, profit-sharing and employee share ownership (Fulcher 1987: p. 137). In a subsequent study, Fulcher described the deregulatory, supply-side policies of the

Social Democrats and their abolition of exchange and import controls as clear evidence of a shift to the right. For Fulcher, 'all this [raised] the difficult question of the degree to which the distinctiveness of the social democratic welfare state [could] be maintained' (Fulcher 1991: p. 302). After the publication of his book, the results of the 1991 election confirmed Fulcher's doubts.

THE ONLY WAY

The implication of both Pontusson's and Fulcher's critiques of the Korpi school is that the latter overestimated the significance of labour's power over the state and underestimated the power of capital. They also also overestimated the radical commitment of the labour movement's leadership. High union membership, strong electoral support for the Social Democrats and opinion polls which indicated widespread support for the welfare state seem to have contributed to a belief among the genuine radicals in the SAP that more of the same would ultimately lead to socialism. This partly explains why Sweden has been going in a direction different from that of its international competitors for some considerable time. Understandably, bravely – but perhaps foolishly – the goals of full employment, the welfare state and 'the strong society' were maintained while other countries were concentrating on productivity and social disarmament. The signs were there to be read in the global economy and they were becoming clearer within Sweden itself. Unfortunately they were camouflaged by the peristent return of Social Democratic governments.

Support for the SAP in the 1980s may have been as much a support for the strong, 'natural' party of government as for its policies. Perhaps the SAP was preferred because the weak and divided parties of the right, judged on their performance from 1976 to 1982, had little to offer. But the composition of the right had slowly been changing since 1970. The Conservatives have doubled their electoral support from 11 per cent in 1970 to 22 per cent in 1991, while the combined support for the Centre and Liberal Parties has been halved from 36 per cent to 18 per cent during the same period. Moreover, throughout the 1980s the neo-liberal tone of the Conservative Party became more strident, while the policies of SAF became more partisan and market-orientated, each insisting that the *only way* out of Sweden's economic difficulties was to reduce the size of the public sector and the burden of high taxation.

If the more radical section of the SAP deceived itself into thinking that its political power was greater than it was, it may also have been guilty of taking too uncritical a view of the public sector and the welfare state. Expansion in itself was neither socialist nor egalitarian. Evidence of waste and overmanning, inefficiency, low productivity and growing inequalities should all have been acted upon sooner. Libertarian left critiques of the Social Democratic technocracy, like that of Ronnby, had not been heeded (Ronnby 1981). In consequence, it has been left to theorists of the right to attack the public sector.

In a series of debate articles in the liberal newspaper *Dagens Nyheter*, the economist Södersten has mounted a formidable attack on waste and inefficiency in central and local government. His claim is that until the massive expansion of the public sector which began in the 1970s, Sweden had experienced decades of consistent and unparalleled economic growth. With the growth of public-sector employment from 25 per cent to 33 per cent of all employment, and the expansion of public-sector expenditure from 35 per cent to over 60 per cent of GDP, Sweden's economic performance has declined (Södersten 1991a). He quotes figures submitted to the government committee on productivity (whose brief excludes a consideration of public-sector productivity) which suggest that productivity in the private sector has declined from an annual rate of 5 per cent in the early 1960s to 1.6 per cent in the late 1980s, with the most rapid decline taking place since 1975 (Södersten 1992a). For the decline in the performance of the private sector, Södersten blames public-sector expansion almost entirely. In his view, the combination of high marginal rates of income tax in the 1970s and the 1980s, coupled with a complicated system of tax allowances, led to middle-class people manipulating the system to make enormous capital gains in the buying and selling of shares, property and housing. The real losers of this system were the manual workers who rented their homes and the value of whose real pay stagnated. Class divisions had increased (Södersten 1991a). This would seem to be confirmed by empirical data referred to in the three previous chapters.

Another principal line of Södersten's critique is the low productivity of public-sector employees. He cites many examples of doctors working much shorter hours than their counterparts in other countries, of overstaffing in health care, child care, the care of the elderly and recreation leaders. He complains that there are so many different forms of leave which are well provided for that on any given day only one third of Stockholm County's work-force turns up for work

(Södersten 1992b). In the private sector, he insists, workers with low productivity would move to jobs with higher productivity. If the Social Democrats had allowed this to happen in the 1980s, when there was an upturn in the economy after devaluation, things might have been different. Instead the public sector was allowed to take up spare labour in times of recession but did not shed it when the economy picked up (Södersten 1992a). The result is a swollen public sector with an insatiable, gargantuan appetite for resources (Södersten 1991b).

His last line of criticism is reserved for ATP, the state earnings-related pension which is always heralded in the Social Democratic literature as the policy which signalled the historic compromise between the working and middle classes. Södersten claims that ATP has led to a decline in personal savings and has deprived the private sector of investment. At the same time the chief losers of the rule which entitles those with 30 years of contributions the right to a full pension, are those manual workers who work from the time they leave school until they retire and whose wages are affected by contributions throughout that period (Södersten 1992b).

If Södersten's argument is valid, then this would explain another development in Sweden which the Social Democrats have under-estimated. While Korpi and others have prided themselves on the a working/middle-class alliance which has given staunch electoral support to the Social Democrats, they have neglected the other working/middle-class alliance. Much of the support for the SAP comes from those who by virtue of their employment or their benefits have a vested interest in the public sector. Meanwhile, disillusioned private-sector manual workers, particularly young ones, who have seen their real pay remain steady or decline, have begun to support the parties of the right.

CONCLUSION

The middle way, based on corporatist cooperation and consensus between government, business and trade unions, provided Sweden with prosperity, security and a reduction in major inequalities up to the 1970s. Ironically, the egalitarian, radical and expansionary policies associated with the labour movement in the 1970s – the socialist way – seem to have brought neither prosperity, greater equality nor socialism. Instead they would seem to have blinded many into believing that Sweden could ignore trends that were occurring elsewhere in the world. The Swedish Fordist economy was becoming less competitive, wages were rising too fast as a consequence of increasing rigidities in the system of pay bargaining, and capital investment was going abroad. The welfare state in these circumstances could not continue in its existing form.

Sadly, the Swedish experiment would seem to have reached the limits of reformism. Decommodification could only go so far. The use of unemployment as a policy device, the privatisation of public services and reductions in welfare benefits, which elsewhere have re-established the primacy of market discipline and social control, are painfully and slowly dismantling 'the People's Home'. Labour, even in Sweden, is in the process of recommodification.

CHAPTER FOURTEEN
Commentary and conclusions

INTRODUCTION

There is an Indian story about a number of blind men who come across an elephant for the first time and try to guess what it is. Unfortunately they each take hold of a part which they mistake for the whole. The one who grabs a leg proclaims that the object is a tree. Another grasps the tail and thinks he has found a rope. A third feels the sharp tusk and declares that he has a knife, and so on. Were the blind men in the story to have pooled their knowledge they might have come to a more accurate conclusion. A similar process goes on in the social sciences generally and the study of capitalist welfare systems in particular, with the qualification that social scientists are partially sighted rather than blind.

The point of this book has been to make a contribution to our understanding of capitalist welfare systems by adding the perceptions of one more partially sighted social scientist. While others must judge the value of the contribution, the onus is on this particular writer to make a case for claiming that insights developed here add something to previous studies. This will be done by relating the principal conclusions of this study to other work in the field. I have chosen to do this through a commentary on Pierson's 'theses'.

In his recent excellent overview of welfare state theory, *Beyond the Welfare State*, Pierson set out a comprehensive summary of the main arguments advanced by others concerning welfare state development and encapsulated these in twelve theses (Pierson 1991). By addressing each of these theses, I hope to show that the inclusion of Japan in a study of welfare systems can make a difference to how we view welfare developments in other advanced capitalist countries. It is important too that this study has been able to include material on Swedish welfare which post-dates the election of the recent bourgeois coalition government. This study does not lay claim to superior insights but rather to the author's good fortune in grabbing a particularly important part of the elephant at a particular point in time.

THE NEGLECT OF JAPAN AND WAITING FOR SWEDEN

Many recent comparative studies of the welfare state have noted changes in the direction of *welfare pluralism* without abandoning the use of the term *welfare state* (Morris 1988; Mishra 1990; Johnson 1987; Pierson 1991; Pfaller *et al*. 1991; Ginsburg 1992). In fairness, it must be said that Esping-Andersen did object to a concept that covered too broad a range of phenomena. Social scientists, he said, had been 'too ready to accept a nation's self-proclaimed welfare state status' and for that reason chose to distinguish between *welfare state régimes* (Esping-Andersen 1990: p. 20). Mere social expenditure was epiphenomenal, he insisted. What was important for him was the degree of decommodification that a particular régime promoted through its welfare policies.

Ironically, Esping-Andersen's own rating system placed Japan amongst the 'corporatist-statist' régimes, a step up from Britain, which languished in the 'liberal' category (Esping-Andersen 1990: p. 52). Similarly, Pfaller's 'synthetic index of welfare statism' placed Japan higher than Britain (Pfaller *et al*. 1991: p. 18). In both cases this probably resulted from the importance of low unemployment in calculating their scores. I would suggest that the literature on the Japanese welfare system referred to in chapters 3–5 lends little support to the idea that it has the comprehensiveness which the British system has in spite of the Thatcherite developments of the 1980s. Moreover, Japanese unemployment rates are not only understated but the lack of social benefits forces many Japanese workers to accept poor employment conditions and low pay in order to survive.

It was argued in previous chapters that Japanese capitalism had deliberately devised a system which prevented the emergence of a labour movement based upon working class solidarity and that this in turn had resulted in a divisive welfare system incorporating strong elements of discipline and control. The Japanese version of welfare pluralism helps to explain why the Japanese economy in the 1970s had such a competitive advantage over other advanced capitalist nations. Members of the Japanese labour aristocracy were not decommodified by high welfare benefits but remained highly dependent on their employers. The rest of the labour force was entitled to benefits and services ranging from the inferior to the non-existent.

It is the contention of this study that an understanding of the changes that have taken place in European welfare systems can best be understood in the context of the growing significance of the Japanese economy for the West. It will be suggested subsequently that where others have attributed welfare changes to general developments such as international competition and the globalisation of the world economy, these in turn can reasonably be reduced to the emergence of Japan and the other successful economies of East Asia, each of which possesses what Jones refers to as an 'oikonomic [or household] welfare state' (Jones 1990: p. 446).

> These are not 'leveller régimes'; they are not participatory democracies; there is no sentimental tradition of indiscriminate, unconditional citizen rights . . . there is no mystique attached to concepts of welfare state or social service *per se*: quite the reverse. It is the pursuit of prosperity which here calls for discipline and duty no less than family ambition. In which cause social services . . . are there to be useful, no more no less . . . the 'no frills' welfare state. Or alternatively . . . welfare capitalism that works.
>
> (Jones 1990: p. 462)

The omission of Japan and the 'little tigers' might help to explain one limitation of recent comparative studies which have focused on European countries and the USA such as Pfaller's *Can the Welfare State Compete?* and Ginsburg's *Divisions of Welfare* (Pfaller *et al.* 1991; Ginsburg 1992).

A further limitation of other studies may simply result from the fact that it is only in the last two years that economic and welfare developments in Sweden have begun to resemble the backlash and retrenchment already familiar elsewhere in the West. Although Olsson was beginning to have his doubts and Ginsburg was suspicious, at the time that they were writing it was far from clear what changes were about to occur (Olsson 1990; Ginsburg 1992). This was particularly unfortunate for Pfaller's book, which compared the relationship between competitiveness and the welfare state, as Therborn's contribution on Sweden made it the exception to the rule. Whereas those who looked at France, Britain, Germany and the USA were able to conclude that a concern for competitiveness had influenced welfare policies, the case of Sweden seemed to imply the opposite (Pfaller *et al.* 1991: ch. 8). A few more months and the hesitancy of their general conclusions would have been unnecessary.

COMMENTARY ON PIERSON'S THESES

The value of Pierson's theses is that they encapsulate a number of theoretical positions in a logical sequence. They embody industrialisation theory; theories about citizenship and social democracy; neo-liberalism; various strands of neo-Marxism; feminist, anti-racist and ecological critiques; and lastly, for want of a better word, pluralism. Each thesis will be taken in turn and related to the findings of this study.

1. *The welfare state is a product of the needs generated by the development of industrial societies*

The concept of an industrial society would now seem to be redundant. It was used to apply to cover command economies as well as those based upon private enterprise. With the changes that have occurred in what was the Soviet Union and Eastern Europe, it is likely that capitalist private enterprise will form the basis of these economies in the future. The collapse of Soviet Communism has made the very concept of socialism problematic. To say something of significance about capitalist welfare systems therefore is to say something about these emerging market economies as well. As to whether industrial societies ever *needed* the welfare state, such a claim is highly dubious. Very few industrial societies ever had a welfare state, if by that term we mean a commitment to full employment; comprehensive, universalistic and adequate social security; and high-quality public services for all. What they and, more relevantly, capitalist societies need are welfare systems. These can take a variety of forms and include various combinations of state, voluntary, fiscal, occupational, private and informal welfare.

If, following Wilensky, we take the first thesis to mean that industrialisation leads to a demand for a certain level of state welfare benefits and services due to the inexorable logic of demography, economic growth and the maturity of state programmes, then we are on safer ground. As Heidenheimer has shown, and as is clear from chapter 3, it is likely that state welfare expenditure in Japan will grow considerably in the next half century. Taking public social expenditure in the year 1980 as 100, by the year 2040, for demographic reasons alone, expenditure in Sweden will increase by 9 per cent, in Britain by 10 per cent and in Japan by 40 per cent – not too long to wait for an equalisation of the competition stakes which will bring about a new convergence of welfare systems.

2. The welfare state is a product of successful political mobilisation to attain full citizenship, in the context of industrialisation

There can be no quarrel with this statement as long as it is understood that it only ever applied to a handful of European countries and then only until the 1980s. Political mobilisation in favour of welfare states is exactly what is under attack in most capitalist societies. The political mobilisation which created highly unionised labour movements has been eroded by technological change and its occupational consequences, employer strategies and political manipulation. Full citizenship does not exist in Japan for outcastes and ethnic minorities or for many ordinary voters whose political clout is weakened by corruption and gerrymandering. Citizenship rights in Britain have been seriously damaged over the last thirteen years. In Sweden, the same process has only just started, with the willingness to contemplate high unemployment as an economic policy. Under the new welfare systems there are full citizens and second-class citizens – two thirds of one and one third of the other.

3. The welfare state is a product of industrial and political mobilisation. It embodies the successes of the social democratic political project for the gradual transformation of capitalism

Like the second thesis, this one is dated. Even in Sweden the expansion of the public sector ceased long ago. Most commentators in the 1980s were agreed that a period of consolidation had been entered. There has been little evidence for some time, either in Sweden or other social democracies, of new measures to transform capitalism. Instead, capitalism in Sweden has begun to transform social democracy in all its manifestations.

Pierson pointed out that the elision of social democracy and the welfare state under capitalism had always been misleading. Too many factors and interests contributed to the Keynesian welfare state for it to be regarded as a purely social democratic institution (Pierson 1991: p. 5). Where the welfare state was most successful it usually involved the cooperation of government, business and trade unions in some degree of liberal corporatism or tri-partism. At times, the governments involved could be conservative or liberal and not necessarily social democratic. What was important was the political mobilisation of a strong labour movement rooted in working-class solidarity, increasingly supported by a public-sector salaried middle-class. The stronger that alliance was, the more pressure could be put on government and business to cooperate in the growth of public welfare. As the working class itself diminished in size and became more fragmented and the remaining public-sector alliance became more radical in its demands, so a new electoral alliance evolved. This consisted of that section of the working class which felt a growing disillusion with the public sector and the ever-increasing demands it made on their pay packets, and those members of the middle class who had always resented the welfare state. Conservative governments and business interests have been able to exploit this discontent and create welfare systems much more amenable to the needs of capital. This occurred throughout the 1980s in Britain and is happening now in Sweden.

The reason it took so long for Sweden to adopt the same welfare path as other European countries can be explained by the success the Social Democrats had over many decades in creating a set of formidable institutions predicated on the conditions of Fordism. Indeed it might be said that Sweden was the most successful of Fordist economies and for that reason has found it most difficult to adapt to a post-Fordist world. The 'Middle Way' at its height represented the optimum way to run an economic system in which centralised national unions based upon extractive and manufacturing industries negotiated with a highly concentrated private sector. Indeed for many years government and unions in Sweden encouraged the concentration of capital through the active labour-market policy.

For a considerable period the historic compromise between capital and labour may have had mutually beneficial results, but the sort of transformation ultimately envisaged by social democrats became increasingly unacceptable to capital.

4. The welfare state is the product of a struggle between the political powers of industrial democracy and the economic powers of capital. Its further development under social democratic hegemony makes possible the gradual transition from capitalism to socialism

This was a common illusion amongst democratic socialists in both Britain and Sweden. In the 1970s, radical members of the British Labour Party were busy developing a number of schemes to extend state control over private enterprise. It had been hoped that the National Enterprise Board would lead to more popular control over the major heights of industry. A Committee of Inquiry into Industrial Democracy had proposed that all firms above a certain size should have equal numbers of representatives of trade unions and shareholders on the managing board. Ideas like these came to little because of the reaction of the British business and political establishments, but they were enough to convince those who already saw corporatism as a form of creeping socialism that something drastic had to be done to reduce the power of the labour movement and welfare bureaucrats and professionals. For much of the rest of the next decade the Labour Party had to divest itself of any socialist aspirations in the most painful manner.

Swedish social democrats also made radical demands in the 1970s. They too wanted representation on the boards of management of private and public organisations and greater control over investment funds. It was thought by some at the time that measures like these would pave the way to socialism. In the event, the Co–determination Act of 1976 and the wage-earner funds established in 1983 were both watered-down measures. Neither added greatly to the powers the labour movement already enjoyed, but they too had the effect on the bourgeois parties and on Swedish business leaders and on parts of the electorate of saying 'enough is enough'. No one would now argue that a transition to socialism was possible in Sweden. It will be enough of a struggle to preserve social democracy. For all those who had thought the transition possible, further decommodification and the growth of the wage-earner funds was essential. The wage-earner funds will shortly be abolished and the *recommodification* of labour is now in the air.

5. The welfare state is an ill-conceived and unprincipled intrusion upon the welfare- and liberty-maximising imperatives of a liberal market society. It is inconsistent with the preservation of freedom, justice and real long-term welfare

The sentiments of this philosophy were used in Britain to good effect to create the illusion that people were gaining more control over their lives. To an extent a greater commitment to the disciplines of the free market were needed in the private and the public sector in order to make the former more competitive and the latter more accountable and efficient. Growth in the public sector had not always resulted in better services or more welfare. Criticisms from the right, like those contained in Anderson's *Breaking the Spell of the Welfare State*, were often valid. The welfare state had assumed an aura of sacredness in some quarters, which made criticism seem wicked and praise obligatory (Anderson 1981). Nor were welfare state professionals and bureaucrats able to come up with satisfactory measures of control and rationing which would have enabled public expenditure to be brought under control. In Britain, free-market ideology struck a resonant and familiar chord. Its place in British political thought had always been a vibrant one.

By way of contrast, in Sweden, the social democratic project had become the nation's project. Anti-state, free-market economics did not thrive. It was accepted that the 'strong society' and a 'strong state' were almost synonymous. Sweden boasted of its 'People's Home'. For people to question the value of the welfare state was to be almost unpatriotic. The people had come to expect well-financed state services; well-furnished, well-equipped public buildings; well-paid public servants. To accept less was to accept the inferior. What this philosophy concealed, however, was the extent to which public-sector workers, in demanding more resources, were often asking for the unjustifiable in pursuit of their own interests. This did not arise out of individual wickedness or greed. It was the consequence of being part of a system which had no self-regulating capacity. It could only grow. While this served the economy well for many years, when the competition was with other Fordist economies similarly engaged in the expansion of their public sectors, it was hopeless in the face of the fierce international competition from Far Eastern countries characterised by low taxation and small public sectors.

But if there was some rational justification for the regeneration of free-market ideas, the fact that their implementation meant the creation of even stronger state powers, even stronger centralising tendencies, even more discipline and control of the work-force, was not so openly discussed. In Britain it entailed the *de facto* creation of a national police force used to break the strength of picketing strikers. It meant giving employers more powers over social security. It meant depriving young people of rights to benefit. It meant establishing a school curriculum which reinforced obedience and discipline rather than the development of individuality and criticism. When British government ministers had talked about the restoration of Victorian values, they were not only referring to laissez-faire liberalism but also to those nineteenth-century values which had underpinned the workhouse punishment of the poor, the neglect of the mentally ill and the acquisition at school of uncritical, patriotic knowledge.

The same sort of mixture was to be found in Japan. On the one hand there was the world's most successful market economy, on the other a government which exploited Confucian values rather than Victorian ones. The end results are not dissimilar. Obedience and loyalty to the group are stressed rather than rights and individuality. The family is expected to provide for the old, the weak and the poor. Rote knowledge and a distorted national history are purveyed in schools.

The Swedes often use the term *historic compromise* to describe significant political alliances. There is none more potent at the moment than the one that prevails between the libertarian and the authoritarian right. The ideology of the former is used to good effect to attack state welfare, while the latter restructures the state in terms of control. A liberal corporatism which embraces the trade unions is rejected but one which includes employers and their organisations is welcomed.

6. The welfare state is a particular form of a developed capitalist state. It functions to secure the long-term circumstances for the accumulation of capital

We can now see that this judgement, popular amongst Marxists in the 1970s, was seriously misleading. With the demise of the welfare state it is obvious that its institution represented a considerable achievement for the labour movements of Britain and Sweden. Capital had to concede the welfare state in order to gain the cooperation of labour. It may be that other factors were involved in the development of the welfare state and other interests were served by it, but as a bargain struck between capital and labour it must in retrospect be seen as a victory for labour. Had it functioned in the long-term interests of capital it might still be with us.

7. The welfare state is a particular form of the developed capitalist state. It embodies the essentially contradictory nature of developed capitalism and is chronically liable to a logic of crisis

This neo–Marxist statement is closer to reality. As Offe pointed out, capitalism seemed to be unable to survive with the welfare state and unable to survive without it (Offe 1984). But capitalism has now resolved that contradiction to a large extent. It is no longer lumbered with a commitment to full employment. Techniques of retrenchment and restructuring have been learnt all over Europe. Even the Swedish government has been able to learn from the experience. Capitalism has found a way out of its dilemma. Yes, it *does* need a degree of state provision in order deal with social problems and to satisfy popular demand but it *does not* have to submit to the collective demands of a strong working/middle-class alliance any more. Moreover, it has gained strong popular support for encouraging other forms of welfare. The middle mass has decided that there are limits to what it is prepared to pay in terms of taxes and social security contributions. In an everyday political sense it can still be said that the system is prone to contradiction and crises of various kinds but these are not system-threatening. Faced with the contradiction and crisis of trying to satisfy ever-increasing demands for state welfare and more public expenditure, capitalist states have reacted by creating more diverse, disaggregated welfare systems and a welfare pluralism which is more amenable to financial, organisational and ideological control.

8. The accommodation of capitalism, social democracy and the welfare state represents the 'exhausted compromise' of the passing phase of organised capitalism

This thesis would seem to refer to Lash and Urry's work *The End of Organised Capitalism* as well as a paper by Offe on *Disorganised Capitalism* (Lash and Urry 1987; Offe 1985). Pierson uses the terms *organised* and *disorganised* capitalism as almost synonymous with *Fordism* and *post-Fordism*. Although both sets of terms attempt to describe the same transition, with the latter concentrating on more recent developments perhaps, my own preference is for the Fordist/post-Fordist distinction. This is partly because I find the term *disorganised* misleading. Lash and Urry insist that they do not mean to imply 'random disorder' but a 'systematic process of disaggregation and restructuration' (Lash and Urry 1987: p. 8). If that is the case then a more appropriate term could have been found. It is particularly inappropriate since it is labour which has become 'disorganised' in reality. Another reason for preferring the Fordist/post-Fordist distinction is that it is closely identified with the concept of 'Japanisation' (Hall and Jacques 1989; Armstrong, *et al.* 1991: ch. 15; Foster and Woolfson 1989). Lash and Urry based their analysis upon developments in the USA, Germany, France, Sweden and Britain. Japan is hardly referred to and does not even earn a mention in the index. This omission leads them almost inevitably to identify the welfare changes taking place as a 'move towards the US incomplete welfare state' (Lash and Urry 1987: p. 281). But competition from the USA could hardly have caused the Europeans to abandon their welfare states. The European model had grown alongside the American welfare system over decades. Competition between them had managed to accommodate increasing state welfare expenditure for many years. What has to be explained is what new phenomenon appeared on the scene to create a sufficient threat to the Americans and the Europeans for them to question their own commitment to public welfare. The answer to that has to be Japan.

This is clearly recognised by some analysts of the welfare state even if only in economic terms. Pfaller, Gough and Therborn actually begin their book with the following quotation from the *Financial Times*: 'For the West, East Asia's growing success poses a growing challenge just as Europe's expansion in the 16th and 17th centuries posed a challenge to China' (*Financial Times*, 30 June 1988, p. 14, quoted in Pfaller *et al.* 1991: p. 1). Later they argue that 'foreign competition weakened an important element of US welfare statism' (Pfaller *et al.* 1991: p. 281). What foreign competition? Obviously not European. The answer is to be found in a footnote: 'The Japanese especially have challenged the other industrialised countries with a series of innovations with regard to firm organisation and firm strategy, each of which outbid the efficiency gains of the preceding one' (Pfaller *et al.* 1991: p. 299). All the more important therefore not to confine your analysis, as critics have apparently said of Lash and Urry, to 'occidental economies' (Pierson 1991: p. 189). Heidenheimer *et al.*, the only comparativists to have included Japan in their analysis of social policy, wondered at the end of the 1980s whether 'the higher cooperative potential of the more corporatist systems will engender greater success in meeting Japanese and other Asian competition on international markets than most British and American industries have so far been able to achieve' (Heidenheimer *et al.* 1990: p. 361).

It is clear then that there is a substantial agreement between different writers that capitalism has entered a new phase and that it does not matter a great deal whether this is referred to as disorganised capitalism or post-Fordism. There is substantial agreement amongst some writers that post-Fordist phenomena are associated with growing competition from Japan and other East Asian countries and that this threat can be dated from the mid-1970s. There are those who believe that as a consequence of this competition Western firms have undergone a process of Japanisation and that Western governments have also had to rise to the threat in some way. However, those writers who note the implications of increased international competition, post-Fordism and Japanisation for the erosion of the welfare state, make no direct connection between the Japanese approach to welfare and the welfare changes which have occurred in the West.

Lash and Urry talk of a fragmented, complex set of social forces behind welfare policies which make it doubtful whether a 'centralised welfare state system can be defended' (Lash and Urry

1987: p. 309). Pierson summarises a similar position when he refers to the Keynesian welfare state as being 'incompatible with this new international political economy' (Pierson 1991: p. 3). Those who share this view feel that the welfare state was rooted in a liberal corporatism which represented a spirit of compromise and consensus, when capital was concentrated and labour movements were characterised by a high degree of working-class solidarity. Governments, labour and business organisations were able to reach agreements about economic, employment and wage policies. Mass production manufacturing was concentrated and vulnerable to industrial action. Management of the economy was a task within the scope of national governments. It is this set of factors which is associated with Fordism.

Post-Fordism, on the other hand, is said to be characterised by batch production, decentralised management operating in smaller production sites, and a reduced ability for national governments to affect the economy and the actions of multi-national enterprises. The proportion of the manual labour force in extractive and manufacturing industries declines. A core of skilled, flexible permanent employees begins to develop interests different from those of the unskilled, insecure peripheral work-force. This new economic order requires a different set of welfare arrangements, a new welfare system. Principles developed in the post-Fordist economy are increasingly applied to the field of welfare – decentralisation, autonomy, flexibility, competitiveness, market orientation, productivity. Providers other than the state are encouraged; the state becomes more of a regulator. Jobs in public welfare are reduced; those that remain become more insecure and more subject to performance criteria. Business people are consulted about welfare reforms in preference to state professionals. The discipline of the present and future labour force becomes a matter of priority; the control of those forces supportive of state welfare, essential. Welfare, like the economy, becomes Japanised.

9. The welfare state is a characteristic form of the developed capitalist state securing the interests of capital and men at the expense of women. It is heavily dependent upon arrangements outside the formal economy and/or public provision through which women provide unwaged/low-waged welfare services

The evidence which demonstrates the ways in which women in a capitalist society are discriminated against in terms of employment, promotion and training is overwhelming. In so far as the welfare state was an intrinsic part of capitalism it often reflected gender inequalities in society at large. But that reflection was approximate rather than precise. The welfare state ameliorated the position of women in many ways and created new opportunities for them. In Sweden, where the welfare state achieved its most developed form, more women were employed, and at rates of pay closer to those of men. They may have been segregated economically in terms of the private and public sector, but in the latter they achieved significant positions of power and responsibility. Their education and training opportunities surpassed those of women in other countries. In terms of their representation in Parliament and government, their political power was significant. The state earnings-related pension scheme (ATP) has been criticised for the way in which it advantaged middle-class, educated women. Parental leave enabled women to undertake the dual responsibility of working in the home and the formal economy (which in all capitalist societies is disproportionately borne by women) with less personal hardship than elsewhere and with the added possibility that it could be shared with their male partners. Women in the Swedish welfare state achieved a considerable degree of independence. It is they who are most worried about the prospects for the future as their jobs are lost, adult education is cut, parental benefit is reduced and the right to a full pension under ATP is made more stringent.

If we look at Japan, a capitalist society in which the welfare state was never allowed to take root, then we find that women play a subordinate role in every sector of society. There are hardly any women in Parliament and only the occasional, token woman in government. Women have no job security and earn half the hourly rate of men. Their husbands treat them as chattels, preferring the company of their male colleagues and bar 'hostesses'. They assume a relatively unshared burden in caring for elderly relatives and children. Their rights to social security are very limited and the support they receive from social services is negligible.

While it is not being argued that Swedish women are about to assume the status of their Japanese counterparts, it is being suggested that the new welfare systems which are developing will pay less attention to the needs of women than did the welfare state.

10. The welfare state is a characteristic of the developed capitalist state, securing the interests of capital and of white people . . . at the expense of ethnic minorities . . .

Ethnic minorites play a marginal role in many types of society. This is as true of Sweden as of Japan, but in Sweden the welfare state has tried to give immigrants, refugees and their families opportunities not only to learn Swedish but also to retain their home language. Measures like these are now under threat. The political forces which are most opposed to the Swedish welfare state are those most vocal in their hostility to the rights of ethnic minorities. In Sweden ethnic minorities have been able to attain citizenship, have rights to most social benefits, and belong to national trade unions which protected their jobs and pay levels. It is hard to believe that the position of ethnic minorities would be any better off in a society which exacerbates dual labour market distinctions, in which unions concentrate on plant bargaining, in which educational opportunities depend more on the purse than ability, and where welfare rights depend more on your employer than they do the state.

11. The welfare state is a particular form of the industrial, capitalist state. Even under social democratic auspices it is vitiated by the logic of unsustainable economic growth and alienating bureaucratic forms

It is clear that many of those who argue for sustainable growth would also like to promote new forms of social development. Their social critiques tend to be anti-hierarchical and anti-professional. They would be much more sympathetic towards a system of welfare which enabled people to be more self-reliant and to operate on the basis of mutual aid. Existing welfare agencies and professional workers are seen more as instruments of social control than as providers of human welfare.

The welfare developments discussed in this book hardly qualify me to pronounce upon Utopian visions, no matter how desirable. Suffice it to say that the sort of welfare pluralism which has been advocated by libertarians of the left did not form the basis of the restructuring which occurred in Britain in the 1980s and is now occurring in Sweden. The welfare pluralism of post-Fordist capitalism is probably even more committed to unsustainable growth than the welfare state of post-war Europe. Post-Fordist economies are intended to be much less subjected to regulation, interference and control from democratically elected bodies. As to the day when it becomes so obvious that something has to be done to curtail the environmental ravages of economic growth, it is far from self-evident that the social response will be of a left libertarian kind. As to the criticism that the welfare state was more concerned with control than welfare, there is much to suggest that the welfare system of Japan, and that which Britain has developed over the past thirteen years, have devised even more effective ways of keeping people under control.

12. The (partially indeterminate) development of welfare states must be understood in a comparative and historical context. Amongst the most important sources of this development are the actions of interest groups, nationally unique political configurations and varying patterns of state organisation

With this thesis Pierson was attempting to summarise the work of those comparativists who place emphasis upon the actions of interest groups and the *competence* and *learning capacity* of individual states (Pierson 1991: p. 99). Such approaches tend to be concerned more with the 'historically unique development of different welfare states' than with their 'generic development' (Pierson 1991: p. 101). Presumably, the changes in the welfare systems of Japan, Britain and Sweden which have already been outlined would, according to the interest group and state-centred schools, have been regarded as the complex outcome of indeterminate, and principally internal, pressures and actions. While such an analysis would be interesting in itself, it would seem to be rooted in a rather narrow conception of societal change. The more interdependent the global economy becomes, the less possible will it be to ignore international influences. While not wishing to deny the uniqueness of different welfare arrangements, there are trends which occur at roughly the same time in different countries that cannot be reduced to national factors or a process of diffusion whereby the civil servants of one country simply borrow a policy idea from another country. The expansion of state welfare programmes in so many countries in the decades following the Second World War had common causes. The retrenchment of those same welfare states in recent years, culminating in challenges to the Swedish system itself, have also had common causes.

There are of course a range of factors which have contributed to the unique development of welfare systems in Japan, Britain and Sweden, many of which have already been alluded to, and it would be foolish to try to suggest that these different circumstances and traditions will be obliterated by international developments. The evidence used in this study, however, suggests that a new convergence is taking place between capitalist welfare systems because of the dynamics of international capitalism on the one hand and demographic changes on the other. While there are clear dissimilarities between the Japanese,

British and Swedish welfare systems, there is a greater resemblance between them now than there was in 1970. Each has, or is moving towards, a welfare pluralism more attuned to the requirements of post-Fordist capitalism. But over the next thirty years, they will become similar in one further respect. Each will be moving towards a population structure in which 20 per cent of the population will be over the age of 65.

THE JAPANISATION OF WELFARE

In conclusion I wish to qualify what is meant by the Japanisation of welfare. The process of 'Japanisation' has been used to describe economic phenomena occurring at two levels, the macro and the micro. At the macro level it has been used to imply that Japan's influence on the global economy has been such as to bring about changes within national economic systems. At the micro level, the characteristics of large enterprises and their relationships with subsidiary companies and trade unions are said to have become Japanised. Japanisation has also been equated with the transition from Fordism to post-Fordism. Murray has referred to the same changes in industrial relations as examples of both Japanisation or post-Fordism (Murray 1989a: p. 46); a study of post-1945 capitalism uses the chapter sub-heading 'From Fordism to Toyotaism' to describe changes in the organisation of production (Armstrong, *et al.*1991); while in a critique of technological determinism, the authors refer to 'new Japanese-style or post-Fordist technologies' (Foster and Woolfson 1989: p. 52).

Moreover, it has already been shown that the economic changes occurring within advanced capitalist countries since the mid-1970s have been accompanied by a trend towards welfare pluralism. Since the publication of the two studies by Morris and Johnson which described these changes, we have been able to observe the same phenomena occurring even in Sweden (Morris 1988; Johnson 1987). It is therefore not unreasonable to suggest that in order to understand the changes that have taken place in Western European welfare systems, in particular those of Britain and Sweden, serious consideration needs to be given to the development and purposes of Japanese welfare pluralism within the context of the nature and requirements of Japanese capitalism. If this book does no more than stimulate others to investigate Japanese social policy more thoroughly than has been possible here, then something of value will have been achieved.

If, as has already been suggested, a new convergence is likely to emerge between the welfare systems of advanced capitalist countries over the next thirty years, then there will be much to learn from the political strategies adopted in Japan, Britain and Sweden.

Notes

1 (Ch. 1, p. 1) 'British' social policy may sometimes apply to the quite different geographical areas – Great Britain, the United Kingdom or England and Wales. For simplicity's sake I have preferred to use the generic, if sometimes inaccurate, term, Britain.

2 (Ch. 3, p. 40) Interview with Tim Fox of the School of Oriental and African Studies (8 January 1992).

3 (Ch. 3, p. 41) Interview with Tim Fox of the School of Oriental and African Studies (8 January 1992).

4 (Ch. 7, p. 120) The seven-year social and economic plan of 1979 stated that: 'If the government tries to satisfy these demands [for health, welfare and education] as it has done previously, it will run the risk of allowing the public sector to grow too large, and make our economy inefficient.' The plan concluded that it would be imperative to construct a 'Japanese-type welfare society [equipped with] a proper system of public welfare built on the basis of the self-help efforts of individuals and co-operation within families and communities' (Tabata 1991: p. 16).

5 (Ch. 10, p. 165) Swedish writers seem to use the term *historical compromise* to describe, first, the cooperation between the SAP and the Agrarian Party in the 1930s; second, the agreement between LO and SAF in 1938; and, finally, the appeal made by the SAP government in the late 1950s and early 1960s to manual and non-manual workers alike.

6 (Ch. 12, p. 207) Swedish Institute literature often refers to at least 2 million participants in study circles. Boucher suggests that an SCB investigation in 1976 showed that this referred to 650,000 individuals, many of whom attended more than one course (Boucher 1982: p. 154).

Bibliography

Abegglen, J. C. (1973), *Management and Worker: The Japanese Solution*, Sophia University, New York.

Amano, I. (1989), 'The dilemma of Japanese education today', in Shields, J. J. (ed.), *Japanese Schooling*, Pennsylvania State University Press.

Anderson, D. (1981), *Breaking the Spell of the Welfare State*, Social Affairs Unit, London.

Anonymous (1983), 'The Japanese-style welfare system', *Japan Quarterly*, vol. 30, July.

Armstrong, P., Glyn, A. and Harrison, J. (1991), *Capitalism since 1945*, Basil Blackwell, Oxford.

Arvidson, L. (1989), 'Popular education and educational ideology', in Ball, S. and Larsson, S., *The Struggle for Democratic Education*, Falmer, Brighton.

Asano, H. and Saito, C. (1988), 'Social service delivery and social work practice for Japanese elders', *Gerontological Social Work: International Perspectives*, Haworth Press, New York.

Ashford, D. (1981), *Policy and Politics in Britain*, Basil Blackwell, Oxford.

Askling, B. (1989), 'Structural uniformity and functional diversification: Swedish higher education ten years after the higher education reform', *Higher Education Quarterly*, vol. 43, no. 4.

Auld, R. (Chairman) (1976), *Report of the public inquiry into the teaching, organisation and management of William Tyndale junior and infant schools*, Inner London Education Authority.

Bacon, R. and Eltis, W. (1976), *Britain's Economic Problem: Too Few Producers*, Macmillan, Basingstoke.

Baerwald, H. (1986), *Party Politics in Japan*, Allen & Unwin, London.

Ball, M. *et al.* (1988), *The transformation of Britain*, Fontana, London.

253

Ball, S. (1990), *Politics and Policy Making in Education*, Routledge, London.

Ball, S. and Larsson, S. (1989), 'Education and society in Sweden', in Ball, S. and Larsson, S., *The Struggle for Democratic Education*, Falmer, Brighton.

Barr, N. *et al.* (1989), 'Working for patients? The right approach?', *Social Policy and Administration*, vol. 123, no. 2.

Barr, N. and Coulter, F. (1990), 'Social security: solution or problem?' in Hills, J. (ed.), *The State of Welfare*, Clarendon Press, Oxford.

Becker, S. and Craig, G. (1989), 'The fund that likes to say no', *Social Work Today*, 8 June.

Becker, S. and Silburn, B. (1990), *The new poor clients: poverty, social work and the social fund*, Community Care.

Benedict, R. (1946), *The Chrysanthemum and the Sword*, Houghton Mifflin, New York.

Beresford, P. and Croft, S. (1984), 'Welfare pluralism: the new face of Fabianism', *Critical Social Policy*, Issue 9.

Bernhardsson, G. (1992), 'Arbetslinjens kollaps', *DN*, 30 January.

Boucher, L. (1982), *Tradition and Change in Swedish Education*, Pergamon Press, Oxford.

Boyd, D. (1973), *Élites and their Education*, National Foundation for Educational Research.

British Medical Journal (1990), 'Decentralising health care in Sweden', vol. 300, 6 January.

Brown, C. (1984), *Black and White Britain: The Third Policy Studies Institute Survey*, Heinemann Educational, London.

Brunnberg, K. (1991), 'Election Year 1991', *Current Sweden*, no. 385.

Buckley, S. (1988), 'Body politics: abortion law reform' in McCormack, G. and Sugimoto, Y., *Japanese Trajectory: Modernisation and Beyond*, Cambridge University Press, Cambridge.

Burgess, T. (1977), *Education after School*, Pelican, London.

Burton, J. (1989), 'A cohesive federation', *Financial Times*, 2 October.

Campbell, J. C. (1989), 'Democracy and bureaucracy in Japan', in Ishida, T. and Krauss, E. S., *Democracy in Japan*, University of Pittsburgh Press, Pittsburgh, Pa.

Carrier, J. and Kendall, I. (1977), 'The development of welfare states', *Journal of Social Policy*, vol. 6, pt 3.

Castles, F. (1978), *The Social Democratic Image of Society*, Routledge & Kegan Paul, London.

Castles, F. and McKinlay, R. (1979), 'The sheer futility of the sociological approach to politics', *British Journal of Political Science*, vol. 9, pt 2.

Childs, M. (1936), *The Middle Way*, Yale University Press, New Haven, CT.

Cole, R. E. (1971), *Japanese Blue Collar*, California University Press, Berkeley.

Coleman, S. (1983), *Family Planning in Japanese Society*, Princeton University Press, Princeton, NJ.

Collick, M. (1988), 'Social policy: pressures and responses', in Stockwin, J. A. A. (ed.), *Dynamic and Immobilist Politics in Japan*, Macmillan, Basingstoke.

Cox, C. B. and Dyson, A. E. (1971), *The Black Papers on Education*, Davis-Poynter, London.

Cummings, W. (1980), *Education and Equality in Japan*, Princeton University Press, Princeton, NJ.

Dale, P. (1986), *The Myth of Japanese Uniqueness*, Croom Helm, London.

Davies, B. (1986), *Threatening Youth*, Open University Press, Milton Keynes.

De Vos, G. A. (1974), *Japan's Minorities*, Minority Rights Group.

Dean, H. (1991), *Social Security and Social Control*, Routledge, London.

Dean, H. and Taylor-Gooby, P. (1990), 'Statutory sick pay and the control of sickness absence', *Journal of Social Policy*, vol. 19, pt 1.

Dean, M. (1986), 'An economic miracle and a welfare mess', *Guardian*, 5 March.

DHSS (1985), *Reform of Social Security*, vol. I, HMSO, London.

Diderichsen, F. and Lindberg, G. (1989), 'Better health – but not for all: the Swedish public health report 1987', *International Journal of Health Services*, vol. 19, no. 2.

Digby, A. (1989), *British Welfare Policy*, Faber and Faber, London.

DN (1990a), 'Skolans krispaket klubbat', 27 April.

DN (1990b), 'Billigare läkemedel löser vårdkrisen', 11 June.

DN (1990c), 'Arbetare dör yngre', 30 November.

DN (1991a), 'Barns hälsa en klassfråga', 21 February.

DN (1991b), 'En svensk demoliserad underklass', 10 March.

DN (1991c), 'Klassskillnader tillbaka', 13 March.

DN (1991d), 'Står jag med på listan?', 1 June.

DN (1991e), 'Alla går tre år i nya gymnasiet', 6 June.

DN (1991f), 'Klarare krav på kunskaper', 11 October.

DN (1991g), 'Hårda besparingar hotar grundskolor', 17 October.

DN (1991h), 'Socialbidragen sänks redan i år', 18 October.

DN (1991i), 'Stockholm tappar jobb', 29 November.

DN (1991j), 'Svensk sjukvård sedd utifrån', 30 November.

DN (1991k), 'Eleverna strejkade mot privat skola', 3 December.

DN (1991m), 'Beställnings jobb av SAF', 17 December.

DN (1992a), 'Regeringen drar in skolmedel', 8 January.

DN (1992b), 'Hårdare tag på högskola', 18 January.

DN (1992c), 'Dyrt spara på gymnasiet', 24 January.

DN (1992d), 'Läroplan oroar miljö grupper', 30 January.

DN (1992e), 'Klass splittras när pengar sparas', 5 February.

DN (1992f), 'Friaskolor får dubbla inkomster', 7 February.

DN (1992g), 'Arbetslösheten sparas i EG låst på högnivå', 18 February.

DN (1992h), 'Regeringen hotar arbetsrätten', 18 February.

Dore, R. P. (1973), *British Factory, Japanese Factory*, Allen & Unwin, London.

Dore, R. P. (1987), *Taking Japan Seriously*, Athlone, London.

Dore, R. P. and Sako, M. (1989), *How the Japanese Learn to Work*, Routledge, London.

Drucker, P. (1978), 'Japan: the problems of success', *Foreign Affairs*, April.

DsA (1988:3), *Labour Market Policy in 1986*, Stockholm.

Duke, B. (1986), *The Japanese School: Lessons for Industrial America*, Praeger, New York.

Eatwell, J. (1982), *Whatever happened to Britain?*, Duckworth, London.

Eccleston, B. (1989), *The State and Society in Post-war Japan*, Polity Press, Cambridge.

Economist (1981), 'Swedish industry's thin upper crust', 4 April.

Economist (1983), 'The ageing of Japanese social security', 14 May.

Economist (1987), 'The nonconformist state', 7 March.

Economist (1988a), 'Europeans seek the right treatment', 16 July.

Economist (1988b), 'Swedish schools: working classes', 12 November.

Economist (1990), 'A survey of the Swedish economy', 3 March.

Education (1991a), 'Parliament', 9 August.

Education (1991b), 'There must be a better way', 13 September.

Education (1991c), 'Parliament', 4 October, p. 278.

Education (1992a), 'Opting out', 17 January.

Education (1992b), 'Parliament', 7 February.

Education (1992c), 'Parliament', 13 March.

Edwards, L. (1988), 'Equal employment opportunities in Japan', *Industrial and Labour Relations Review*, vol. 141, no. 2.

Elander, I. and Montin, S. (1990), 'Decentralisation and control', *Policy and Politics*, vol. 18, no. 3.

Elliott, J. (1978), *Conflict or Cooperation? The Growth of Industrial Democracy*, Kogan Page, London.

Elmér, Å. (1983), *Svensk socialpolitik*, Liber, Lund.

Elmér, Å. (1986), *Svensk socialpolitik*, Liber, Lund.

Englund, T. (1989), 'Educational conceptions and citizenship education', in Ball, S. and Larsson, S., *The Struggle for Democratic Education*, Falmer, Brighton.

Esping-Andersen, G. (1985), *Politics against Markets*, Princeton University Press, Princeton, NJ.

Esping-Andersen, G. (1987), 'Citizenship and socialism: decommodification and solidarity in the welfare state', in Rein, M., Esping-Andersen, G. and Rainwater, L., *Stagnation and Renewal in Social Policy*, M. E. Sharpe, New York.

Esping-Anderson, G. (1990), *The Three Worlds of Welfare Capitalism*, Polity Press, Cambridge.

Esping-Andersen, G. and Korpi, W. (1984), 'Social policy as class politics in post-war capitalism', in Goldthorpe, J., *Order and Conflict in Contemporary Capitalism*, Clarendon Press, Oxford.

Evandrou, M. *et al.* (1990), 'The personal social services', in Hills, J., *The State of Welfare*, Clarendon Press, Oxford.

Falkingham, J. (1989), 'Dependency and ageing in Britain', *Journal of Social Policy*, vol. 18, pt 2.

Field, F. (1989), *Losing Out: The Emergence of Britain's Underclass*, Basil Blackwell, Oxford.

Fisher, P. (1973), 'Major social security issues: Japan 1972', *Social Security Bulletin*, March.

Folksam (1988), 'Vår trygghet 1988–89', Stockholm.

Folksam (1990), 'Vår trygghet 1990–91', Stockholm.

Foreign Press Centre (1988), *Social Security in Japan*, Tokyo.

Foster, J. and Woolfson, C. (1989), 'Corporate reconstruction and business unionism', *New Left Review*, no. 174, March/April.

Fujimura-Fanselow, K. (1989), 'Women's participation in higher education in Japan', in Shields, J. J. (ed.), *Japanese Schooling*, Pennsylvania State University Press.

Fujita, K. (1987), 'Gender, state and industrial policy in Japan', *Women's Studies International Forum*, vol. 10, no. 6.

Fukushima, T. (1989), *Japanese Social Structure*, University of Tokyo Press.

Fulcher, J. (1987), 'Trade unionism in Sweden', *Economic and Social Democracy*, vol. 9, pp. 129–40.

Fulcher, J. (1987), 'Labour movement theory versus corporatism: social democracy in Sweden', *Sociology*, vol. 21, no. 2.

Fulcher, J. (1991), *Labour Movements, Employers and the State*, Clarendon Press, Oxford.

Furniss, N. and Tilton, N. (1977), *The Case for the Welfare State*, Indiana University Press, Bloomington.

Gamble, A. (1988), *The Free Economy and the Strong State*, Macmillan, Basingstoke.

Garon, S. (1987), *The State and Labour in Modern Japan*, University of California Press, Berkeley.

George, V. and Wilding, P. (1976), *Ideology and Social Welfare*, Routledge & Kegan Paul, London.

Ginsburg, N. (1992), *Divisions of Welfare*, Sage, London.

Glennerster, H. (1990), 'Social policy since the Second World War', in Hills, J. (ed.), *The State of Welfare*, Clarendon Press, Oxford.

Glennerster, H. and Low, W. (1990), 'Education and the welfare state', in Hills, J. (ed.), *The State of Welfare*, Clarendon Press, Oxford.

Glennerster, H. *et al.* (1991), 'A new era for social policy', *Journal of Social Policy*, vol. 20, pt 3.

Glyn, A. and Sutcliffe, B. (1972), *British Capitalism: Workers and the Profit Squeeze*, Penguin, Harmondsworth.

Gough, I. (1979), *The Political Economy of the Welfare State*, Macmillan, Basingstoke.

Gould, A. (1981), 'The salaried middle class and the corporatist welfare state', *Policy and Politics*, vol. 9, no. 4.

Gould, A. (1982), 'The salaried middle class and the welfare state in Sweden and Japan', *Policy and Politics*, vol. 10, no 4.

Gould, A. (1984), *Swedish Educational Leave in Practice: The Gothenburg Experience*, Discussion Paper 12, Association for Recurrent Education, Nottingham.

Gould, A. (1988), *Conflict and Control in Welfare Policy*, Longman, London.

Gould, A. (1989), 'Cleaning the People's Home: recent developments in Sweden's addiction policy', *British Journal of Addiction*, vol. 84, no. 7.

Government Statistical Service (1991), *Educational Statistics for the UK*, HMSO, London.

Green, D. G. and Lucas, D. (1992), 'Private welfare in the 1980s', in Manning, N. and Page, R., *Social Policy Review 4*, Social Policy Association.

Gregory, J. (1987), *Sex, Race and the Law: Legislating for Equality*, Sage, London.

Gretton, M. and Jackson, M. (1976), *William Tyndale: The Collapse of a School – or a System*, Allen & Unwin, London.

Greve, J. (1978), *Low Incomes in Sweden*, background paper to Report no. 6, Royal Commission on the Distribution of Incomes and Wealth, HMSO, London.

Guardian (1990), 'Pensions opt out: costs soar', 3 January.

Guardian (1992), 'The Election', 12 March.

Hall, S. and Jacques, M. (1989), *New Times*, Lawrence & Wishart, London.

Ham, C. (1988), 'Governing the health sector: power and policy-making in the English and Swedish health services', *Millbank Quarterly*, vol. 66, no. 2.

Härnqvist, K. (1989), 'Comprehensiveness and social equality', in Ball, S. and Larsson, S., *The Struggle for Democratic Education*, Falmer, Brighton.

Hartmann, J. (1985), 'New forms of youth participation and work in Sweden', *International Social Science Journal*, vol. 37, no. 106.

Hawkins, J. N. (1989), 'Educational demands and institutional response: *Dowa* education in Japan', in Shields, J. J. (ed.), *Japanese Schooling*, Pennsylvania State University.

Heckscher, G. (1984), *The Welfare State and Beyond*, University of Minnesota Press.

Heclo, H. (1974), *Modern Social Politics in Britain and Sweden*, Yale University Press, New Haven, CT.

Heclo, H. and Marsden, M. (1986), *Policy and Politics in Sweden*, Temple University Press, Philadelphia, PA.

Hedborg, A. and Meidner, R. (1984), *Folkhems Modellen*, Rabén & Sjögren.

Heidenheimer, A., Heclo, H. and Adams, C. (1990), *Comparative Public Policy*, St Martin's Press, New York.

Hill, M. (1990), *Social Security Policy in Britain*, Edward Elgar, Aldershot.

Holgersson, L. (1981), *Socialvård*, Tiden.

Holland, S. (1975), *The Socialist Challenge*, Quartet Books, London.

Houghton, V. (1974), *Recurrent Education*, Ward Lock Educational, East Grinstead.

Huntford, R. (1971), *The New Totalitarians*, Allen Lane, London.

ILO (1988), *The Cost of Social Security 1981–3*, Geneva.

Inoue, K. (1979), 'Structural changes and labour market policies in Japan', *International Labour Review*, vol. 118, no. 2, March/April.

Japan Statistical Yearbook (1990), Statistics Bureau, Management and Coordination Agency, Tokyo.

Japan Statistical Yearbook (1991), Statistics Bureau, Management and Coordination Agency, Tokyo.

Jenkins, C. and Sherman, B. (1979), *The Collapse of Work*, Eyre Methuen, London.

Johnson, N. (1987), *The Welfare State in Transition*, Harvester, Hemel Hempstead.

Johnson, N. (1990), *Reconstructing the Welfare State*, Harvester, Hemel Hempstead.

Jones, C. (1990), 'Hong Kong, Singapore, South Korea and Taiwan: Oikonomic welfare states', *Government and Opposition*, vol. 25, pt 4.

Jonsson, I. and Arman, G. (1989), 'Social segregation in Swedish comprehensive schools', in Ball, S. and Larsson, S., *The Struggle for Democratic Education*, Falmer, Brighton.

Jonzon, B. and Wise, L. R. (1989), 'Getting young people to work: an evaluation of Swedish youth employment policy', *International Labour Review*, vol. 128, no. 3.

Jordan, B. (1981), *Automatic Poverty*, Routledge & Kegan Paul, London.

Jordan, B. (1982), *Mass Unemployment and the Future of Britain*, Basil Blackwell, Oxford.

Judge, K. (1982), 'The growth and decline of social expenditure', in Walker, A., *Public Expenditure and Social Policy*, Heinemann Educational Books, Oxford.

Kahn, H. (1971), *The Emerging Japanese Superstate*, Deutsch, London.

Kamata, S. (1983), *Japan in the Passing Lane*, Allen & Unwin, London.

Kargl, I. (1988), 'The hospitalisation of the mentally ill in Japan', in Nish, I. (ed.), *Contemporary European Writing on Japan*, Norbury, Ashford.

Kawashima, Y. (1987), 'The place and role of female workers in the Japanese labour market', *Women's Studies International Forum*, vol. 10, no. 6.

Kiefer, C. (1988), 'Care of the aged in Japan', in Norbeck and Lock, *Health, Illness and Medical Care in Japan*, University of Hawaii Press.

Kitazawa, Y. (1986), 'Who will bear the burden?', *AMPO Japan–Asia Quarterly Review*, vol. 18, no. 2–3.

Klein, R. (1989), *The Politics of the National Health Service*, Longman, London.

Korpi, W. (1978), *The Working Class in Welfare Capitalism*, Routledge & Kegan Paul, London.

Korpi, W. (1983), *The Democratic Class Struggle*, Routledge & Kegan Paul, London.

Korpi, W. (1989), 'Power, politics and state autonomy in the development of social citizenship', *American Sociological Review*, vol. 54.

Kuroda, T. (1978), 'The demographic transition in Japan', *Social Science and Medicine*, vol. 12A.

Laczko, F. (1988), 'Partial retirement: an alternative to early retirement?', *International Social Security Review*, vol. 41, no. 2.

Lash, S. and Urry, J. (1987), *The End of Organised Capitalism*, Polity Press, Cambridge.

Lawrence, T. L. (1985), 'Health care facilities for the elderly in Japan', *International Journal of Health Services*, vol. 15, no. 4.

Lee, H. K. (1987), 'The Japanese welfare state in transition', in Friedmann, R., *Modern Welfare States*, Wheatsheaf, Hemel Hempstead.

Le Grand, J. *et al.* (1990), 'The National Health Service: safe in whose hands', in Hills, J. (ed.), *The State of Welfare*, Clarendon Press, Oxford.

Leichter, H. M. (1979), *A Comparative Approach to Policy Analysis*, Cambridge University Press, Cambridge.

Linton, M. (1984), 'By all accounts they should be bust', *Guardian*, 9 October.

Linton, M. (1985), *The Swedish Road to Socialism*, Fabian Tract No. 503, Fabian Society.

Lister, I. (1974), *Deschooling: A Reader*, Cambridge University Press, Cambridge.

Lock, M. (1984), 'Licorice in Leviathan: the medicalisation of the care of the Japanese elderly', *Culture, Medicine and Psychiatry*, vol. 8, no. 2.

Lundqvist, S. (1975), 'Popular movements and reforms 1900–1920', in Koblik, S., *Sweden's Development from Poverty to Affluence 1750–1970*, University of Minnesota Press, Minneapolis

Lynn, R. (1988), *Educational Achievement in Japan: Lessons for the West*, Macmillan, Basingstoke.

MacCormack, J. and Sugimoto, Y. (1988), *Japanese Trajectory*, Cambridge University Press, Cambridge.

McCormick, K. (1989), 'Towards a lifelong learning society: the reform of continuing vocational education and training in Japan', *Comparative Education*, vol. 25, no. 2.

Maclure, S. (1989), *Education Reformed – A Guide to the Education Reform Act*, Hodder & Stoughton, London.

McNab, C. (1989), 'Minority education in the Swedish comprehensive school', in Ball, S. and Larsson, S., *The Struggle for Democratic Education*, Falmer, Brighton.

Mann, K. (1989), *Growing Fringes: Hypotheses on the Development of Occupational Welfare*, Armley Publications, Leeds.

Mann, K. (1992), *The Making of an English 'Underclass'?* Open University Press, Milton Keynes.

Maruo, N. (1986), 'The development of the welfare mix in Japan', in Rose, R. and Shiratori, R. (eds), *Welfare State: East and West*, Oxford University Press, Oxford.

Millar, J. and Glendinning, C. (1989), 'Gender and poverty', *Journal of Social Policy*, vol. 18, pt 3.

Ministry of Foreign Affairs (1978), *Social Security in Japan, Facts about Japan*, Public Information Bureau, Tokyo.

Ministry of Health and Welfare (1985), *National System of Old-age, Disability and Survivors' Benefits in Japan*, Tokyo.

Mishra, R. (1977), *Society and Social Policy*, Macmillan, Basingstoke.

Mishra, R. (1990), *The Welfare State in Capitalist Society*, Harvester, Hemel Hempstead.

Moore, B. Jr (1973), *Lord and Peasant in the Making of the Modern World*, Penguin, Harmondsworth.

Moores, K., Booth, P. and Duncan, K. R. (1987), 'Sheltered employment strategies in five countries', *Policy and Politics*, vol. 21, no. 2.

Morishima, M. (1982), *Why has Japan Succeeded?*, Cambridge University Press, Cambridge.

Morris, R. (ed.) (1988), *Testing the Limits of Social Welfare*, Brandeis University Press, Boston.

Murray, R. (1989a), 'Fordism and post-Fordism', in Hall, S. and Jacques, M., *New Times: The Changing Face of Politics in the 1990s*, Lawrence & Wishart, London.

Murray, R. (1989b), 'Benetton Britain', in Hall, S. and Jacques, M., *New Times: The Changing Face of Politics in the 1990s*, Lawrence & Wishart, London.

Nakagawa, Y. (1979), 'Japan, the welfare super-power', *Journal of Japanese Studies*, vol. 5, no. 1.

Nakane, C. (1973), *Japanese Society*, Pelican, London.

Noguchi, Y. (1986), 'Overcommitment in pensions', in Rose, R. and Shiratori, R., *The Welfare State: East and West*, Oxford University Press, Oxford.

Ny Start för Sverige (1991), Moderaterna, Stockholm.

O'Connor, J. (1973), *The Fiscal Crisis of the State*, St James Press, London.

OECD (1985), *Measuring Health Care 1960–83*, Paris.

OECD (1987), *Financing and Delivering Health Care*, Paris.

OECD (1991), *National Accounts 1960–1989*, Paris.

Offe, C. (1984), *Contradictions of the Welfare State*, Hutchinson, London.

Offe, C. (1985), *Disorganised Capitalism*, Polity Press, Cambridge.

Ogawa, N. (1982), 'Economic implications of Japan's ageing population', *International Labour Review*, vol. 121, no. 1.

Ohta, T. (1988), 'Work rules in Japan', *International Labour Review*, vol. 127, no. 5.

Olsson, S. (1986), 'Sweden' in Flora, P. (ed.), *Growth to Limits*, vol. I, Walter De Gruyter.

Olsson, S. (1987), 'Towards a transformation of the Swedish welfare state', in Friedmann, R., *Modern Welfare States*, Wheatsheaf, Hemel Hempstead.

Olsson, S. (1988), 'Decentralisation and privatisation in Sweden', in Morris, R., *Testing the Limits of Social Welfare*, Brandeis University Press, Boston.

Olsson, S. (1989), 'Sweden', in Dixon, J., *Social Welfare in Developed Market Countries*, Routledge, London.

Olsson, S. (1990), *Social Policy and Welfare State in Sweden*, Arkiv, Lund.

Øyen, E. (1986), *Comparing Welfare States and their Futures*, Gower, Aldershot.

Panitch, L. (1981), 'Trade unions and the capitalist state', *New Left Review*, no. 125, January/February.

Parkin, F. (1971), *Class, Inequality and Political Order*, MacGibbon & Kee, London.

Parry, R. (1986), 'United Kingdom', in Flora, P. (ed.), *Growth to Limits*, vol. II, W. de Gruyter.

Patrick, H. (ed.), (1976), *Japanese Industrialisation and its Social Consequences*, University of California Press, Berkeley.

Peacock, A. (1991), 'Welfare philosophies and welfare finance', in Wilson, T. and Wilson, D. (eds), *The State and Social Welfare*, Longman, London.

Pempel, T. J. (1978), *Patterns of Japanese Policymaking*, Westview Press, Colorado.

Pempel, T. J. (1990), 'Polarities of "responsible capitalism"', in Dankwart, A. R. and Erickson, K. (eds), *Comparative Political Dynamics*, Harper & Row, New York.

Persson, I. (ed.) (1990), *Generating Equality in the Welfare State: The Swedish Experience*, Norwegian University Press.

Pfaller, A., Gough, I. and Therborn, G. (eds) (1991), *Can the Welfare State Compete?*, Macmillan, Basingstoke.

Philip, A. B. (1978), *Creating New Jobs: A Report on Long Term Job Creation in Britain and Sweden*, Policy Studies Institute.

Pierson, C. (1991), *Beyond the Welfare State*, Polity Press, Cambridge.

Pinker, R. (1986), 'Social welfare in Japan and Britain', in Øyen, E., *Comparing Welfare States and Their Futures*, Gower, Aldershot.

Pinker, R. (1991), 'On rediscovering the middle way', in Wilson, T. and Wilson, D., *The State and Social Welfare*, Longman, London.

Pontusson, J. (1984), 'Behind and beyond social democracy in Sweden', *New Left Review*, vol. 143, January/February.

Pontusson, J. (1987), 'Radicalisation and retreat in Swedish social democracy', *New Left Review*, vol. 165.

Powell, M. and Anesaki, M. (1990), *Health Care in Japan*, Routledge, London.

Rampton, A. (Chairman) (1981), *West Indian Children in our Schools*, Interim report of the Committee of Inquiry into the Education of Children from Ethnic Minority Groups, HMSO, London.

Reid, I. (1989), *Social Class Differences in Britain*, Fontana, London.

Rose, R. (1989), 'Welfare: the Lesson from Japan', *New Society*, 28 June.

Rose, R. and Shiratori, R. (1986), *Welfare State: East and West*, Oxford University Press, Oxford.

Ronnby, A. (1981), *Socialstaten*, Studentlitteratur, Lund.

Rubenson, K. (1989), 'Swedish adult education policy in the 1970s and the 1980s', in Ball, S. and Larsson, S., *The Struggle for Democratic Education*, Falmer, Brighton.

Rubinstein, D. (1979), *Education and Equality*, Penguin, Harmondsworth.

SAF-Tidningen (1992), *Lokal lönemarknad*, no. 7, 28 February.

Scase, R. (1977), *Social Democracy in Capitalist Societies*, Croom Helm, London.

SCB (1986), *Statistisk Årsbok*, Stockholm.

SCB (1990), *Statistisk Årsbok*, Stockholm.

SCB (1992), *Statistisk Årsbok*, Stockholm.

Schoppa, L. (1990), 'Education reform in Great Britain and Japan', in *Conference Proceedings of the American Political Science Association*.

Seldon, A. (1981), *Wither the Welfare State*, Institute for Economic Affairs, London.

Shenfield, A. (1980), *The Failure of Socialism*, Heritage Foundation, Washington, DC.

Shirai, T. (1984), 'Recent trends in collective bargaining in Japan', *International Labour Review*, vol. 123, no. 3.

Showler, B. (1976), *Public Employment Services*, Longman, London.

Simmons, C. (1990), *Growing Up and Going to School in Japan*, Open University Press, Milton Keynes.

Simon, B. (1988), *Bending the Rules*, Lawrence & Wishart, London.

Sjöström, K. (1979), *Socialpolitik eller Socialism?*, Arbetarkultur, Lund.

Sked, A. (1987), *Britain's Decline*, Basil Blackwell, Oxford.

Smith, D. (1987), *The Rise and Fall of Monetarism*, Penguin, Harmondsworth.

Social Trends 1991, HMSO, London.

Socialstyrelsen (1985), *Social Bidrag*, Stockholm.

Södersten, B. (1991a), 'Sverige: dårarnas paradis', *DN*, 27 January.

Södersten, B. (1991b), 'S skapade ett klassamhälle', *DN*, 28 January.

Södersten, B. (1992a), 'Därför går det så illa', *DN*, 3 January.

Södersten, B. (1992b), 'Yrkesgrupper utan berättigande', *DN*, 4 January.

Soeda, Y. (1991) 'The development of the public assistance system in Japan 1966–83', in *Annals of the Institute of Social Sciences*, Institute of Social Sciences, Tokyo.

Statistisk Årsbok 1992, SCB, Stockholm.

Ståhlberg, A.-C. (1991), 'Lessons from the Swedish pension system', in Wilson, T. and Wilson, D. (eds), *The State and Social Welfare*, Longman, London.

Steinhoff, P. G. (1989), 'Protest and democracy', in Ishida, T. and Krauss, E. S., *Democracy in Japan*, University of Pittsburgh Press, Pittsburgh, PA.

Stephens, J. D. (1979), *The Transition from Capitalism to Socialism*, Macmillan, Basingstoke.

Steslicke, W. E. (1988), 'The Japanese state of health: a political–economic perspective', in Norbeck, E. and Lock, M., *Health, Illness and Medical Care in Japan*, University of Hawaii Press.

Stevens, R. (1988), 'The Japanese working class', in Tsurumi, E., *The other Japan*, Sharpe.

Sugimoto, Y. (1986), 'The manipulative bases of consensus in Japan', in McCormack, G. and Sugimoto, Y., *Democracy in Contemporary Japan*, Sharpe, New York.

Sumama, K. (1978), 'The Japanese family in relation to people's health', *Social Science and Medicine*, vol. 12A.

Sundström, G. (1988), 'Social work an old age care in Sweden', *Journal of Gerontological Social Work*, vol. 12, pts 1–2.

SvD (1989a), 'Svenska skolan får gott betyg men underkänt i matematik', 12 May.

SvD (1989b), 'Tio år i kö med utsliten och värkande höftled', 6 August.

SvD (1989c), 'Kampanj skall locka pappor till barnledigt', 15 August.

SvD (1989d), 'Arbetsskador ökar oroande', 26 September.

SvD (1992), 'Socialbidragen under existensminimum', 19 February.

Swann, M. (Chairman) (1985), *Education for All*, Report of the Committee of Inquiry into the Education of Children from Ethnic Minority Groups, HMSO, London.

Swedish Institute (1988), *Fact Sheet: Labour Market Policy*.

Swedish Institute (1989), *Fact Sheet: The Care of Elderly in Sweden*.

Swedish Institute (1990a), *Fact Sheet: Adult Education in Sweden*.

Swedish Institute (1990b), *Fact Sheet: Labour Market Policy*.

Swedish Institute (1991), *Fact Sheet: Social Insurance in Sweden*.

Tabata, H. (1991), 'The Japanese welfare state: its structure and transformation', in the *Annals of the Institute of Social Sciences*, Institute of Social Sciences, Tokyo.

Takahashi, T. (1973), 'Social security for workers', in Okochi, K., Karsh, B. and Levine, S. B., *Workers and Employees in Japan*, University of Tokyo Press.

Takahashi, T. and Someya, Y. (1985), 'Japan', in Dixon, J. and Kim, H. K. (eds), *Social Welfare in Asia*, Croom Helm, London.

Takashima, S. (1988), *Unemployment and its Impact on Social Work in Japan*, paper presented to the World Conference of Social Workers, Stockholm.

Tasker, P. (1987), *Inside Japan*, Penguin, Harmondsworth.

Taylor, R. (1989), 'Mediator in an economic arena', *Financial Times*, 2 October.

Taylor, T. (Chairman) (1977), *A New Partnership for Our Schools*, Report of the Committee of Enquiry into the Management and Government of Schools, HMSO, London.

Thorslund, M. and Johansson, L. (1987), 'Elderly people in Sweden: current realities and future plans', *Ageing and Society*, 7.

Tintner, M. (1989), *State Imperfect*, MacDonald Optima, London.

Tomasson, R. (1970), *Sweden: Prototype of Modern Society*, Random House, New York.

Townsend, P. and Davidson, N. (1982), *Inequalities in Health: The Black Report*, Penguin, Harmondsworth.

Toyoda, Y. (1988), 'Japanese social work' (letter sent to the author).

Toyoda, Y. (1990), 'The study of old age as a problem for women' (unpublished paper sent as a personal communication to the author).

UK National Accounts 1991, HMSO, London.

UN Statistical Yearbook 1987 (1991), New York.

UNESCO Statistical Yearbook (1981, 1983 and 1988).

Urry, J. and Wakeford, J. (1973), *Power in Britain*, Heinemann, London.

Vågerö, D. and Lundberg, O. (1989), 'Health inequalities in Britain and Sweden', *Lancet*, 1 March.

Vaizey, J. and Sheehan, J. (1968), *Resources for Education*, Allen & Unwin, London.

Verba, S. *et al.* (1987), *Élites and the Idea of Equality*, Harvard University Press, Cambridge, MA.

Viewpoint (1987), *Forgotten Millions*, Central Television Documentary shown on 31 March.

Viklund, B. (1977), 'Rising with one's class, not above it', *Current Sweden*, no. 153, Swedish Institute, Stockholm.

Vinterhed, K. (1991), 'Svårare vara fattig', *DN*, 10 December.

Vogel, E. (1979), *Japan as Number One: Lessons for America*, Harvard University Press, Cambridge, MA.

Watanuki, J. (1986), 'Is there a "Japanese-type welfare society"?', *International Sociology*, vol. 1, no. 3.

Webb, A. and Wistow, G. (1987), *Social Work, Social Care and Social Planning*, Longman, London.

Wernersson, I. (1989) 'Gender equality – ideology and reality', in Ball, S. and Larsson, S., *The Struggle for Democratic Education*, Falmer, Brighton.

White, M. (1987), *The Japanese Educational Challenge*, Free Press, New York.

WHO (1978), *Social and Biological Effects on Peri-natal Mortality*.

WHO Statistics (1988), Geneva.

Wicks, M. (1987), *A Future for All*, Penguin, Harmondsworth.

Wiener, M. (1981), *English Culture and the Decline of the Industrial Spirit*, Cambridge University Press, Cambridge.

Wilensky, H. (1975), *The Welfare State and Equality*, University of California Press, Berkeley.

Willetts, D. (1992), *Modern Conservatism*, Penguin, Harmondsworth.

Wilson, D. (1979), *The Welfare State in Sweden*, Heinemann.

Woodsworth, D. E. (1977), *Social Security and National Policy: Sweden, Yugoslavia, Japan*, McGill, Montreal.

Worsthorne, P. (1978), 'Too much freedom', in Cowling, M., *Conservative Essays*, Cassell, London.

Index